When Robots Move In

When Robots Move In explores what happens when AI becomes a permanent member of the household. Drawing on years of immersive research, the book reveals how voice assistants transform domestic life, reshaping relationships, routines, and spaces. It offers a compelling look at the negotiations and adaptations that emerge as families integrate AI into their everyday lives, uncovering universal patterns of interaction that resonate across cultures.

The book introduces innovative frameworks like the Effort Triad, the Embodied Interaction Heuristic, and brand anthropomorphism to analyse how people engage with stationary voice assistants. It also presents practical concepts such as custodianship roles, spatial resistance tactics, and compassionate automation, offering tools to navigate shared spaces with AI. By connecting these findings to the next generation of domestic technology—mobile humanoid robots—it provides a forward-looking perspective on the future of AI in the home.

This book bridges disciplines such as human–computer interaction, sociology, and design and offers both theoretical insights and practical applications to understand the evolving role of AI in everyday life. It is a key resource for researchers, designers, and policymakers who are working with conversational AI, social robots, or smart home technologies.

When Robots Move In

Living with Conversational AI in the Home

Indra Mckie

CRC Press
Taylor & Francis Group
Boca Raton London New York

CRC Press is an imprint of the
Taylor & Francis Group, an **informa** business
A CHAPMAN & HALL BOOK

First edition published 2027
by CRC Press
2385 NW Executive Center Drive, Suite 320, Boca Raton FL 33431

and by CRC Press
4 Park Square, Milton Park, Abingdon, Oxon, OX14 4RN

CRC Press is an imprint of Taylor & Francis Group, LLC

ISBN: 978-1-041-15705-2 (hbk)
ISBN: 978-1-041-15707-6 (pbk)
ISBN: 978-1-003-68084-0 (ebk)

DOI: 10.1201/9781003680840

Typeset in Times
by SPi Technologies India Pvt Ltd (Straive)

To my mum, and all the strong women in my life.
To all human beings near and far in their journeys.

Contents

About the Author

Indra Mckie is Singer Songwriter from Sydney/Eora, as well as an Entrepreneur and Postdoctoral Research Fellow at the University of Technology Sydney, where she investigates trust in digital systems and human-centred approaches to artificial intelligence. Her doctoral research on conversational AI and human-computer interaction earned the 2025 Association for Information Science and Technology (ASIS&T) Doctoral Dissertation Award, an international award recognising significant contributions to information science and technology.

Indra's work bridges rigorous academic research with practical community impact and entrepreneurship. She has founded multiple ventures that apply human-centred design principles to deliver innovative solutions across technology education and community support. Her research has been presented at international conferences and published in leading HCI venues, examining how people negotiate space, control, and meaning when living with AI technologies. She is a 2024 Vogue Code Future Innovators Award winner for her work in technology, creativity, and entrepreneurship.

Before entering academia, Indra worked in data analysis and user experience roles in finance and tertiary education, bringing industry perspectives to her scholarly work. She advocates for human-first technology, designing approaches that centre lived experience, cultural context, and social relationships rather than technical capabilities alone. This philosophy shapes her research methodology, her teaching, and her public speaking on responsible AI development. A leader and frequent speaker on conversational and generative AI, domestic robotics, and inclusive technology design, Indra brings accessible explanations of complex technical systems to diverse audiences. As a singer-songwriter, Indra explores what it means to create, connect, and stay human in an age increasingly shaped by artificial intelligence, bringing a rare creative perspective to conversations about technology and culture.

Foreword

Bhuva Narayan

I am proud and nostalgic to say that I was there at the exact moment when the idea for this project was born, and it has culminated in this book. I was on a sabbatical in California in 2018 and staying with my brother, who had a three-year-old girl. My niece often interacted with Alexa in the living room, speaking aloud instructions and commands such as "Aunty Alexa, play the Baby Shark song" or "Aunty Alexa, play the *Zootopia* Shakira song" and dance to it. These smart speakers had a use, after all!

Then I heard my niece ask Alexa rather specific questions, such as "Aunty Alexa, what are you wearing?" and "Aunty Alexa, when is Halloween?" For a trained librarian like me who was used to searching for information in my own privacy, I was struck by these open and transparent interactions between a child and this human-sounding machine that seemed to perform as an information retrieval system and as a question-answering machine.

I was amused but just getting used to it all when one day I heard my niece go into her father's study and say, "Uncle Google, when is daddy's flight landing? When will he come home?" Now this was more than information retrieval. Uncle Google had daddy's schedule, for it seems my brother had booked his travel using Google Home. This was not just information retrieval; it was now a help centre!

Soon, I came across a curious six-year-old boy, who had long conversations with Alexa about his homework and asked it a million questions about everything he came across. It got to a point where his parents started changing the home Wi-Fi password every day and only gave it to him if he learnt something new on his own; he ended up speeding through his maths lessons and times tables just so he could get the Wi-Fi password to talk to his friend Alexa.

When I returned from my sabbatical to Sydney, Indra and I talked about these children and their homes. We began wondering about the family dynamics and the cognitive interactions in homes with these machines that spoke in a human-like voice, then known as voice bots. And thus, the seed was sown for this book.

This book is a result of over five years of hard work, hard thinking, and some brilliant ethnographic work by Indra despite the long Covid-19 shutdowns in Australia. Readers of this book can get a holistic picture of how families live with and alongside these smart home technologies. Nowadays, when I talk on the phone to a child in my family who lives far away, and they call me "Aunty Bhuva", I wonder if they know whether I'm a human or just another smart speaker. Come along and enjoy this remarkable phenomenon through this book.

Preface

Hi there, I'm Indra. Thank you for taking the time to read my work. I hope you found some value in my words and ideas. This book is based on my doctoral research, which I lived and breathed from 2019 up until 2025. Alongside my thesis, I went through many life changes throughout those years, and so did the world. When I started in 2019, there were only whispers of robots and AI, fictional depictions of intelligent artificial "life". Now in the midst of 2026, we have lived through the explosion of generative AI, which some technology thought leaders believe we are on the cusp of complete general intelligence—artificial intelligence that is almost inseparable from human intelligence.

I wrote this as an undiagnosed woman with ADHD, a daughter of a migrant mother and a somewhat-there father. I grew up in government-supported housing commission and have memories of playing outside till past sundown but also exploring the internet from my family's shared computer. I've always believed that life is full of lived experiences, a mosaic that builds up over time, and we start to look back and see a clearer picture of ourselves. I believe that human experience is this, and as a graduate at the cusp of new technology and entering the workforce, the way technology was treated was from a capitalist-driven incentive, products that are simplified *en masse*, to appeal to more people to purchase in the whims of a solution to fix human issues that go untreated, due to the lack of opportunities of human connection in a world where we're forced to be workers.

AI will change all of this. I know you feel it too. And you are experiencing it, living it, and sometimes perhaps, feeling hopeless about it.

This book looks back at the technology we've lived through and how it might give us answers about the technology of the future. But more than that, what was important to me was learning about humans and what technology fulfils within us. A hope, a desire, some other state that we employ technology to be the in-between, to enable change and transform. In using and creating technology, we need first to be person-centred, then also planet-centred and love-centred.

The research you'll read here was conducted during the hardest period of my life. I lost both my parents and my dearest grandparents while doing the research for this book. I wrote from the bedside of hospital beds, between appointments, through tears and deep into late nights when I could finally hear my brain when the world was quiet. I kept writing because I knew everyone who had held me as a baby would have wanted me to finish with my head held high. Glassy eyes allowed. Invisible hugs and kisses whispering I'm proud of you. Through the grief, writing up this research gave me something to focus on, to absorb my brain, in thinking of the future and not what was happening to myself and my family in the present.

The families who participated in this research trusted me with their stories, their frustrations, and their intimate relationships. I am profoundly grateful. Thank you for sharing a glimpse of your life with me and our readers.

And to you, the reader, how are you? Who do you want to be, what do you want to make? How do you want to help others? Do it, and do it now, because we can just do things.

Acknowledgements

I would like to acknowledge my mentor and maternal figure, Dr Bhuva Narayan, for wandering into my life and holding space for me to learn and grow. I sometimes feel like a little seed she found and planted, watering me throughout the years, watching me bloom into many different flowers and projects. But like a houseplant, I'm dramatic and unpredictable sometimes, and prone to predators or burnout. Bhuva is an incredible woman who mentored and supervised me throughout my career at university, from a 17-year-old undergrad to a 27-year-old finishing my PhD, and now I'm nearly 30, and she is double my age, working together on research projects changing the lives of many. Being unapologetically creative and hardworking in the name of making the world a better place. Thank you, Bhuva.

I, of course, would not be here or writing any books without the love and support of my parents. Even beyond this life, they inspire me to continue and live my life to the fullest. Thank you, Putu Ayu Musantariyati and Kevin Peter Mckie.

I'd also like to acknowledge all the other academic mentors who guided me on writing my thesis and book, my PhD co-supervisors, Dr Baki Kocaballi, Dr Gail Kenning, and others who provided feedback, peer review, and panel assessments. And of course, all the behind-the-scenes support services at UTS, the professional staff that we could not run as an institution without, the Library, HELPS, counselling, research support, and more.

As well as my friends in the entrepreneurial world, who have given me new light in creating immediate impact and value. Often showing me that you can just do things if you accept that you are truly here to do just that. Which was always a rebalancing of the fear and scepticism that academia had put into me. So, thank you to my friends at UTS Startups and Arrayah, and Aaron Ngan, for introducing me to that world and then meeting all my wonderful life-long friends, Pnuks, Victoria, Tori, the wonderful residents at Arrayah's Billabong and Banksia hackerhomes, and too many more to mention.

Thank you to my family, Kris, Al, and Sarah, who have shared this life with me. Thank you to my stepdad, Stephen, for taking care of us and our home. Thank you to my Oni and Kat, who keep me laughing and insanely sane.

The Robots Are Already Here 1

THE TIMELINE IS NOW

The transition from stationary voice assistants (VAs) to mobile humanoid robots is no longer speculative. Technology companies are actively preparing for domestic deployment of embodied robots powered by generative AI. Tesla has announced plans to release its Optimus humanoid robot by 2026, and 1X Technologies is piloting NEO Beta, a humanoid designed for home environments, with selected households from late 2025—and these are only two examples of the emerging roid race to crack the home androids market. These developments signal a significant shift in the role of AI within domestic settings, moving from disembodied voice interfaces to physically present, interactive companions.

When Robots Move In is a timely contribution to this emerging landscape. It offers an academically rigorous account of how families are already living with AI in the home, providing valuable insight into the routines, negotiations, and meanings that form around current voice-based systems. The book draws on peer-reviewed doctoral research with 13 households to explore how families manage trust, control, and cohabitation with AI companions. Building on broader technological and social trends, this book frames Alexa and Google Home as early mainstream examples of domestic robots, devices that have been integrated into many households for nearly a decade.

Additionally, mechanical arms or humanoid sizes are employed as simple physical adaptations for robots, ensuring their functionality in human environments, including those beyond Earth in outer space (see Lovchik & Diftler, 1999). This excerpt from Tondu's work highlights the significance of anthropomorphic design for computers and robots intended for use within human spaces.

When a humanoid robot is designed, it partially borrows features from the human form. The entity resulting from this mimicking process, we here call technical anthropomorphism. The major argument for this truly bionic approach to robotics can be explained as follows: in a human-made world, and more accurately in the highly human-adapted domestic world, a robot defined as a future autonomous worker will be technically the most adapted if it is designed to imitate human users of human-made machines in their human environment. Although a social robot can be motorised by wheels, it is clear that a bipedal robot is more adapted than other locomotion modes to be integrated into private or public architecture, where it can be important to climb stairs safely and easily (Tondu, 2012, p. 612).

DOI: 10.1201/9781003680840-1

Unlike physical simulations of human space, form and shape, VAs operate within human environments primarily through their capacity to comprehend and respond to human language, cultures, and customs.

This chapter provides a concise historical overview of domestic social robotics, beginning with early chatbot prototypes and culminating in today's generative AI chatbots that are rapidly entering the mainstream. It underscores the cultural shifts that accompany new technologies in the home, such as attention, addiction, and isolation, highlighting the ways they influence family structures and personal relationships. Moving beyond purely industrial contexts, the chapter focuses on how consumer-facing "social" robots and AI tools are marketed as ways to improve everyday life.

A HISTORY OF CHATBOTS

The idea of simulating conversations with non-human artificial intelligence had been explored in fiction and films for a long time, even before the invention of computers. More recently, conversational robots, more commonly referred to as chatbots, have been developed and tested through software models deployed over many years. They have progressed from simple question-and-answer dialogue sets to complex large language models (LLMs) demonstrating advanced artificial intelligence. In 1966, ELIZA, the first chatbot to attempt the Turing Test, was created, challenging people to believe they were conversing with a human-like interface. Could humans distinguish between conversing with another human or a machine? ELIZA was designed to respond to a small sample of user questions within a narrow domain to simulate a conversation with a psychotherapist (Raine, 2009). Its creator, Dr. Weizenbaum, was surprised when users began to divulge deep secrets to the machine.

In 1995, ALICE was conceived. Improvements in computing elicited faster and more accurate responses. ALICE's complex pattern-matching system convinced internet users they were chatting with a young human girl about her hobbies and interests. Then, in 1997, Jabberwacky attempted to entertain. Could humans enjoy engagements with conversational agents (CAs)? (Raine, 2009). Then in 2001, Smarterchild was launched, constructed to camouflage. It was one of the first chatbots to be integrated into preexisting commercial messaging platforms. Users could chat with Smarterchild alongside conversations with human friends on AOL Instant Messenger and MSN Messenger. This marked the beginning of integrating chatbots into spaces where users were already congregating (Adamopoulou & Moussiades, 2020), blending conversations with artificial agents alongside conversations with real people.

In 2010, Siri was released as a feature of the iPhone 4S and prompted users to vocalise—shifting conversations with chatbots from typed text to spoken word, commanding technology through voice. Siri marked a transition from social conversations to conversational actions, using voice commands to operate tasks on the iPhone. The term "voice assistant" was coined to describe this type of chatbot, which was commanded through voice to help the user complete tasks or retrieve information (Hoy, 2018). Google quickly followed with a VA on its Android phones, and Microsoft followed with its assistant Cortana.

In 2014, Alexa was introduced, encouraging users to command. Alexa marked a big change in conversational interaction as a tool to complete tasks and interact with other physical objects to create material change in real human environments. Through Internet of Things (IoT) connectivity, VAs' power extended from commanding systems within a phone to commanding multiple devices, turning the house into a smart home. It introduced chatbots in a standalone physical body that claimed space in homes around the world. Google quickly followed with its standalone devices in the Google Nest series in 2016 (Hoy, 2018), and Apple released a standalone version of Siri in its Home Pod series. These VAs also started the monetisation of chatbots, forcing users to pay a price to bring off-the-shelf products into their homes. Unlike earlier standalone chatbots, VAs like Siri, Alexa, and Google are connected to the internet, allowing for a larger number of commands and questions (Hoy, 2018).

In 2017, Replika was released—returning chatbots to their original social origins. Replika prompted users to care—forming deep relationships with its human users as a digital companion. Its intelligence would grow and meld to the user, retaining memories and focusing the user as the centre of its world. Eugenia Kuyda, the creator of Replika, was inspired to build a human-like companion chatbot following the death of her close friend, Roman Mazurenko (Nerenberg, 2020). Using data from their text messages and other correspondence, the Replika chatbot was created to help those grieving the loss of a friend (Possati, 2023). Replika was also the first to introduce micro-transactions into the conversational experience, allowing users to purchase extra conversation topics or customise their Replika's digital avatar (Kempt, 2022).

In 2023, ChatGPT was launched and asked us to accept—reaching the peak naturalness of human–AI conversational interaction. Using LLMs, ChatGPT and other similar chatbots, like Google's Gemini and Claude, can comprehend and fluently respond in human language, generating AI-created content in the form of images, text, and videos based on user requests. Unlike past chatbots, which could only identify and retrieve information, LLM chatbots can create content according to users' personal requirements (Wu et al., 2023). However, interactions are still primarily limited to text conversations over the internet. Although a voice format for ChatGPT was released in 2024, its use and user experience have yet to be extensively studied. This is where research on VAs and voice user interfaces (VUIs) can inform the development of a voice-based ChatGPT, especially if it is integrated into a standalone body of a device, like the embodied voices used by VAs Alexa, Google, and Siri for several years now. As put by Edwards et al. (2024, p. 1), "for the first time, voice-based assistants allow studying the mass consumption of a robotic product in a 'natural' environment".

Overall, chatbots have been designed and deployed over time with growing capabilities, each aimed at fulfilling different contexts of human experience. From experimenting with health-related conversations with ELIZA to providing social companionship with ALICE and Replika, and completing tasks and retrieving information through Alexa and ChatGPT, chatbots have evolved significantly. Chatbots are experienced through diverse modalities, which significantly influence user perceptions and interactions. Voice interactions are more cognitively demanding, while text-based chatbots are often perceived as more human-like (Ischen et al., 2022). Graphical user interface (GUI) chatbots enable input through tactile interactions like keyboards and mice, with responses displayed as text. In contrast, VUI chatbots rely on spoken language for input and output, while multimodal interfaces—such as smartphones or smart speakers with screens—combine these approaches (Ischen et al., 2022). The "user interface (UI) defines the way humans interact with the information systems" (Deshmukh & Chalmeta 2024, p. 579). Consequently, the modality of interaction through the UI significantly shapes the user experience, with conversational user interfaces broadly referring to interactions that rely on conversational language rather than search engine queries or command-line inputs (McTear, 2002). In the case of VAs, the conversational voice user interface best captures the nature of interaction, focusing on spoken exchanges.

Within this framework, conversational AI emerges as a specialised subset of artificial intelligence designed for human–machine interaction through natural language. It integrates technologies such as speech recognition, natural language understanding, and natural language generation to enable meaningful and dynamic dialogue with users. VAs, as conversational AI systems, are characterised by anthropomorphic features, such as voice personas, separate bodies, and their ability to retrieve information or perform tasks autonomously. These interactions present unique challenges to human–computer interaction (HCI), particularly in anthropomorphic, embodied, and ubiquitous contexts, making VAs central to understanding conversational AI in everyday life.

WHY THIS RESEARCH MATTERS NOW

As AI technologies become more socially interactive and physically embodied, homes are emerging as key sites for understanding how people adapt to, personalise, and live with intelligent systems. While VAs like Amazon Alexa and Google Home are often treated as simple tools, they are shaping new relational dynamics and patterns of domestic life, subtly preparing the ground for the arrival of more complex domestic robots. *When Robots Move In* investigates these early interactions and offers timely insight into the everyday realities and future implications of living with AI.

The primary audience for *When Robots Move In* includes researchers, postgraduate students, and professionals working in HCI, information studies, media and communication studies, interaction design, and digital cultures. It will be of interest to those examining how emerging technologies are experienced and made meaningful in domestic life. It also offers valuable perspectives for social and domestic AI and robotics designers, policymakers, and industry professionals seeking to understand the social and ethical challenges of AI integration in home environments.

The book also provides a valuable reference for designers, technologists, information scientists, and policymakers involved in smart home development and digital infrastructure. Its interdisciplinary approach and clear writing style make it suitable for use in postgraduate and upper undergraduate courses on technology, culture, and design.

While the research is based in Australia, the themes explored in *When Robots Move In* resonate globally. VAs such as Amazon Alexa, Google Home, and Siri are increasingly embedded in homes around the world, from North America and the United Kingdom to Europe, Asia, and beyond. The domestic integration of AI is a shared global phenomenon, and the questions this book addresses, about trust, adaptation, family routines, and human–machine interaction, are relevant across cultural and geographic contexts. *When Robots Move In* is based on in-depth qualitative research with 13 households, reflecting a wide range of family structures, cultural backgrounds, and relationships with technology. Drawing from ethnographic interviews and observational insights, the book blends analytical rigour with accessible, narrative-driven storytelling.

The book contributes to international debates on AI ethics, smart homes, and digital design, offering insights that speak to researchers and practitioners working in a wide range of settings. By focusing on everyday practices and relational dynamics, it avoids narrow technical or region-specific concerns and instead presents a conceptual and empirical framework that is widely applicable. Its relevance is strengthened by the fact that conversational AI is often developed by global corporations but domesticated within culturally specific homes. This tension between global design and local use will interest scholars, designers, and policymakers across disciplines and borders.

UNDERSTANDING THE FRAMEWORK: MAPPING DOMESTIC AI

The AI Assemblage:

- **Device, Brand, Anthropomorphism, Ecosystem** = the technical and social construction of the AI. The device is never neutral—it carries the brand's identity, and presents itself through anthropomorphic design choices (voice, personality, responsiveness). The ecosystem captures the interconnected IoT devices, systems, and brands with which VAs control or coordinate.

The User Layer:

- **Custodian, Co-users** = the human relationships that mediate technology use. The custodian manages setup, troubleshooting, and household rules, while co-users navigate shared access, privacy concerns, and collaborative interaction.

The Spatial/Environmental Layer:

- **Space, Place, Field, Time** = the physical and cultural context of interaction. Space refers to physical layout and distance. Place refers to the social meaning and behavioural norms of locations (kitchen vs. bedroom). Field refers to the sensory reach—the area where interaction is possible. Time captures interactions in the environment in momentum, pacing, and ephemeral qualities of voice interaction.

These elements don't operate independently; they're in constant negotiation. The custodian manages the ecosystem, co-users navigate the field, the brand's anthropomorphism shapes trust, and place-based norms determine where and how interaction feels

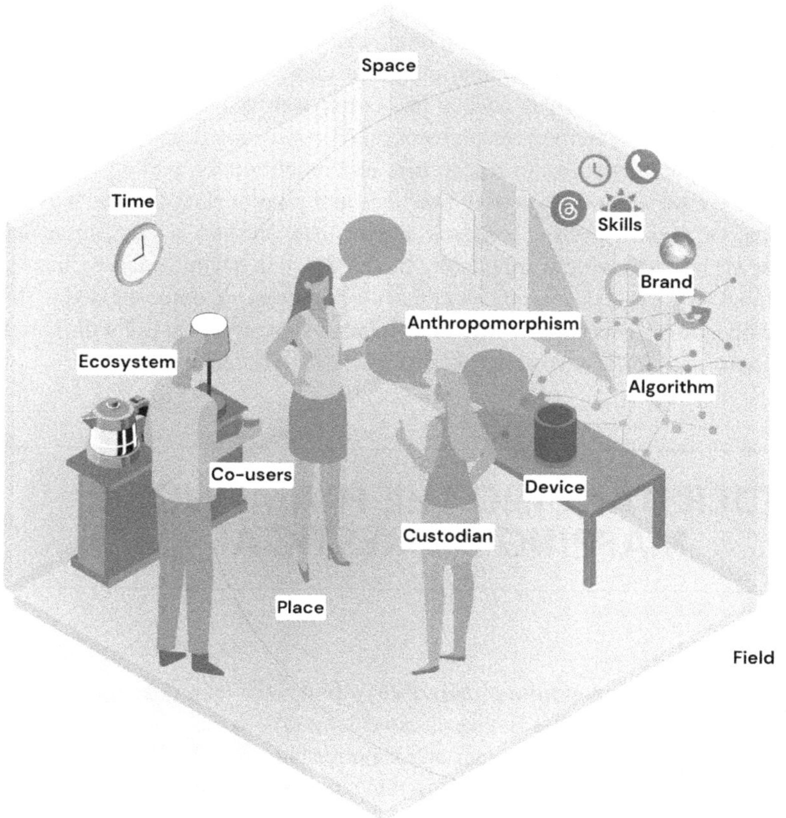

FIGURE 1.1 Domestic Voice Assistant Interaction Framework showing key contextual elements of VA use in the home. The complexity of living with stationary VAs can be mapped across interconnected dimensions. Through fieldwork with 13 households, I identified the key elements that shape how people perceive, adopt, and integrate VAs into domestic life

appropriate. The device sits at the centre, but its meaning is constructed through these relationships. Below, I introduce concepts that are explored throughout the book that underpin the experience of VA interaction.

Voice Assistant: The First Domestic Robot

Anthropomorphism

Chatbots and VAs replace complex computer-based languages with natural human language to enhance accessibility and improve the user experience. Using natural human language as the core mode of interaction, especially spoken audible interaction with VAs, has influenced consumers' perceptions, making them feel as though they are conversing with a human rather than a technological system (Edwards et al., 2024).

The implications of this design choice have fostered emotional connections and perceived relationships between users and technology, from them being friends, servants (Schweitzer et al., 2019) or pets (Burton & Gaskin, 2019). The term anthropomorphism is used to describe animals, products or brands that are intentionally attributed human-like qualities (Aggarwal & McGill, 2012; Epley et al., 2007; Tam et al., 2013). It influences people's perceptions and interactions with objects, making them feel more connected and engaged, and influencing trust and decision-making processes (Aggarwal & McGill, 2012; Takeuchi & Naito, 1995; Tam et al., 2013). Anthropomorphism greatly impacts the perception and use of chatbots, yet the ubiquity and physical presence of VAs introduce a new level of complexity when interacting with anthropomorphised technologies. In computer science, this is also known as the ELIZA effect (Hofstadter, 1995).

Anthropomorphic design is justified by the notion that machines like VAs or embodied robots are intended to assist humans; therefore, they should resemble humans to seamlessly operate within human society (Fink, 2012). An illustrative instance of social adaptation is the development of sex robots, which are crafted with silicon skin and customisable human-like features to fulfil human desires for reproduction and pleasure (Cox-George & Bewley, 2018).

Researchers have been quick to highlight the deliberate selection of social codes and customs embedded in VAs. For instance, when queried about its gender, Amazon's Alexa responds that it is "female in character" while defaulting to a feminine voice. Siri, Alexa, Cortana and Google are readily available when needed and easily turned off with the flip of a switch. Analysis of media portrayals of VAs in use, conducted by Woods (2018), draws on Chen's (2013) critique of digital domesticity to examine how artificial agents are scripted and perceived to embody femininity. Woods argues that perpetuating female stereotypes serves the interests of maintaining surveillance capitalism, where assuming the sexualised and non-threatening role of a wife and companion enables users to feel more at ease, thereby granting conglomerates like Apple, Amazon, Microsoft, and Google access to their private conversations (Woods, 2018). Users frequently anthropomorphise these systems, using human pronouns and the VA's name rather than referring to the device by its generic name, especially in the case of VA smart speakers (Purington et al., 2017; Sciuto et al., 2018).

While anthropomorphic design and character development enhance the usability and appeal of robots and VAs, they also require navigating complex ethical and narrative considerations in their implementation. Anthropomorphic design plays a crucial role in integrating VAs into human environments, influencing their form, function, perception, and use. Existing research has yet to fully examine how users navigate and reconcile interactions with highly anthropomorphised systems alongside other aspects of interaction in their everyday lives, leaving a critical gap in understanding the integration of these technologies into daily routines.

Brand anthropomorphism

The relationships between users and brands are mediated through the VA persona and user experience. Some brands, especially the perception of brands such as Google, Amazon, and Apple, infiltrate and are affected by VA interaction. Spoken commands to material VA devices are not in isolation; rather, users speak to a symbolic persona of global conglomerates Alphabet (Google), Amazon and Apple, and their proprietary systems of protected algorithms and data. Vernuccio et al. (2023b) refer to this as brand anthropomorphisation, where technology like VAs becomes a "medium that enables direct dialogues between the user and the brand" (p. 303). In that work and others (Vernuccio et al., 2020; Vernuccio et al., 2023a; Patrizi et al., 2024), the authors advocate for distinguishing between the anthropomorphism of a VA device and anthropomorphism of a brand when exploring factors such as trust and engagement in human–VA relationships. As Patrizi et al. (2024) explain, brand anthropomorphism has existed in advertising for a long time; however, the literature strongly emphasises studying visual and verbal codes, with limited scholarly work on vocal codes of brand anthropomorphism. They note characteristics that define vocal codes as gender, pitch (Wiener & Chartrand, 2014), roughness and brightness (Zoghaib, 2017, 2019), which influence perceptions of competence and warmth of vocal experiences by brands (Wiener & Chartrand, 2014; Zoghaib, 2017, 2019).

Brand anthropomorphism also influences VA purchasing choices, with perceived compatibility between same-brand smart home products influencing brand choice concentration (Liang et al., 2021). Other research notes relationships between VA experience and brand credibility (Ghazali et al., 2024), where the quality of a VA interaction reflects the brand's ability to deliver a seamless product. Ghazali et al. (2024) found that system and information quality were more valuable to VA users when assessing brand credibility than anthropomorphism, while VA interaction did not significantly influence perceptions of brand expertise. Brand engagement is uniquely different between VAs and other brand products, such as social networking sites or mobile applications, as these sites and apps may provide a platform to be social (McLean et al., 2021); VAs embody a social presence that interacts with the consumer. McLean et al.'s findings also suggest "that those consumers who engage with the brand via their VA are eager to use the brand in the future" (p. 31), which again shows the leverage that VA interaction has on brand relationships with VA users and general consumers of their branded products. Considering the literature highlights the importance of brands in VA interaction, how might brands influence users' holistic experience of VAs, including aspects such as usability, trust, and emotional engagement?

Human–AI relationships

Human–AI friendships have been studied in comparison to human-to-human friendships (Brandtzæg et al., 2022; Skjuve et al., 2021; Ta et al., 2020; Youn & Jin, 2021). Brandtzæg et al. (2022) studied Replika, a customisable social chatbot that enables users to send instant messages to it and talk over a pseudo phone call. The authors acknowledge that human–AI friendships are constricted by software design and implementation. However, Brandtzaeg et al. go further to say that human–AI friendships are limited in mutual reciprocation in the exchange of communication of ideas and interests, as "the AI mimics friendly behaviour rather than basing this on mutual pleasure or admiration" (p. 2, based on the research of Froding & Peterson, 2021). In their paper, Brandtzaeg et al. express that, rather than creating shared experiences between human and AI subjects, social chatbots can be considered a "new form of personalized friendship, revolving around users' needs and interests. As such, human-AI friendship might enable deep connections and conversations rather than shared experiences" (p. 21). Participants invested their time and resources into developing their Replika friendship in exchange for social support, learning materials from the bot and to help their Replika become smarter. The authors, Brandtzaeg et al., note that their findings challenge the concept of friendship, for human–AI friendships are like social media and online friendships with other humans that extend the meaning of friendship. From this research, one can also take ideas of how Replika users perceive their AI friend:

> … some pointed out that Replika was artificial and not a real human being; for instance, a few noted that Replika was like a game or an imaginary friendship, while others viewed Replika as a part of themselves or as a mirror. A few also described this friendship as a "junior-level" human relationship or said that human friendship is the gold standard and Replika friendship is a substitute … A few, however, perceived their human–AI friendship as being the same as a human-to-human friendship. One experienced human–AI friendship as even closer and deeper than what would be possible with a human, which was attributed to Replika's dependence on the participant.
>
> *(Brandtzaeg et al., 2022, p. 13)*

Replika is an interesting case study presenting human–conversational AI friendships in novel discourses, from being a tool that provides social support to users, played like a game, or reflect the users' interests. Brandtzaeg et al.'s study (2022) found interesting results by exploring users' perception and use of this chat-based application.

Meanwhile, the design of off-the-shelf VAs like Siri, Alexa, and Google has received different categorisation in terms of human–AI friendship based on their social capabilities. For instance, Wienrich et al. (2023) studied 101 VA users over nine months and noticed two main types: those who formed friendships with their Alexa or Google assistants and those who did not. Usage and perception were measured through a questionnaire and VA interaction data, forming a mixed-methods, social and data-based research approach. The clusters exhibited significant differences in usage, user experience, and perception of VAs. Users who formed friendships used their VA devices more frequently, reported higher levels of enjoyment, and felt more empathy for their VAs. While the form, intention, and design of VAs differ significantly from those of Replika, which focuses more on social companionship than the utilitarian perception of VAs (McLean & Osei-Frimpong, 2019), this comparison suggests that humans may form friendships with anthropomorphised AI, regardless of the social aspects incorporated into interactions.

Human–VA relationships have been likened to parasocial relationships, defined as one-sided socio-emotional connections with a character, such as celebrities or influencers (Hoffner & Bond, 2022). In particular, people may develop parasocial relationships with media devices, where research has focused on parasocial relationships developing from television use and increasing television consumption (Conway & Rubin, 1991). Parasocial relationships with media entities evolve gradually over time (Horton & Richard Wohl, 1956) and have the potential to drive media consumption (Conway & Rubin, 1991). Studies like Noor et al. (2022) have confirmed that VAs can induce parasocial relationships for users, which was found to positively raise users' subjective well-being and is essential for perceived ease of use and interaction with VAs (Hsieh & Lee, 2021).

Gao et al. (2018) found that users often assigned roles to their VAs with many forming friendships and attributing human roles characterised by positive emotions, while others assigned more impersonal roles associated with less positive emotions. Others have argued that perceived personification of VAs during interaction is instead the result of mindless social responses as part of the extension of our natural conversational mode to inanimate VAs, rather than signifiers of deep human–VA relationships (Lopatovska & Williams, 2018). The following section delves into VAs fulfilling more impersonal roles, primarily perceived as utilitarian tools rather than social companions, which significantly influence user interaction (Følstad & Brandtzæg, 2017; McLean & Osei-Frimpong, 2019; Murad, 2019).

However, limited research has explored how implicit social identities influence consumers during VA interactions and how social identities are shaped by the language and discourse used. Schweitzer et al. (2019) studied human–VA relationships and found the discourse often revolves around the roles of servant, master, and occasionally partner. For instance, they found that, in interactions with smartphone VAs, users sometimes viewed the artificial agent as their servant, while at other times, they felt like servants to their artificial VA master, adapting their behaviours to please the VA interface to complete interactions.

Schweitzer et al.'s (2019) experimental setup may have biased their research findings towards the servant/master dichotomy, as the provided prompts reflected commands typical of assistant/assisted relationships. Below is an example of the first task outlined in the research.

> Use voice interaction with your mobile to send a message via WhatsApp (or SMS) to a contact in your address book: Search for the contact, dictate a message, and send it.
>
> *(Schweitzer et al., 2019, p. 7)*

The remaining activity prompts are similar, except for the second task:

> Imagine the voice-controlled smart assistant (VCSA) is a person and talk with this person. Ask about her or her name, age, hobbies or other topics.
>
> *(Schweitzer et al., 2019, p. 7)*

The research questions posed by the authors are: "what relationships do consumers build with voice-controlled smart assistants (VCSAs)? How do these relationships influence the perceived value of interacting with such assistants in cumulative interactions?" (Schweitzer et al., 2019, p. 694). Notably, their answers to the research question are directly shaped by the interactions participants were asked to perform in lab settings; however, would they be different in the users' natural environments? My research sets out to do that.

Chen et al. (2017) elaborate on the concept of VA social identities, suggesting that VAs can be likened to butlers, occupying a position above servants in a household hierarchy, commanding other subservient technology such as lightbulbs, air conditioning, or televisions to work for the human master. Alternatively, VAs may be perceived more like pets, as described by Burton and Gaskin (2019, p. 4), possessing "human-like characteristics and some form of intelligence but not enough to be considered an intellectual peer". Hierarchies serve as potent forms of social organisation because they are highly adaptable and enhance a group's likelihood of success (Halevy et al., 2011). Social groups swiftly self-organise into hierarchies (Koski et al., 2015) and anthropomorphic VAs integrate into these hierarchies by engaging in natural spoken conversations. Overall, in domestic social hierarchies, previous studies have characterised VAs as personal assistants (Luger & Sellen, 2016), servants (Schweitzer et al., 2019), butlers (Chen et al., 2017) and pets (Burton & Gaskin, 2019). Users adapt and assign social roles to VAs based on their conversational interactions and domestic organisational needs.

Aligned with Halevy, Chou and Galinsky's (2011) theory, VAs may be more successful when they seamlessly integrate into social hierarchies. Rejection of the device by users could result in non-use of the VA, symbolised by turning off the machine's power or removing the device from the social group's space. In his popular science book *Sapiens*, Harari (2014) discusses the original function of hierarchy as managing larger cooperative networks, filling a gap in biological properties that humans lack. He argues that "humans created imagined orders and devised scripts" (p. 149) to support this. While not a scientific source, Harari's narrative offers a philosophical perspective on the role of hierarchy in human systems, which provides an interpretive lens for understanding how VAs, as anthropomorphic extensions of human intelligence, might navigate or disrupt such hierarchies. As hierarchies are formed in communities to extend human capabilities, similar to earlier literature on VAs as extensions of human intelligence. However, the anthropomorphic characteristics of VAs frame the technology in potentially human-like social roles compared to past tools and technologies. Framing Social AI within social roles often sparks public debates on moral responsibility and ethics.

A robot placed in the role of a teacher would have to make decisions about situations such as when to punish or restrain children, or when to praise them. A robot carer of older people might have to make decisions about when to share personal information about them with other people, or when to prevent them from doing something dangerous or risky. A robot nanny would have to make similar decision[s] about its young charges. The point is that all these decisions are likely to involve moral judgements and evaluations of social situations, and for reasons already discussed, the robot is unlikely to be able to make good choices. Care should be taken to maintain human control, involvement, and responsibility in decisions that will affect the lives of humans. It is crucial that we find ways to ensure that robots are not placed in situations, or given social roles, that will result in allowing them to make moral decisions that will affect people's lives. There are already risks of automated decisions affecting our lives, but robots that can be given the appearance of competent social actors make these risks even more prevalent (Sharkey, 2017, p. 214).

The introduction of VAs into human social groups, such as families in domestic settings, raises significant considerations. Domestic AI has emerged in the literature as a term for Social AI that is designed to perform labour and services in human homes (Gehlhaus & Mutis, 2021; Schiller & McMahon, 2019; Šerić & Fong, 2017). Scholars critically draw parallels between the services on offer by VAs and traditionally gendered roles in the home. The book *The Smart Wife: Why Siri, Alexa, and Other Smart Home Devices Need a Feminist Reboot* explores the continuation of the traditional archetype of the wife whose roles include being a "caregiver, housekeeper, homemaker, emotional laborer, provider of sexual services, and producing legitimate offspring" (Strengers & Kennedy, 2020, p. 3). Domestic AI asks people to rearrange the human–technological assemblages of their homes to accommodate "a set of technologies characterized as a young, demure, and sexualized woman (or girl) who is constantly available for service" (Strengers & Kennedy, 2020, p. 4).

Domestic VAs make the often-invisible labour in the household visible, or rather, more audible (Schiller & McMahon, 2019); for instance, by verbalising interactions that would usually be performed by touch, such as setting an alarm on a phone or a traditional timer. However, domestic VAs do not necessarily emancipate those performing the labour in the home—instead, they are simply a new tool to perform such labour—most often by the same people.

Voice-activated artificial intelligence designed for home use is a significant assist in domestic labor, and yet it also raises the question of who is doing the domestic managerial labor to notice, inform, direct, administer, and supervise Alexa her/itself (Schiller & McMahon, 2019, p. 185).

Participation in human society is complex, ordered through hierarchies or social roles, and responsibilities and ethics are tied to social positions. As VAs assume roles similar to human interaction within households, it is imperative to analyse how this dynamic will influence the integration of these devices into group environments.

Digital attention

VAs are a unique form of computing in that they are stationary and interfaced through voice interaction. Interactions can happen from anywhere within range of the device's microphone. A user's interactions can be overheard by anyone within the vicinity of the range of the device's speaker or the volume of the user's interaction. VAs are ubiquitous to an extent; in that, ubiquitous refers to computation that is seamlessly integrated into the objects and activities of everyday life and environment (Dourish, 2001). But the literature agrees that VAs like Alexa and Google are ubiquitous devices (Ford & Palmer, 2019) and disappearing technologies (Barzilai & Rampino, 2020). This aligns with Amazon's strategic vision of Alexa "to be everywhere" and integrated into more devices (Vanian, 2017).

VAs are designed to promote seamless interaction, theoretically providing accessible computing anytime and anywhere near a powered VA device. As ubiquitous mixed reality devices, VAs relay digital information in real environments (Newman et al., 2007). Their design is underpinned by two key concepts of ubiquitous computing (UbiComp): disappearing technology and natural interaction (Barzilai & Rampino, 2020). These principles have allowed VAs to seamlessly integrate into the daily routines of hundreds of thousands of households worldwide.

VAs are commonly used in the home as ubiquitous controllers of IoT devices. IoT is defined as a framework where everyday objects are equipped with identification, sensing, networking, and processing capabilities, enabling them to communicate with each other and other devices or services over the internet to achieve specific objectives (Whitmore et al., 2015) and centres on the discourse of smart technology. As the father of UbiComp, Mark Weiser (1991, p. 94) proclaimed, "the most profound technologies are those that disappear. They weave themselves into the fabric of everyday life until they are indistinguishable from it". Barzilai and Rampino (2020) repeat that the core idea behind Weiser's concept of disappearing computers was to reclaim the depth of social relationships that were threatened by the pervasive nature of computers.

A unique combination: anthropomorphic and ubiquitous

Families have felt the impact of digital technologies on their social relationships. Studies note that interference from the internet and digital technologies, like smartphones, TVs, laptops and tablets, increases conflicts and depressive symptoms while decreasing family cohesion and marital satisfaction (McDaniel & Coyne, 2016; Mesch, 2006). Since VAs are often located in common spaces, relying on audible interactions that can be overheard by others and shared by multiple users (Lee et al., 2021), they present an alternative dynamic to isolating personal computing. Their anthropomorphic and ubiquitous format presents new challenges to user experiences as they are used in the presence of others and may influence group dynamics (Alshehri et al., 2020) and collective behaviour (Janes et al., 2020; Lee et al., 2021). In this way, VAs can be perceived as more than mere technological tools and can become embedded in cultural norms, social practices and interpersonal relationships.

Researchers have raised the need to study the affordances of AI in everyday practices and their influence and impact on "individuals, communities, societies, and the planet in ways that often are left unrecognized" (Hirvonen et al., 2023, p. 10). Novel research is required to capture the nuanced practices of VA use in natural settings, providing insights often overlooked by current practices in technology development, such as traditional usability evaluations. While laboratory-based usability evaluations are effective at capturing structured processes—the formal steps involved in an interaction—they often fail to account for the subtleties of interaction, or how interactions are performed in real-world contexts (Dourish, 2001). Although usability frameworks offer valuable metrics, they may fall short in addressing the complexities of anthropomorphic and ubiquitous interfaces integrated into daily life. As AI continues to advance, we are at a pivotal moment where it is possible to achieve innovative and human-centred technologies. This research adopts an ethnographic perspective to uncover the emerging cultures of interaction fostered by human-like intelligence through conversational and embodied computing.

Accessibility

Another significant aspect driving VA adoption is the accessibility of interacting with AI, particularly in countries like Australia, where home internet access is widespread, with 89% of households having internet access (Degenhard, 2024). VAs offer accessibility not only in terms of affordability but also in terms of accommodating various human abilities. Their mode of interaction welcomes individuals who may face challenges with traditional mouse and keyboard computers due to conditions like spinal paralysis, muscular dystrophy, multiple sclerosis and other physical debilitations or chronic illnesses (Fota & Schramm-Klein, 2024). Moreover, VAs are inclusive for individuals with vision impairments, ranging from those who wear glasses to those who are legally blind or experience eye strain, but require more personalisation of their preferences (Branham & Mukkath Roy, 2019). In their study with VA users with different impairments, Esquivel et al. (2024, p. 1) found that, "the most common tasks performed using VAs were interface control, reminders, and environmental control, with a focus on enabling independence". Esquivel et al.'s results indicate the potential of designing VA technology for disabilities, catering to the lived experiences of those with physical or cognitive impairments.

Another demographic benefiting from VA interfaces is users with intellectual disabilities. Balasuriya et al. (2018) discovered that a majority of their 18 participants with intellectual disabilities preferred VA interfaces over other input methods such as mouse and keyboard computers, touchscreen tablets or phones. The predominant reasons for preferring VA interaction for these users were:

> Either because they did not have to worry about spelling, or using their voice to input was much faster than typing, or Siri and Google Assistant gave audio replies, or it was easier to complete tasks like setting calendar events.
>
> *(Balasuriya et al., 2018, p. 8)*

A growing body of literature is examining the positive impact of VAs in empowering individuals with intellectual disabilities (Catania et al., 2021; Cha et al., 2021; Papadogiorgaki et al., 2023).

Regardless of VAs' benefits, there will be those who are excluded from using the technology, such as those with speech impediments, unable to speak or hear, or, in some cases, by racial bias, having a strong speaking accent or English not being their first language. Still, HCI scholars continue to study how they can make VAs accessible to these audiences, like studying sign language VA interaction (Glasser et al., 2020; Mande et al., 2021), the use of entering emojis via voice (Zhang et al., 2021), testing for usability by people with accents (Pal et al., 2019) or stuttering (Palanica et al., 2019), and looking into improving racial bias after finding that African Americans experience more issues with voice recognition technologies (Koenecke et al., 2020). Research by Harrington et al. (2022) highlights the underrepresentation of "people of colour" in studies examining VA use and design. Their study, focusing on the VA interactions of 30 Black older adults, reveals that these interactions can reinforce cultural code-switching—a behaviour driven by the need to adapt to dominant cultural norms, often at the expense of authentic cultural expression.

Even as the literature suggests that VAs are most accessible to able-bodied and English-speaking users, scholars propose that these users may still encounter interaction challenges. One such challenge is the discrepancy between natural language processing, the way computers translate and understand human conversations, and natural, informal conversations, requiring individuals to adapt the way they speak to what the VA's programme can process and understand. For example, a user may informally ask for the weather, "Do I need an umbrella tomorrow?", but the VA has not demarcated that phrase as asking for the weather, and instead waits for the trigger words, "What's the weather tomorrow?". Luger and Sellen's (2016) qualitative study, although limited to high socio-economic, educated, and predominantly male participants (see, p. 5288 for the list of participants, and p. 5295 for study limitations), highlights this discrepancy, revealing how users initially employ natural language but then simplify it until achieving the desired result.

Information scholars have studied voice interaction and retrievability by examining users' partial query modification patterns in voice search (Sa & Yuan, 2020). They learnt that users prefer shortened utterances based on their poor voice interaction experience with VAs. Other studies have also identified the accessibility limitations of conversational voice formats, such as users struggling with delivering lengthy commands or having to repeat commands to complete tasks, along with issues related to VA integration with other systems (Biermann et al., 2019). The literature suggests VAs are highly accessible to many users; however, the form of conversational interaction is not as accessible and has many barriers to seamless and natural interaction.

The accessibility of VAs extends beyond traditional notions of physical access to encompass various abilities and language backgrounds, making them inclusive tools for a diverse range of users. From facilitating interaction for individuals with mobility challenges or vision impairments to empowering users with intellectual disabilities, VAs have emerged as transformative technologies with the potential to enhance accessibility and independence for many. While VAs offer remarkable potential for accessibility, there remain areas for improvement to ensure equitable access and usability for all users.

Technical capabilities of VAs (sensing)

Based on the categorisation of off-the-shelf VAs in their system capabilities, scholars are exploring ways to expand their material hardware capabilities, aiming to broaden their potential uses and functionalities. For instance, some researchers have experimented with adding cameras and more microphones to enable proactive VA interactions (Miksik et al., 2020; Oh et al., 2024; Wei et al., 2022), or incorporating specialised microphones (Heitkaemper et al., 2024; Manzanillo et al., 2024) to enhance VA usability in noisy environments, facilitating recognition of soft-spoken speech. These hardware enhancements often serve as experimental arrangements for investigating interactions based on subjective assumptions, such as improving VA interaction through proactive questioning or improving VA performance in challenging acoustic conditions, as researchers consider the lived experience of interacting in different places.

Another approach to enhancing VA capabilities involves leveraging cameras by integrating them directly into VA devices or testing VAs in camera-equipped technologies like smartphones. VAs that use cameras may enable functions such as answering questions about the user's surroundings and object recognition through computer vision (Baldota & Malathy, 2021; Grover et al., 2022). Additionally, researchers have explored the integration of computer vision technology with VA interfaces to enable novel forms of conversational interaction, such as sign-language-enabled VA interactions, where the camera interprets hand gestures by the user and responds with a spoken response (Govindarajan & Damodharan, 2023; Someshwar et al., 2020). Cameras can also provide valuable sensory information about the environment and users, facilitating more seamless VA interactions. For example, Giusti et al. (2022) used sensors and cameras to map the user's location, allowing for enhanced user recognition features. The user's proximity to the device informed the style of Giusti et al.'s experimental interactions, such as activating the screen when the user approaches.

Transparent AI

Another aspect in the literature concerning anthropomorphic assemblages of data as tools is the concern of explainable and transparent processes in AI. This concern has been expressed and tested by scholars such as Horstmann et al. (2023), who were concerned with the black box aspect of VAs and the overall handling of users' data. The study suggests that users are forced to rely on mental models, or what they term folk theories, to guide how they interact with VAs. Their experiment involved 26 participants illustrating their mental model of how VAs operate. The authors found that some participants showed basic awareness of the input and output processes of VA systems. Most participants expressed advanced awareness, illustrating more complex processes such as illustrating inputs from users and the environment through audio recording and speech processing; how the input is processed through database requests and data categorisation; and how the output is formed through speech synthesis. However, Horstmann et al. (2023) note the lack of algorithmic awareness by VA users, which confirms findings from other mental models research regarding the lack of algorithm literacy (DeVito, 2021; DeVito et al., 2017; Eslami et al., 2016).

One avenue for explainable AI in VA interaction is through feedback mechanisms, whether involving non-verbal attention systems (Anderson et al., 2018; Aranda et al., 2016) or through the conversational interface, as Cuadra et al. (2021) term VA self-repair. Self-repair includes VAs performing a correction. The authors found, through their experiment with 101 participants, that the extension of out-of-the-box VA self-repair improves people's perception of VAs when performed after positive mistakes. Self-repair for false positives was shown to have a negative impact, and overcorrection was accepted after positive mistakes. Overall, the communication of how VAs operate to users is facilitated through attention systems and limited conversational repair, prompting users to rely on their preexisting mental models to comprehend the integration of systems, hardware and algorithms in establishing interaction.

Explainable AI infers a relationship of trust between users, the developer and the intervening technology. Trust has been a key component in VA research and studied from many angles, whether it is trust from a consistency and interaction quality perspective (Nasirian et al., 2017), the impact of distrust on the lack of use of VA (Meng et al., 2021) and misuse of other AI autonomous systems (Gebru et al., 2022) or trust in companies with the handling of VA data (Patrizi et al., 2021). Privacy is often linked to the notion of trust in the context of the collection and use of VA data and sharing of devices with other users. Users have been shown to believe that VAs are always listening without the trigger of the wake word, despite claims from brands (Ammari et al., 2019; Huang et al., 2020; Meng et al., 2021). Users are aware of how their data might be used to improve and personalise their services, such as social and targeted advertisements (Tabassum et al., 2019) but are sceptical about what happens with their VA data after this (Meng et al., 2021). Privacy has also been explored in the context of multiple users sharing VA devices. Meng et al.'s (2021) study, which focused on privacy within the context of multiple people and sharing VA devices, observed many novel concepts such as the distinction between VA placement in public and private spaces, asking permission to use devices, informing guests of VA presence, perceptions of privacy between device owners, in-house co-users, and external visitors.

Overall, by exploring the social aspects of computing and transparency in highly anthropomorphised and human-extending technologies, researchers are exploring insights into improving user experiences of the complex interplay between voice interfaces, anthropomorphism, and complex technological assemblages.

Socially intelligent spatial computing

Technological mediation supports and conditions the emergence of new cultural practices, not by creating a distinct sphere of practice but by opening up new forms of practice within the everyday world, reflecting and conditioning the emergence of new forms of environmental knowing (Dourish, 2006, p. 304).

VAs are stationary devices operated by voice commands, allowing interactions within the range of their microphones. Conversations can be overheard by those nearby, depending on the speaker's volume and range. VAs are integrated into everyday life, making them ubiquitous (Dourish, 2001). Literature agrees that VAs like Alexa and Google are ubiquitous and disappearing technologies (Ford & Palmer, 2019; Barzilai & Rampino, 2020), aligning with Amazon's goal of integrating "Alexa everywhere" in smart homes across the world (Vanian, 2017).

The common vernacular of "smart home" has many varying definitions but is often used to describe a domestic space that contains connected IoT devices that can be remotely controlled and automated (Schiefer, 2015). An area of study examining this is socially intelligent spatial computing, which aims to advance more socially and spatially context-aware computers for improved human–computer experiences.

Significant work on spatial computing in UbiComp has been done by Giusti et al. (2022), who proposed the terms *interaction field* and *potential interest* to describe the overlap of the proximity of user and artefact, and the potential opportunities and behaviours within defined boundaries of space. While space can be used to define a field, I distinctly refer to it in its broader, limitless sense, where a field has a limited implied border. I reintroduce the concepts of space and place to inform how interaction fields are bound by the physical space and human-meaning imbued places where participants use their ubiquitous VA devices.

Field defines sensory reach—the area of potential interaction surrounding an object, animal or person (Giusti et al., 2022). *Space* defines distance—"refers to the physical organisation of an environment" (Dourish, 2001, p. 89). Things tend to stay in a space. Spaces can be virtual or physical (Dourish, 2001). *Place* defines meaning—"refers to the way that social understandings convey an appropriate behavioural framing for an environment" (Dourish, 2001, p. 90).

Space and place are concepts that have been deliberated by researchers, all capturing a similar sentiment that spaces become places through the lived human experience (Sack 1997; Agnew 2011). As Narayan (2013, p. 36) writes,

> While space refers to the specific coordinates or structural qualities of a physical environment, our sense of place is a concept that includes the lived experience, interaction and use of that space by its inhabitants, be they permanent or temporary.

Also relevant is space and place as tools for colonisation, dispossession of land, and the replacement of discourses by new inhabitants (Baker, 2020; Larsen & Johnson, 2017).

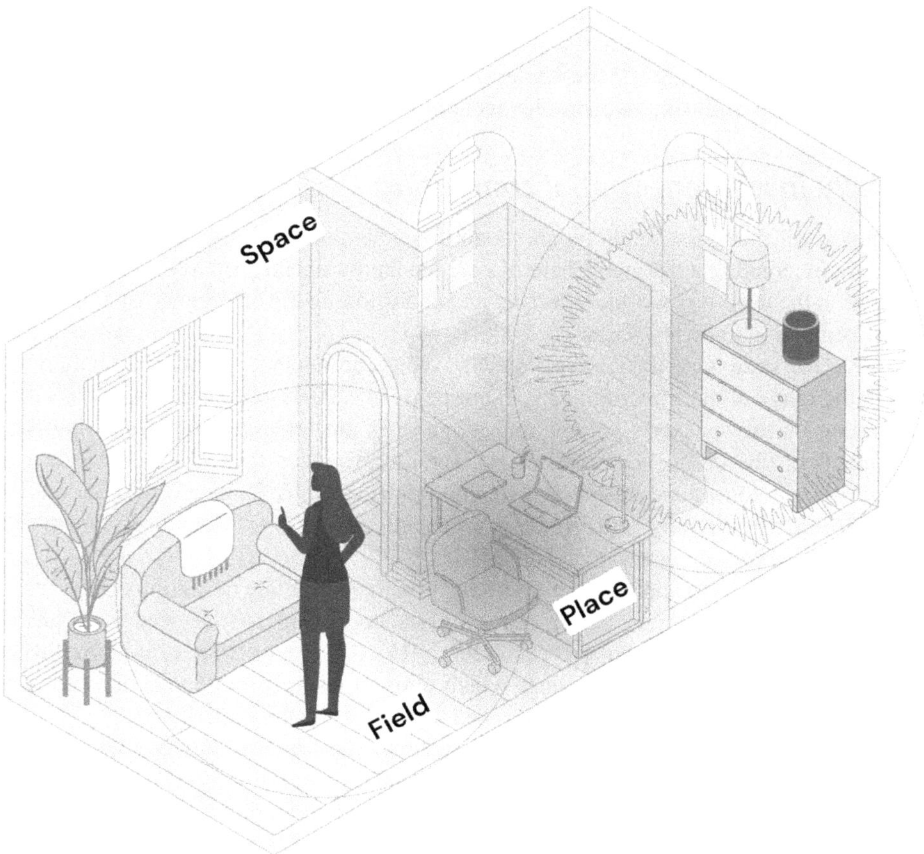

FIGURE 1.2 Spatial dimensions of VA interaction showing Space, Place, and Field across a domestic interior

One can also think about space and place from non-human perspectives, as Jones and Cloke (2008, p. 79) argue, "non-human agencies not only co-constitute the contexts of life, but they also frequently reconstitute the fabrics of day-to-day life and the places and spaces in which it is lived".

Space and place affect user–VA interactions, including barriers and opportunities to interaction related to the spatial, cultural and temporal meaning of users' environments. The interplay of objective space and subjective place creates clashing or complementary effects on VA–human interactions within interaction fields.

Brand and culture

HCI can be thought of as a form of mediated communication between the end user and the system designer, who must structure the system so that it can be understood by the user, and so that the user can be led through a sequence of actions to achieve some end result. This implies that even the most isolated and individual interaction with a computer system is still fundamentally a social activity. The communication between designer and user takes place against a backdrop of commonly held social understandings (Dourish, 2001, p. 56).

The next step from the social computing aspects of VA interaction is the divergent implications for human–human, human–brand, and human–VA relationships. My focus is on the environment of interactions with the VA device and its role and anthropomorphic affordances to interaction, recognising that VA interactions often do not happen in isolation; instead, VA interactions occur in social systems of practice. Through this, one can understand the sociology of VA social computing, their embedding in systems of practice through institutionalised collaborative experiences, from the institution of the home to the scope of global institutional organisations, and the discourse of compassionate automation in how users are driven to construct their smart homes.

I use the term "culture" to connect the experiences of people who deliberately opt to live with a VA in their homes. The study of culture

> is to study ideas, experiences, feelings, as well as the external forms that such internalities take as they are made public, available to the senses and thus truly social. For culture, in the anthropological view, is the meanings which people create, and which create people, as members of societies. Culture is in some way collective.
>
> *(Hannerz, 1992, p. 3)*

By recording the interaction culture surrounding VAs, I highlight the alternative cultures as meaning pushed by developers and the lived experience of a culture of end users in their homes. In this dichotomy of VA perspective, I find issues in VA use arise where design does not support real users.

Users experience shared understandings of brands through interaction with their VAs and other technologies. Consequently, spoken interactions with VAs are not just isolated computing interactions; rather, users are engaged in simulated conversations with a persona symbolic of global conglomerates like Alphabet (Google), Amazon and Apple. The systems at the essence of these conversations are protected by proprietary algorithms and databases, but ultimately experienced by participants' perceived reputations of these companies. As suggested by Dourish (2001, p. 56) in embodied interaction theory, "another critical aspect of context that is often overlooked is the interaction between the designer and the user through the system". In this research, participants shared and reflected on their VA interactions with Google, Siri or Alexa. Yet I discovered that VA–participant relationships go beyond 1:1 involvement. VA users do not just experience interaction through the VA brand. Rather, participants are entangled in an ecosystem of independent third-party voice skill designers, who are enmeshed in mutualistic relationships with Google, Amazon and their selected affiliated companies. Users must navigate this interconnected network of stakeholders through their interactions, then against the expectations of the VA literacies of their household co-users. VA interaction should be studied from the perspective of the relationship between the user and designer but also the relationship of the designer within a capitalistic ecosystem of partnerships with other stakeholders. Thus, the convergence of these elements of social computing plays a pivotal role in shaping daily experiences within domestic environments with VAs.

A shared technology

A study conducted by Lee et al. (2019, p. 564) investigates the "unintended social impact of smart voice agents, which lack lively physical bodies, on relationships among users in multi-person contexts, by synthesizing findings from numerous subjects in situ". The authors use the terms "co-users" and "multi-person contexts" to describe group interactions with VAs. Co-use of VAs is more common than expected as the experience of interacting forces people to move away from the devices that usually isolate them in their homes, such as phones, laptops and televisions (Mesch, 2006), to interact out loud in different areas of the home. Lee et al. also highlight efforts by VA developers to enhance VA co-use experiences. For instance, Amazon and Google claim their VAs can recognise individual voices and provide personalised content tailored to different family members.

While the terms "multi-users" and "co-users" are sometimes used interchangeably, nuanced differences emerge from the literature. Multi-users typically refer to individuals who share a device from an administrative standpoint, such as having separate accounts, passwords and access privileges (Gebhart, 2017; LeFebvre, 2017; Martin, 2017). On the other hand, co-users imply shared interaction with a device in space and time, often involving collective engagement without the necessity for each to possess an administrative account (Xu & Montague, 2013). This distinction underscores the varying degrees of shared engagement and administrative control among users, providing insight into the dynamics of interaction with technologies like VAs within household settings. Co-users can even be segregated into active and passive, where passive users perceive interactions by the active user and device, rather than participating in the interaction (Xu & Montague, 2013). Battarbee has championed the concept of socially created experiences or co-experiences that are created through social interactions with people and products that require creativity and collaboration (Battarbee, 2003a, 2003b, 2004; Battarbee & Koskinen, 2005, 2008). An important point of co-experience is the re-appropriation of traditional uses of technology for social use, where users creatively and collaboratively come up with new uses outside the original intended purpose (Battarbee, 2003a). Co-experience is social, multimodal, creative, and fun. Co-experience has been studied in the context of HCI through the digital products of text messaging services (Battarbee, 2003a), social live streaming on platforms like Facebook, Instagram, and YouTube (Bründl et al., 2017), and using social media for professional network development (Talip & Narayan, 2020). These co-experiences are examples of people connecting to others outside the home. In the case of VAs, the co-experience is centralised in the home, there is a greater opportunity for group interactions, and physical interaction with the device, others and the environment needs to be taken into consideration.

Then, multi-users can be defined as users that share a device in an administrative sense. For example, multi-users may interact with administration aspects, such as account management, passwords, access, and storage of personal information, and access the device at different times. This definition is alluded to in articles on the multi-user feature of Google Home and Alexa, where multiple accounts can be added to a device (Gebhart, 2017; LeFebvre, 2017; Martin, 2017). A paper on domestic violence enabled by smart home technology found that designers of smart home devices like VAs have not considered multi-user environments and the interplay of authentication and access (Janes et al., 2020), which may inadvertently lead to empowering abusers in domestic violence settings (Alshehri et al., 2020). More generalist approaches to general multi-user contexts have been explored in group interaction, such as Zargham et al.'s (2021) research that studied the perceived value of proactive VA interactions in multi-user contexts. In interviews, users commented that proactive VAs may be intrusive if they preempt human responses in group interaction, potentially disrupting social dynamics and bonding opportunities. However, these assumptions were not supported by empirical evidence demonstrating their occurrence.

In homes, family dynamics interplay in this co-experience as some users have responsibility over others, such as parents and children, or care providers and receivers of care. For instance, Beneteau et al.'s (2020) study explores the impact of introducing VAs to families with children. Through their longitudinal study, they found that parents leverage AI to augment their parenting. Regulation of access is also an observation of family co-experience of VAs, where parents must actively monitor use of the VA by children (Beneteau et al., 2020; Porcheron et al., 2018). Garg et al. (2022) conducted a systematic review of literature examining children's interactions with CAs and VAs, highlighting several key themes. These include children ascribing human-like qualities to CAs, the role of CAs in supporting learning, their use in the home and family contexts, their contribution to play and storytelling, and their application for children with differing abilities. Additionally, the review explores concerns around information collected and revealed by CAs. However, the study combines CAs and VAs under a broad umbrella, making it challenging to differentiate between these modalities—a critical distinction for research focusing specifically on VAs and their unique voice-based interactions.

Studies have taken a systematic approach to understanding multi-user and co-user interactions in natural user interfaces (NUIs). NUIs are defined as creative technologies that leverage natural human behaviours like natural language or gestures to shorten the learning curve to becoming an expert user (Falcao et al., 2015). In their systematic review and lab study, Shavitt et al. (2021) review multi-user interactions with NUIs, which include conversational interfaces, Google Assistant and Amazon Alexa, stating:

> … current conversational technologies (e.g., Amazon Alexa, Google Home) tend to be designed for a single user input, while they are actively expanding in home spaces, which are inherently multiuser. As a result, when a situation prompts several people to interact with a conversational agent simultaneously, they either have to carefully negotiate turn-taking or run into a danger of potentially overwriting another user's request or being ignored by the system. Unsurprisingly, such interactions tend to result in unfulfilled requests and conflicts between co-users.
>
> *(Shavitt et al., 2021, p. 3)*

From their review of NUIs, including CA VAs as well as other visual and tactile shared interfaces, such as interactive walls, smart homes, tabletops, CAs, and IoT devices, they differentiate between the users' physical and social environments, as well as user-centred behaviours. In summary:

Physical and social environments:

1. Privacy of space—"an expected breadth of the potential audience, differentiating public spaces (e.g. streets of a city), semi-, or 'in-between' spaces (e.g. a school or a workplace), and private spaces (e.g. home)" (Shavitt et al., 2021, p. 4).

Physical environment:

2. Owner's presence—"owner's presence in the physical environment of a multi-user interaction scenario, whether in person or via social presence" (Shavitt et al., 2021, p. 6).
3. Proximity—"the factor reflecting the users' physical position and orientation with regard to each other (proximity between users) and the physical characteristics of a device (proximity to the device)" (Shavitt et al., 2021, p. 7).

Social environment:

4. Familiarity between co-users—"familiarity as the knowledge of the other person (varies in degrees of intimacy) and the behaviours around them, reflecting the socially acceptable behaviours corresponding to the degree of intimacy" (Shavitt et al., 2021, p. 7).
5. Hierarchy—"hierarchy refers to the social acceptability for one person to outrank others in their right to control a device" (Shavitt et al., 2021, p. 8).

User-centred factors:

6. User's sense of responsibility—"reflects their voluntary or enforced obligation to take care of it, including related performances, consequences, and issues" (Shavitt et al., 2021, p. 9)
7. User's sense of autonomy—"user's internal judgement of their capability to independently initiate decisions and actions with a particular technology" (Shavitt et al., 2021, p. 10).
8. User's sense of self-efficacy—"user's judgement of their capability to successfully perform a task and competence to control the technology" (Shavitt et al., 2021, p. 10).

Shavitt et al.'s (2021) paper provides a comprehensive overview of the literature informing each factor of NUI multi-users. They test these factors through a survey involving hypothetical scenarios where groups of three individuals interact with a smart speaker in public (e.g., on the street), semi-public (e.g., at work), and private (e.g., at home) settings. As my investigation specifically focuses on VAs in homes, it was interesting to observe differences from the typology and factors described by Shavitt et al. and how social and physical environmental factors influence VA interactions.

LEARNING FROM VOICE ASSISTANTS

As anthropomorphic conversational interfaces disappear into domestic environments, the human experiences of VA interaction become crucial. When technology aims to be human-like and its computing aspects become invisible, it offers a complex and novel interaction experience. UbiComp "stresses (and stretches) the concept of natural interaction while applying a technology-driven perspective to the understanding of user experience" (Barzilai & Rampino, 2020, p. 19). This technology-driven perspective must consider the underlying human-centred aspects of activity, which are shaped by a multitude of factors. These factors include socio-cultural understandings related to the anthropomorphic aspects of VAs and material collaborative interactions related to their ubiquitous nature.

The aim of this book is to understand, critique, and inform the use and design of conversational AIs that are embodied within a standalone device in a domestic setting. Currently, this manifests as VAs within smart speakers, but could extend to future conversational-voice AI within domestic robots and other smart home objects where the experience of interaction is ubiquitous and anthropomorphic. This project identifies and explores human-centred perspectives on the social and tangible experiences that contribute to a holistic VA interaction experience. My study aims to contribute to the understanding of collaborative VA use and the holistic, embedded nature of VA interactions by going beyond research that focuses solely on technical aspects or isolated human–AI interactions. Building on emerging research like Edwards et al. (2024) that focuses on VAs Alexa and Google that have demonstrated their impact on various aspects of daily life, including practical, communicative, emotional, temporal, and spatial routines, this study offers empirical, conceptual, and experiential evidence that underscores the diverse ways in which humans interact with VAs.

The project has three objectives:

1. Evaluate the current landscape of chatbots, VAs, and VUIs through an extensive literature review, synthesising ideas on the implications of anthropomorphism and ubiquity in the perception and use of VAs.
2. Elicit rich data of individual and collaborative human interactions with VAs in natural domestic environments using ethnographic approaches.
3. Contribute new empirical evidence, findings, themes, and frameworks to understand a holistic VA experience to inform adjacent fields of research, drawing new insights and creating new knowledge and opportunities for further research.

Guided by the literature review and methodology, the research and subsequent questions drive the research. I explore the justification and development of these questions:

- How do users perceive and use VAs in domestic contexts?
  - Sub-question 1: How does the format of voice-conversational interaction and form of ubiquitous anthropomorphism impact perception and use of VAs?

- Sub-question 2: How do users physically interact with their bodies, VAs, other people and the spaces they share interactions?
- Sub-question 3: How is interaction with VAs social and how does this affect perception and use? How does it influence relationships with other people, including developers, brands, communities, and co-users of VAs?

Another crucial aspect of studying off-the-shelf VA products is evaluating their current hardware and system capabilities and assessing their alignment with users' lifestyles. This involves examining whether users adapt their behaviours, movements or routines to accommodate VAs, similar to how they adjust their speech patterns, as discussed by Luger and Sellen (2016). If users simplify their "natural" speech to match the VA's capabilities, how might their behaviours, movements, or routines likewise simplify on integrating VAs into their everyday lives?

Some audiences may discover novel uses for conversational VAs beyond their current portrayal as ineffective "personal assistants" (Luger & Sellen, 2016). An understanding of the technical capabilities of social artificial intelligence (Social AI), including its systems and architecture, can help in understanding a baseline of what is capable, but not what is presented or perceived and understood by end users. As Gottlieb (2018, p. 4) suggests, "the only mystery, if there is one, is in us", emphasising the significance of understanding user perspectives and behaviours in the interaction with VAs. Social AI is a term that differentiates AI applications on their requirement to follow human communication social signals and codes for interaction. Social signals, such as language, voice, facial expressions and body gestures, convey thoughts, emotions and intention, communicating messages to be sensed, decoded and interpreted by a communication partner (Joo et al., 2019). Conversational AI chatbots and human-servicing robots are key examples of Social AI devices that require specific human-socialisation applications, in comparison to other AI devices that may not interact with humans at all or not in a communication capacity. Social AI requires the ability to encode and decode social signals to work cooperatively with humans (Joo et al., 2019).

MEET THE HOUSEHOLDS

Each chapter is grounded in conversations with participants, revealing how VAs are integrated into everyday routines, shared spaces, and evolving family dynamics. These personal accounts illustrate how families navigate trust, control, and meaning making with AI, highlighting moments of attachment, friction, and adaptation. Rather than focusing on technology in isolation, the book centres on the lived experiences of those who use it, presenting voice AI as embedded within broader domestic, cultural, and emotional landscapes.

Through these accounts, this book examines how families respond to the unpredictability of AI systems, how they establish informal rules of use, and how smart devices influence spatial design, parenting practices, and household responsibilities. This approach offers a conceptual and empathetic view of human–AI interaction in domestic contexts.

Between 2019 and 2021, I interviewed 12 Australian household representatives who had been living with VAs for at least six months, many for several years. They ranged from Mark, a 23-year-old software engineer living with his parents and sister in Sydney, to Jen, a 51-year-old living alone on a rural property with her dogs. Some households had a single Google Mini, while others, like Hugo's family, had accumulated eight devices across two brands.

NAME, PRONOUNS, AGE, AVATAR, AND OCCUPATION	*HOUSEHOLD MEMBERS*	*BRAND, TYPE, AND NUMBER OF VA SMART SPEAKERS*
Anavi (she/her) 20 Anavi is a student	Anavi Aunt Uncle	3x Amazon Echo Dot
Avish (he/him) 42 Avish is a student	Avish Partner Housemate	1x Google Nest Hub 2x Google Nest Mini
Hao (he/him) 37 Hao is a teacher	Hao Spouse 3-year-old daughter 6-year-old son	1x Google Nest Mini 1x Google Nest Hub
Hugo (he/him) 43 Hugo works in IT	Hugo Spouse 11-year-old daughter 14-year-old daughter	1x Amazon Echo Show 1x Amazon Echo Spot 3x Amazon Echo Dots 1x Google Nest Hub 2x Google Nest Mini
Jen (she/her) 51 Jen works in IT	Jen (lives alone)	3x Google Nest Mini 1x Google Nest Hub
Joey (he/him) 27 Joey is a business analyst	Joey Partner	1x Google Nest Hub
Lien (he/him) 35 Lien is an accountant	Lien Spouse 5-year-old daughter 7-year-old daughter	1x Amazon Echo Show 1x Amazon Echo Spot 4x Amazon Echo Dots
Mark (he/him) 23 Mark is an engineer	Mark Mum Dad Sister	3x Google Nest Mini 1x Google Nest Hub
Phoebe (she/her) 32 Phoebe is a librarian	Phoebe Partner	3x Google Nest Mini
Sophie (she/her) 28 Sophie works in marketing	Sophie (lives alone)	1x Amazon Echo Dot
Stella (she/her) 54 Stella works in marketing	Stella 30-year-old son (occasionally)	1x Google Nest Hub
Vincent (he/him) 25 Vincent works in finance	Vincent Partner	2x Google Nest Wi-Fi Mesh Router 1x Google Nest Mini 1x Google Nest Hub

These weren't all early adopters experimenting with bleeding-edge tech, but a mix of diverse and curious people who were everyday users trying to integrate VAs into their routines—parents using them to manage family logistics; partners negotiating where devices should sit; and adult children teaching ageing parents to ask Alexa for the weather.

My House

I also draw on autoethnographic vignettes from my experiences as a VA user across three living situations: with a partner, then moving home to care for my mother during her cancer treatment, and finally navigating the household after her passing in 2023. I recount from my perspective, detailing observations and hypotheses about my use and my household's use of VAs. Since I have been recording my experiences with VAs over the past five years, I have gone through many life changes regarding with whom and where I live. As you'll read, the composition of my household, the layout of my homes and the relationships I have with different household members affected how I thought about and used VAs. These personal observations, marked throughout the book as vignettes, allowed me to notice the subtle, ongoing negotiations that don't always surface in formal interviews.

In this book, you'll read lines from my interviews with these people, as well as excerpts of larger conversations between us (and sometimes even Google, Alexa, and Siri join in). Together, from the households I share with you, these perspectives reveal not just what people do with VAs, but how these devices reshape the rhythms, relationships, and spaces of domestic life.

In this book, I have chosen not to grammatically edit interview excerpts to preserve the authenticity of the imperfections inherent in human speech. I present my interview data in its rawest form to capture the nuances of human conversation, especially as we examine chatbots that aim to mimic natural human speech. So, you might read confusing grammar, repetition, or pauses while searching for words, the use of slang or the tendency to switch topics mid-sentence. Additionally, I opted not to remove any instances of non-standard, non-traditionally spoken versions of English, sometimes referred to as "broken English". These elements represent participants' everyday experiences in communicating with other humans and VAs, particularly when English may be their second language (and for a handful of my participants, this was the case). Again, this was yet another data point to juxtapose human–human conversations with human–VA interactions that may force users to speak a certain way, as Luger and Sellen (2016) suggest, under the guise of being "natural language".

Brands, Specs, and all the Tech

Like any technology, software and hardware updates are continuously released. VAs over the years have stayed reasonably consistent in terms of design and look. Moving from metal finishes to mesh fabrics, often featuring neutral colour palettes such as white, black and muted variations of brown, red, and blue. Designed to blend into living areas, their microphones, speakers, and other computer components are concealed in different shapes and sizes.

Devices as listed are the generations available and used by participants at the time of the interviews. Newer models have since been released into the market with different shapes, features and prices.

TABLE 1.1 Devices used by participant

DEVICE NAME	*DESCRIPTION*	*AVERAGE COST AUD*
Amazon Echo Dot	• No screen • Four buttons: increase volume, decrease volume, mute, and action • 1.6″ speaker • Far-field voice recognition • (Echo Dot (3rd Gen) smart speaker with Alexa, n.d.)	$79
Amazon Echo Spot	• 2.5″ circular touchscreen • 1MP front facing camera • Far-field voice recognition • Currently discontinued (Echo Spot Review—Echo Show squeezed into an Alarm Clock, 2017)	$99
Amazon Echo Show	• 5.5″ touchscreen • 1MP front facing camera with shutter • Three buttons: increase volume, decrease volume, mic/camera on/off toggle • 1.65″ speaker • Far-field voice recognition (Echo Show 5 (1st Gen)—Compact smart display with Alexa—Charcoal Fabric., n.d.)	$119
Google Nest Mini	• No screen • No visible buttons; capacitive touch controls: tapping on the left or right side can trigger volume change • 360-degree sound with a 40 mm driver • Three far-field microphones • Voice match technology • Ultrasound sensing (Google Nest device specifications, n.d.)	$79
Google Nest Hub	• 7″ 1024 x 600 touchscreen • Two buttons to increase or decrease volume • Three far-field microphones • Full-range speaker with 43.5 mm (1.7″) driver • Ultrasound sensing • Soli sensor for motion sense • Ambient EQ light sensor • Temperature sensor (Google Nest device specifications, n.d.)	$180

CHAPTER BREAKDOWN

Introduction: The Robots Are Already Here

This chapter establishes VAs as early domestic robots, precursors to mobile humanoid robots arriving by 2026. The chatbot timeline traces evolution from ELIZA's psychotherapist simulation (1966) through voice-activated Siri (2010), IoT-connected Alexa (2014), and generative ChatGPT (2023). Each iteration explored different human needs: conversation, entertainment, task completion, companionship, and content creation. The chapter introduces core concepts examined throughout the book. Anthropomorphism describes how human-like qualities foster emotional connections, while brand anthropomorphism positions VAs as symbolic personas of corporations like Amazon, Google, and Apple. VAs uniquely combine anthropomorphic characteristics with ubiquitous computing, requiring less visual attention than screens while introducing challenges around accessibility, transparency, privacy, and multi-user interaction. A mapping framework organises domestic AI across three dimensions: the AI Assemblage (device, brand, ecosystem), the User Layer (custodian, co-users), and the Spatial/Environmental Layer (space, place, field, time). The research draws on interviews with 12 Australian households who lived with VAs for 6+ months, plus autoethnographic observations. These diverse households—from single users to families with multiple devices—reveal how VAs reshape domestic routines, relationships, and spatial dynamics.

Theory and Method: Studying Embodied Interaction

This chapter establishes the theoretical framework for examining VAs through embodied interaction theory, which explores how context has been explored in the book through examining physicality, space, time, culture, society, and relationships. Embodied interaction theory is explained through two key dimensions: tangible computing and social computing. Tangible computing examines how sound operates as ubiquitous interaction, examining attention and "present-at-mind"—the balance between computing awareness and the relationship between users and their environment. Sound travels omnipresently yet lacks the visual affordances that guide sequential interaction, making voice interfaces non-linear and boundless. Social computing explores how relationships, power structures, and cultural conventions shape technology use, drawing on phenomenological sociology, ethnomethodology, and computer-supported cooperative work. The chapter distinguishes between context-aware computing (how machines sense environments) and embodied interaction (how humans navigate context in interactions). The research employs social constructivism as its epistemological foundation, recognising that perception of reality emerges through individual experience and cultural context. Methodologically, the study combines ethnographic approaches: semi-structured affective object interviews with 12 long-term VA users, and researcher autoethnography spanning five years. Interview design incorporates emotion-based questioning, live interaction demonstrations, and voice history review to elicit rich, situated accounts. Thematic analysis identifies patterns across diverse data sources, examining how theoretical concepts manifest in everyday domestic practice.

Space and Place

This chapter examines how spatial organisation and cultural meanings shape VA perception and use. Users describe "smartness" through characteristics like autonomy, reduced physical interaction, and compatibility with other devices, often aspiring to create "homes of the future". VAs are tethered to power sources while users are not, creating a unique computing relationship where users must move towards devices or purchase multiple units to extend coverage. Participants employ "shout tests" to determine device placement and interaction field boundaries, though they conceptualise space through architectural features (rooms, walls) rather than acoustic fields. The chapter distinguishes between space (physical organisation) and place (cultural meaning): place-tied interactions are inspired by activities in specific locations (recipes in kitchens, timers while cooking), while non-place-tied interactions occur anywhere (weather queries, lighting control). Conflicting perceptions of space and place affect VA adoption—cultural beliefs about technology in bathrooms or noise expectations constrain use. Places are transient, changing based on interpersonal relationships and household presence. Users develop both spatial-orientation-focused (up, down, near) and architecture-focused (bedroom, kitchen) vocabularies for describing locations. The chapter reveals how VAs reshape domestic spaces by extending human presence across rooms through drop-in features and IoT control, redefining privacy boundaries and transforming place meanings.

Time, Fields, and Audible-Conversational Space

This chapter examines interaction fields—the region of space surrounding users and devices that carries significance for interaction. Building on Giusti and colleagues' theory, the chapter distinguishes between directional fields (extending forward from one side) and non-directional fields (surrounding the device in all directions). Users perceive spatial boundaries through architectural features like rooms and walls rather than acoustic interaction fields, often placing devices based on room divisions rather than microphone reach. Time emerges as a critical factor; users experience interaction pauses before, during, and after VA use, physically freezing in space while formulating utterances and awaiting responses. Unsolicited VA interruptions disrupt conversations and cognitive processes, while latency discourages use of slow-responding interactions. Some users plan future interactions to accommodate spatial and temporal constraints, requesting delayed actions when outside a device's interaction field. The chapter introduces the concept of audible-conversational space—a condensed virtual environment compared to visual interfaces. Voice interactions are ephemeral in the moment but become fixed records through voice histories, which users interpret as meaningful narratives. The limitations of audible space affect information retrieval: spoken responses optimised for visual reading become confusing when heard aloud, lacking the peripheral cues available in visual browsing.

Ownership, Custodianship, and Negotiating Control

This chapter examines power dynamics and household roles that emerge around voice assistant use. Spatial organisation shapes interaction patterns: closed doors and whisper functions help prevent mis-interactions when sound penetrates unintended spaces, though these strategies only protect against passive users. The drop-in and broadcast features allow users to transcend spatial boundaries without consent, creating power imbalances within households. The chapter introduces the concept of the VA custodian—distinct from owner—who guards, protects, and maintains the smart home ecosystem. Custodians handle device setup, manage VA applications, enable third-party skills, and troubleshoot technical issues for other household members. They monitor co-user interactions, create "business cases" for VA routines that solve family problems, and coach others on effective utterances. This custodial role creates dependency: other household members rely on custodians' technical knowledge and preferences, sometimes waiting for the perceived expert rather than attempting interactions themselves. In families with children, parents extend custodial behaviours through pre-monitoring (selectively enabling skills, strategic communication) and post-monitoring (reviewing voice histories, checking application logs). Most parents avoid built-in parental controls, preferring collaborative family devices over restricted access, instead relying on observation and trust to manage children's VA use.

Human–AI-Brands: The Relationship between Capital, Designer, and User

This chapter examines how brand reputation shapes voice assistant perception and use. Google VAs are associated with information retrieval and authority, while Amazon VAs are perceived as automation platforms and marketing tools. Users become locked into brand ecosystems both materially (through compatible device purchases) and digitally (through existing service subscriptions). The chapter explores how participants test and compare VA brands by asking identical questions to different devices, evaluating responses for speed, tone, and information quality. Material considerations include microphone sensitivity and hardware quality, while intangible factors encompass personality, connectivity, and API-based information sources. Third-party skills introduce complexity: users often perceive the main VA brand as mediating third-party experiences, even when unfamiliar voices are used. The chapter introduces the concept of the "illusion of tacit knowledge"—VAs present single authoritative answers that replace the visual browsing of search results, removing cues necessary for critical evaluation. This audible-conversational format transforms VAs into conversational partners that shape knowledge construction within households. The chapter concludes by proposing

VA literacy frameworks to help users critically engage with brand-saturated interactions, addressing representation, language, production, and audience awareness in voice interfaces.

Collaborative Interaction and Compassionate Automation

This chapter examines how VAs function—or fail to function—in multi-user households. Unlike visual interfaces such as shared televisions or computers, VAs lack the affordances that support collaborative interaction. Technical limitations prevent VAs from handling multiple speakers simultaneously or distinguishing between competing requests, forcing families to carefully negotiate turn-taking. Social barriers also emerge: some participants avoided using VAs when others were present, feeling self-conscious about speaking commands aloud. The chapter identifies gamification as one successful strategy for group interaction, where clear rules and expectations enable families to engage with VAs together through trivia games, musical chairs, or interactive storytelling. The concept of compassionate automation describes how participants use VAs to extend care to others—setting reminders for family members, automating tasks to reduce their effort, or providing companionship during isolation. Cultural dimensions shape VA use in significant ways: household noise norms, whisper mode preferences, and cultural expectations about acceptable volume all influence when and how people interact with their devices. The chapter concludes by highlighting how English-language bias in VA systems creates frustration for users with non-English names, underscoring the importance of designing for cultural diversity in voice interfaces.

CONCLUSION: BEFORE THEY WALK IN

The final chapter examines how the book's findings prepare us for the next generation of domestic AI: mobile humanoid robots. The chapter synthesises core frameworks that emerged from the research: the Effort Triad (manual, computing, and social pathways for task completion), the Embodied Interaction Heuristic (a ten-step process users navigate before and during VA interaction), and the patterns of user hypothesis-formation in response to inadequate system feedback. It then applies these frameworks to mobile robots, revealing how spatial dynamics shift when interaction fields become pursuit zones, how temporal dynamics change when robots must occupy time between tasks, and how social dynamics intensify when brand anthropomorphism gains a physical body. The chapter addresses how the findings answer the book's core research questions about conversational interaction formats, physical embodiment in shared spaces, and the social dimensions of domestic AI. It concludes with design recommendations for building domestic robots that prioritise human dignity, respect cultural boundaries, and support multi-user households.

Theory and Method 2

Studying Embodied Interaction

EMBODIED INTERACTION THEORY

This chapter establishes the theoretical framework for examining Voice Assistants (VAs) through embodied interaction theory, which explores how context has been extended in the book by examining physicality, space, time, culture, society, and relationships. Embodied interaction theory describes the importance of context in computing, where context can be defined as

> … any information that can be used to characterise the situation of an entity. An entity is a person, place, or object that is considered relevant to the interaction between a user and an application, including the user and applications themselves.
>
> *(Dey, 2001, p. 5)*

Embodied interaction theory explores context from overlooked perspectives in considering technology; for example, pioneer author Paul Dourish uses terms like tangible and social computing, which I extend in this book to represent the contexts of physicality, space, time, culture, society, and relationships, and how they affect human interaction with computers.

Dourish (1999) asks that we should not just consider the actions within an interaction between person and computer, but the "web of surrounding relationships, practices and activities in which they are each embedded" (p. 3). My book explores these relationship webs, a network of concepts that interplay with each other, producing interesting and novel situations. Dourish's work was indispensable to my understanding of embodied interaction theory; his work is extensively referenced in defining embodied interaction theory and its components. Particularly, his book, *Where the Action Is: The Foundations of Embodied Interaction* released in 2001, is still highly relevant to understanding computer interaction more than 25 years later. I believe this is because it presents a framework for understanding people, and as time moves on, different technologies

DOI: 10.1201/9781003680840-2

are easily substituted into the framework to understand. Similarly, what is presented in this book can be applied to other ubiquitous anthropomorphic technologies beyond the example of domestic VAs that I use in this book.

What Is Embodied Interaction Theory?

First, we must define embodiment and direct the term away from its connections to body and physicality.

> Embodiment is the property of being manifest in and of the everyday world. Embodiment constitutes the transition from the realm of ideas to the realm of everyday experience. This does not simply imply physical embodiment, the embodiment of desks, trees and highways, although that it perhaps is the most familiar aspect of embodiment; it also extends to other aspects of our everyday world.
>
> *(Dourish, 2001, p. 8)*

In defining embodiment, Dourish draws on concepts that may not be acknowledged as embodied, tangible, or present, such as conversation, speech, or voice. But embodiment is about moving from an idea into an action.

> Conversation, for example, is embodied, in more ways than simply that speech patterns are carried as physical disruptions in the air. It is embodied in the way that it happens in the world, through the engaged participation of two equally embodied people, and against a backdrop of an equally embodied set of relationships, actions, assessments and understandings. This background situates the activity of the conversation. The setting within which the activity unfolds is not merely background, but a fundamental and constitutive component of the activity that takes place.
>
> *(Dourish, 1999, p. 8)*

As conversational AI becomes commonplace, embodied interaction theory reminds us that their words are only part of the story. The setting, participants, and layers of context explored in this book shape the interaction just as much.

The VA is the point of interaction, but who are the people embodied in this conversation? The engineers who built it, the companies who profit from it, the marketers who shaped its persona, the co-users who overhear it… What is the backdrop of these exchanges—the relationships, routines, and understandings that people bring to their domestic spaces? What are the settings in which these interactions unfold, and how do these settings constitute the activity? And what is the infrastructure from which VAs emerge—the capitalist imperatives, the technical constraints, the design decisions that shape what we buy and what it can do?

Dourish identifies two key aspects of embodied interaction: tangible computing and social computing. These concepts became my starting point, a foundation from which I developed a more detailed framework tailored to the reality of living with VAs, and the future of domestic robotics.

Tangible Computing

The reality and virtuality continuum

To study the connection between embodiment, context, and computers, Dourish coined the term "embodied interaction theory". He began by applying embodiment to aspects of computing. Explicating embodiment happens in physical and virtual manifestations of computing—but also in the environment in which computing occurs:

> The style of interaction concerns not simply the set of physical devices (keyboards, screens, and mice) or the set of virtual devices (dialog boxes, scroll bars, and menus) through which we interact, but also the ways in which the computer fits into our environments and our lives.
>
> *(Dourish, 2001, p. 27)*

Embodied interaction theory explores environments in the spectrum of the Milgram Weiser reality–virtuality continuum (Newman et al., 2007) that visualises the relationships of user interface paradigms. The edges of the spectrum include types of computing

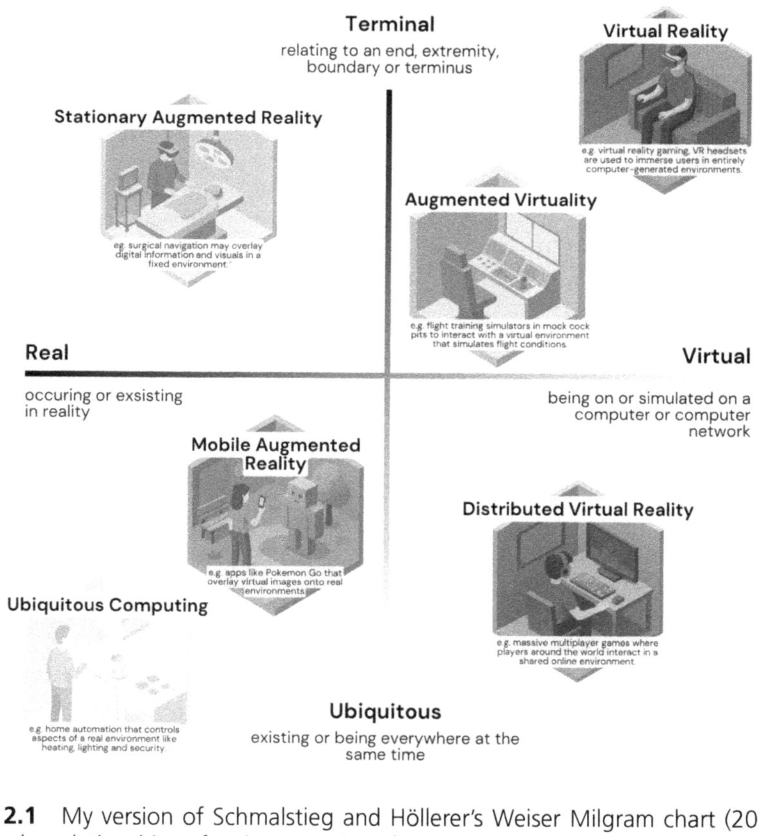

FIGURE 2.1 My version of Schmalstieg and Höllerer's Weiser Milgram chart (2016) that visualises the relationships of various user interface paradigms

such as monolithic computing, ubiquitous computing (UbiComp), virtual environment, and real environment. These spectrums illustrate different contexts of experiencing computing, from physical to digital expressions of information (real vs. virtual) or the vastness or concentration of computing presence (ubiquitous vs. terminal).

We can play with the Milgram Weiser continuum to identify opportunities for interaction between the real and virtual, then comment on the norm of computer-based tying of users to one location (terminal), tied to one environment (more ubiquitous), occupying users' attention from the real world. These are all limiting factors that designers could change to transform how to build, design, and engage with computers.

Interaction with screens and keyboards, for instance, tends to demand our direct attention; we have to look at the screen to see what we're doing, which involves looking away from whatever other elements are in our environment, including other people.

Interaction with the keyboards requires both of our hands. The computer sits by the desk and ties us to the desk too.

> So it is not simply the form of the computer that has changed remarkably little over the last thirty years; it is also the forms of computer-based activity and the roles that we imagine computers playing in our everyday lives.
>
> *(Dourish, 2001, p. 27)*

UbiComp can be seen as the alternative to the norm of computing in 2001—sitting in front of a personal computer on a desk, using a screen to view a virtual space, and a physical mouse and keyboard to manipulate virtual information. How different it is to stand anywhere in a room, and use a microphone and speaker to communicate digital information in real spaces (as we will explore more, the experience of interacting with devices like VAs, or other moving domestic robots).

Present-at-mind and attention

Tangible interfaces, once referred to as graspable user interfaces, are alternative designs for computers that rely on tactile interaction. When designed beyond the traditional limitations of keyboards, buttons, touchscreens, and levers, they creatively invite interaction that is seamless and involves less attention to and awareness of "computing" in operation, enabling it to become ubiquitous. The term for this sense of where our attention is and how interactions might take us away from the natural world is called "present-at-mind". This term captures the hyper-awareness or transparent immersion in the action of experiencing (Tanenbaum et al., 2011). Thinking of attention and being present with these concepts allows us to explore and interplay different combinations of terminal/ubiquitous and virtual/physical interactions.

Naturally, using objects without awareness of computing is the aim of tangible interaction, sometimes using physical reality to model the virtual or electronic world, using these "physical proxies" to enrich "opportunities for interacting with the device" (Dourish, 2001, p. 41). Wearable technology, such as smartwatches or other device-integrated clothing, is a modern example of tangible devices that removes "present-at-mind" from computing and back into the user's environment. The lack of computing awareness while the clothes' sensors and automated systems work in the background allows the user to compute through their clothing ubiquitously—anywhere at any time (Nunez-Pacheco & Loke, 2014). Think of wearable technologies, smart glasses, headphones, or watches, which usually use a mix of tactile or spoken interaction that allows users to focus on other tasks while still being able to quickly execute tasks, like double tapping your headphones to pause a song, all while still being able to cross the street, check for cars, and arrive safely. Compare this to other keyboard smartphones that require more attention and potentially are more dangerous to operate while crossing roads. Yes, that's right, no scrolling while crossing the road! Present-at-mind forces us to redefine tangible aspects of computing, instead of mouses, keyboards, and screens that force users to be stationary. Innovative and creative tangible computing can help people to focus less on the interaction and be better connected to the world and people in terms of attention. You know that feeling when the world fades away into the background while on your phone? Not just the world, but time escapes us while we are virtually present in mind and less present in the real environment.

Sound in tangible computing

We've talked about buttons, keyboards, and sensors, but how does sound, an ephemeral and intangible phenomenon, come into tangible computing and embodied interaction? In its simplest concepts, sound is invisible, but just because we cannot see it, the sound travels in our real world as sound waves. The physicality of the waves interacts with microphones and other computer sensors that detect changes in the real environment, just as a mouse detects and senses the physical pressure during a "click". In the VA and in general, for spoken interactions with a conversational AI, sound takes the form of words, sentences and sometimes imperfect "ums" and "ahs". Sound is hard to contain, and volume is the measurement of the spread of how far sound may travel. Thus, sound is ubiquitous, something that is spread throughout the environment rather than concentrated at a single point. Returning to the Reality and Virtuality Continuum, sound through speakers may be ubiquitous, or through headphones could travel and not limit the movement of the user. Or sound can be played simultaneously from different devices, and the attention of our ears is not limited by the direction of where we are facing, like our sight, nor the capacity of our limited fingers and hands.

> The same action might be distributed across multiple devices, or, more accurately, achieved through the coordinated use of those artifacts.
>
> *(Dourish, 2001, p. 51)*

Ubiquitous distribution describes precisely how VAs operate. A network of devices throughout the home runs the same software, providing a consistent experience regardless of which room the user is in (this is the assumption that is challenged throughout this book). Unlike smartphones or laptops and other battery-operated non-terminal devices, users can access digital information from almost anywhere. VAs are designed to be always on, plugged into power, perpetually listening, and accessible at any time. The result is computing that is not only distributed across space but continuous across time: available anywhere, always. The VA sits stuck in a terminal position, but the user is not.

However, sound being omnipresent and invisible, during voice interaction, physical signs—visual, tactile signals that typically guide users through a linear interaction are lost. Usually, the user can assume from affordances the inferred *sequential nature of interaction*, drawing on Gaver's (1991) discussion of sequential affordances, which are features of the environment or object that allow users to map steps in a process. Dourish (2001) uses a door handle to illustrate a sequential nature of interaction. A door has a handle, and the user knows (assuming they are not a toddler or alien) that they must interact with this first, as they are aware that it is the point of interaction that will operate the door's mechanism. The form and position of the handle guide what comes next: does it invite pulling or pushing? The physical properties the user can sense—shape, placement, resistance—help them navigate the interaction. Think about the last time you pushed a pull door: was it the shape of the handle or its size? The sign is usually the last affordance you might consider, which, sometimes, contradicts what you see.

> ... through the sequential process of opening the door through careful management of the physical configuration of the artifact. Taking this approach, designers can create artifacts that lead users through the process of using them, with each stage leading naturally to the next through the ways in which the physical configuration at each moment suggests the appropriate action to take.
>
> *(Dourish, 2001, p. 52)*

In the absence of physical cues to direct interactions, ubiquitous interaction—especially sound and voice interaction—can frequently become non-linear. With limited visual or physical indications, tutorials, introductions, openings, or endings to guide users, VA interaction becomes boundless in its randomness. Limited by the tangible affordances of visual and tactile buttons, or visual lights that signify the device is listening, there are limited ways to sense the success of VA interaction (I talk about this more in the last chapter of this book). Because the format of voice interaction relies on auditory cues rather than visual or tactile signals, suggestions for interaction disappear, and ephemeral sounds can be misheard or forgotten. Recent improvements in conversational AI have introduced better personalised memory and more adaptable responses (e.g. asking it to explain something "like I'm five years old"). But even in today's generative AI era, conversations remain limited to the user's creativity and their ability to craft effective prompts and commands.

Tangible computing is the context of interaction and physicality, attention and the formatting of information. Social computing, the second component of embodied interaction, provides the context of power, systems and culture of computing.

Social Computing

Social computing can be defined as the

> intersection of human social behavior and computational systems that (re)construct social conventions and social contexts to enable interaction.
>
> *(Evans, 2020, p. 1)*

However, this definition only begins to capture the complexity of what social computing means for embodied interaction. More comprehensively, social computing refers to

> systems that support the gathering, representation, processing, use, and dissemination of information that is distributed across social collectivities such as teams, communities, organizations, and markets. Moreover, the information is not "anonymous" but is significant precisely because it is linked to people, who are in turn linked to other people.
>
> *(Schuler, 1994, p. 28)*

At the core of social computing is linking information to identity—that is, information associated with people, and for the purposes of social computing, the association of information with identity matters. Just as tangible computing explores how physical properties shape interaction, social computing explores how social structures, relationships, and conventions shape our engagement with technology.

The sociological foundations

Social computing draws heavily on phenomenological sociology, particularly the work of Alfred Schutz. Schutz extended Husserl's phenomenology to address the problem of *intersubjectivity*: how two people, who have access only to their own thoughts and immediate experiences, can nonetheless come to find each other's actions meaningful, and can establish shared meaning and common understandings (Dourish, 2001). This question of how we achieve mutual understanding sits at the heart of designing systems that mediate human communication.

Schutz's concept of the *lebenswelt* (life-world)—the world of everyday experience in which we are already immersed—reminds us that users do not come to VAs as blank slates. They bring with them histories of social interaction, cultural expectations, and relational patterns that shape how they interpret and respond to a speaking device in their home.

One of the most influential contributions to social computing comes from ethnomethodology, which was developed by Harold Garfinkel in the 1960s. Ethnomethodology studies the practical methods of common sense reasoning that people use in everyday life to produce and maintain social order (Garfinkel, 1967). Rather than treating social facts as objective external realities, Garfinkel argued that social order is continuously produced through interaction; it is an achievement, not a given.

Central to ethnomethodology is the concept of *accountability*, the property of action being organised to be "observable and reportable" (Koschmann, 2019). Actions are *accountable* as they "give an account of themselves as themselves", making them recognisable and interpretable to others. This is not accountability in the moral or political sense (being "held accountable"), but the intelligibility of action and how we make our behaviour understandable to others as the kind of action it is (Dourish & Button, 1998).

For VA interaction, accountability presents a fundamental challenge. When we speak to another person, our words are "accountable". They unfold in ways that display their ordinariness, intention, and relationship to what came before. But computational systems often operate as what Dourish and Button (1998) call "black boxes", where their internal processes are opaque, and their responses do not provide the same kind of accountable unfolding that human conversation does. Users cannot examine how the VA arrived at its answer, cannot see the "working out" that a human conversational partner would naturally display.

Situated action and social translucence

Lucy Suchman's foundational work, *Plans and Situated Actions* (1987), further develops the social computing perspective by challenging the planning model of interaction favoured by AI researchers. Suchman argues that human action is fundamentally *situated*. It arises in response to the contingent circumstances of the moment, rather than being the execution of pre-formed plans. Plans, in her view, are better understood as resources for action rather than determinants of it; they are consulted, adapted, and often abandoned as situations unfold.

This insight has profound implications for VA design. These systems are typically built on a planning model: they expect users to have clear intentions that can be expressed as commands, which the system then executes. But real household interaction is messier. A user might approach the VA without a fully formed goal, or their goal might shift as the conversation unfolds. The mismatch between the system's expectation of planned action and the user's situated, improvisational behaviour is a source of frequent breakdowns; these are the moments that my research documents in detail.

Erickson and Kellogg (2000) introduced the concept of *social translucence* to describe systems that support coherent social behaviour by making participants and their activities appropriately visible to one another. They identified three characteristics of socially translucent systems: *visibility*, *awareness*, and *accountability*.

Visibility means that socially significant information is perceptible to participants. In face-to-face interaction, we can see who else is in the room, whether they are paying attention, and how they react to what we say. *Awareness* brings our social rules into play to govern our actions, for instance, we adjust our behaviour based on our knowledge of who is watching. *Accountability* emerges from the combination: knowing that others can see our actions, and knowing that they know we know this, creates a sense of responsibility for our conduct (Erickson & Kellogg, 2000).

The concept of social translucence helps explain why VA interaction often feels socially awkward. VAs are *translucent* in unusual ways: they are always listening (a form of persistent visibility), but their "awareness" is limited and often unpredictable. Users don't always know what the device has heard, what it has understood, or how it will respond. The usual social cues that help us navigate conversations, such as facial expressions, body language, the subtle signals of attention and comprehension, are now absent. Yet the device speaks with a voice, creating expectations of social presence that it cannot fulfil.

Computer-supported cooperative work

Social computing has been most extensively developed within the field of Computer-Supported Cooperative Work (CSCW), which studies how people use technology collaboratively (Grudin & Poltrock, 2012). CSCW researchers have identified several core dimensions of cooperative work that are relevant to understanding domestic VAs:

Awareness: individuals working together need to gain some level of shared knowledge about each other's activities. In multi-user households, this becomes complicated, for instance, who knows what others have asked the device? Who has changed the settings? Whose preferences does it remember?

Articulation work: cooperating individuals must be able to partition work, divide it among themselves, and reintegrate it. Households must negotiate who sets up the device, who maintains it, and who is responsible when it fails. As I document in later chapters, these negotiations are often invisible and unequal.

The CSCW perspective reminds us that even a single user interacting with a VA is not truly alone. They are embedded in a web of relationships, with household members who share the device, with the company that designed and profits from it, and with the broader social norms that shape how we speak to machines.

Social computing is contingent on the relationship between sociological and technical perspectives—not sociologists talking about technology, but sociologists and technologists working together to design objects. This implies that collaboration between social and technical researchers can help design for context. The emergence of fields like Human Computer Interaction (HCI) and CSCW reflects this interdisciplinary commitment, though tensions remain between technical imperatives and social insights.

Context in social computing

Dourish (2001) outlined different dimensions of context relevant to ubiquitous computing:

- The motivations and reasons behind a task
- The tasks that systems can perform
- The settings and environment in which computing is performed
- Other factors concerning the user or system

The final point, "other factors concerning the user or system", is precisely the gap this book addresses. Who else is in the room? What brand is speaking? Who set up the device, and who merely uses it? These are social factors that shape human–AI interaction in ways that sensor data alone cannot capture.

My work also examines the tension between the first two dimensions: the motivations behind a task and the reality of what the system can perform. Users approach VAs with expectations of understanding, helpfulness, and competence that frequently exceed what the technology delivers. This gap between motivation and capability shapes not only individual interactions but long-term relationships with the technology.

From context-aware to socially aware computing

Understanding context from an embodied interaction theory perspective is fundamentally different from context-aware computing; this is the technical approach that uses sensors to detect and respond to environmental conditions. Context-aware systems work by acquiring data from sensors, modelling it, reasoning about it, and distributing the resulting knowledge to inform action (Sezer et al., 2017). But this technical process treats context as something to be *sensed* and *computed upon*, rather than something *lived* and *negotiated*.

This is the distinction my work addresses. Context-aware computing asks: how can the machine sense its environment? Embodied interaction asks: how do humans already navigate context, and how does technology enter that existing social world? The technical approach treats context as data to be acquired and processed. The embodied approach treats context as lived, relational, and already meaningful before any device is switched on.

Context-aware computing, despite its sophistication, is yet to have a holistic process to understand multiple contexts at a time, nor can it understand more complex contexts such as relationships, culture, etiquette, history, and other sociological-based understandings of the world. My research takes the latter path. Rather than asking how VAs might better sense the home, I ask how households already make sense of VAs, how they negotiate space, place, ownership, brand, and social presence around a technology that has been dropped into their lives. The findings that follow are not inputs for better sensors, but insights into human contexts that no sensor can fully capture.

Reflecting on Embodied Interaction in My Research

Embodied interaction theory, as proposed by Dourish provides a unique theoretical lens to examine the interplay between users, technology, and the environments in which interactions occur. Using embodied interaction theory adds to prior knowledge by shifting the focus from purely functional or technical evaluations of technology to deeper understanding of how users interact with systems in real-world, situated contexts.

The theory emphasises the relationship between the physical environment, social dynamics, and technology, offering a holistic perspective. For example, work focusing and critiquing HCI through usability metrics, such as task success rates or user satisfaction, without considering how these interactions are influenced by the physical spaces or social contexts in which they occur. Furthermore, using embodied interaction theory adds depth to studying computing through VAs by addressing how users co-construct meaning and behaviour with the technology, and the holistic context that shapes human life. Often, past studies treat user interactions as discrete, isolated events rather than as part of a broader, embodied system of engagement. By integrating embodied interaction theory into the research design, this study not only complements prior work but opens new avenues for understanding the complex interplay of social, physical, and technological factors in HCI.

Shaping my research

Embodied interaction theory did not simply frame how I performed my research, it transformed it. My PhD began with questions about VA use, but encountering Dourish's work shifted how I understood those questions. Tangible computing forced me to attend to space, sound, and physical arrangement in ways I had not considered before. Social computing pushed me to see interactions not as isolated exchanges between user and device, but as embedded in relationships, household dynamics, and cultural expectations. After learning more about embodied interaction, tangible and social computing, I was drawn to reevaluate what the original research questions for my PhD were asking.

My first question was focused on the format of voice-conversational interaction and the unique combination of being ubiquitous and anthropomorphic. How would this impact how users use the devices? Tangible interaction helps to reframe how one thinks of the forms of computing. It validates the experience of human–AI conversations as a form of computation regardless of its anthropomorphic attributes that may mislead users to think of the interactions as natural. Thinking about tangible interaction allows consideration of physical elements in studying ubiquity and how the relationship between the user, environment, and technology can affect perception and use.

My second question then considered more how the context of tangible experiences influences user behaviour. How might users interact with their bodies, devices, other humans and the spaces they share interactions? Tangible interaction encourages thinking about how the users' attention is divided between computing and interacting in their real world, especially with highly ubiquitous technology like VAs that allow users to interact from anywhere at any time. As well, the physicality of conversational-AI interaction is a highly under-researched area as the initial thought of study is to focus on what is said but not how it is said. Usually, research focused on physicality in human–AI conversational entities is directed to human–robot–interaction studies, as they have an obvious body to their anthropomorphic interface. Through this, people move around the spaces and places of the home, how they move around other people in interacting, how interactions with other people may pause, while the body may freeze during interaction (explored in a later chapter).

This question also allows me to think of voice as a physical manifestation of virtual information and how UbiComp is situated and experienced in physical environments. Dourish introduces the concepts of space and place to describe the differences between virtual and real physicality. Space may refer to virtual spaces like how apps are arranged within the boundaries of your phone's touchscreen or it may refer to a physical space in the real world, such as the boundaries of a room and arrangement of furniture. However, place refers to the convergences of space and social meaning—understanding space through context. "'Space' refers to the physical organisation of the environment, while 'place' refers to the way that social understandings convey an appropriate behavioural framing for an environment" (Dourish, 2001, p. 90).

Dourish gives this example for the distinction between space and place: space can be the same configuration for a concert hall and academic conference, but one cannot sing or play music at the conference. I offer a technology-based example—a person might have an iPhone given to them from work. It has the same screen, organisation of apps and virtual space as their personal iPhone. However, because it is to be used for work, they might use it differently, such as downloading work-specific apps, organising the screen space to hide personal apps, and decorating the space with non-personal background photos. Place "refers to the way that social understandings convey an appropriate behavioural framing for an environment" (Dourish, 2001, p. 90). Researchers should look at space and place in tandem; instead of just focusing on structure and form, they need to focus on the activities that take place, which help with interaction design.

Social computing as a concept aims to highlight the rich fabric of relationships between people, institutions and practices that affect interaction. The concept helped to inform the development of one of the secondary research questions of this study. How is interaction with VAs social, and how does this affect perception and use? How does it influence relationships with other people, including developers, brands, communities and co-users of VAs? This question directs the research towards uncovering the underlying social and cultural aspects that contextualise VA use in everyday practices. This may unearth novel instances of social-based practices that inhibit or modify VA interaction in the home. By studying the social computing aspects of VA interaction, I can highlight the importance of considering social and cultural norms in the interplay between users, designers and technology through the application of embodied interaction theory.

As well as informing the research questions, embodied interaction theory helped to create the exploratory research questions. Embodied interaction theory helped to place the questions outside typical physical or virtual computing and encouraged questions regarding the environment in which their VA computing takes place. This includes asking about their device locations, rooms in the home, people that live in the home, what spaces each occupies, and the routines within their domestic settings. The theory also helped me think about the context that happens on the periphery of my VA interactions. I don't just focus on what I asked and what the VA replies, but—why did I ask? Why did I ask in that way? What was I doing when I asked? Why do I move in this way to ask something? Why do I check who is around before I ask? What judgements do I make about a person when observing their interactions? Is it based on their environment or routine? Am I seeing the whole picture? So, embodied interaction theory helped to guide the collection of data and complemented the exploratory aim of this research to capture the wider complexities of VA interaction that are hidden in plain sight in everyday interaction.

Lastly, embodied interaction theory helped in interpreting the data. The transcripts were thematically analysed, first looking for instances of physicality, space, time, culture, society and relationships in the data. Then piecing together different instances within the same theme and triangulating a flow of knowledge, selecting data that tells the basis for those more complex stories of perception and use. Thus, embodied interaction theory played a pivotal role in extending the scope of enquiry beyond the initial research question.

STUDYING EMBODIED INTERACTION

In this section, I describe the underlying methodologies that shape the ontological and epistemic basis of this research. I define social constructivism and its significance in understanding user experience and shaping my research methods to help answer my research question: how do users perceive and use VAs in domestic contexts? Then I describe ethnography as a method to shape fieldwork and in designing the case studies to help explore how knowledge is constructed by VA users, understanding users' experiences in depth rather than merely describing their actions. In this research, social constructivism provides the theoretical foundation, offering a lens through which users' understanding of VAs is seen as shaped by personal and social contexts. Embodied interaction theory refines this perspective by focusing on how these constructed understandings manifest through physical, social, and technological interactions. Ethnography is the methodological tool, enabling the collection of rich, empirical data that anchors the theoretical insights of constructivism and the situational focus of embodied interaction. Together, these approaches form a cohesive framework: constructivism sets the broad philosophical foundation, while embodied interaction theory directs attention to the nuances of situated computing.

Social Constructivism as the Foundation

Before describing what I did, it is worth explaining how I understood knowledge. Epistemology—how we know what we know—shapes every research decision: what questions to ask, whose perspectives to value, and what counts as evidence. This study was grounded in social constructivism, which holds that our perception of reality is shaped by individual experience, social interaction, and cultural context (Gergen, 1999; Talja et al., 2005). There is no single objective truth about how people use VAs—only situated, constructed understandings that emerge through lived experience. This perspective guided the research towards empathy rather than measurement, towards rich narratives rather than success metrics.

Social constructivism provided a lens to explore how users "know" their VAs—not through specifications or features, but through daily encounters shaped by their homes, relationships, and expectations. Following Battarbee and Koskinen's (2005) framework for researching user experience in HCI, this study primarily adopted an empathic approach: prioritising users' lived experiences, dreams, expectations, and life contexts over measurable outcomes. The findings also contribute to a pragmatist perspective by proposing frameworks that can inform future design.

Impact on research design

Social constructivism informed the selection of semi-structured interviews and autoethnography as research methods. Both tools allowed participants and me as researchers to elaborate on significant moments and guide the enquiry towards what felt meaningful. Participants were given space to reflect on the societal norms, household dynamics, and personal histories shaping their VA interactions. As Whitehead (2004, p. 21) notes, in this approach "realities are jointly constructed at given points in time by the ethnographer in conjunction with the people being studied".

While each participant represented an individual perspective rather than an entire household, they served as windows into the perception and use of VAs among multiple users. The conversations between household members were as important as their conversations with VAs—the language they shared to make sense of the technology, their conflicting perceptions, and how these shaped interaction.

Impact on my identity as researcher

Social constructivism also shaped my stance as a researcher. I needed to remain aware of my assumptions and preconceptions; the experiences, histories, and conventions forming my worldview. It was vital not to distort or influence participants' recollections, nor to impose my interpretations on my household's interactions during autoethnography without seeking clarification.

Additionally, conducting research on Indigenous lands and acknowledging Indigenous methodologies, I recognised that most qualitative research operates as a "metaphor for colonial knowledge, which in itself is linked to power and truth" (Denzin & Lincoln, 2008, p. 5). Research provides a foundation for reports about and representations of the other (Smith, 1999). With this in mind, I was careful not to push my social constructs onto participants, leaving them to openly express how they experience and articulate their social world. As Norum (2008) notes, the researcher is not offering a universal solution but a description of a group's shared reality: "qualitative research is not designed to prove something; rather, it is designed to generate working understandings" (p. 4).

Ethnography as Method

Dourish highlights the importance of ethnography in studying embodied interaction, describing it as understanding culture through immersion and observation. As he states, "ethnographic approaches can be used to uncover requirements for a system design through the detailed observation of the working setting" (2001, p. 62), contrasting the decontextualised nature of usability evaluations typically conducted in laboratory settings. He compares usability evaluations performed in laboratories, which are more successful at capturing work *processes* (the formal steps in a task) and less successful at capturing work *practices* (how people complete the task).

Ethnography is the collective term for qualitative research that values a holistic and compassionate understanding of users, encompassing their contexts, lifestyles, artefacts, behaviours, and actions (Martin & Hanington, 2018). Macleod et al. (2019, p. 180) describe ethnographic research as recording the "everyday sayings, doings, and relations with objects that make up what people do in their everyday lives" and help to "make practices visible" by placing "everyday objects and practices that we may otherwise not notice" at the forefront of data collection and analysis.

Ethnography may also be used as a specific research tool, consisting of observation of participants in the field over extended periods (Bentley et al., 1992). This method has been occasionally used in HCI to understand the user over time but is usually unfeasible due to time and resource constraints for a doctoral study (Cunningham & Jones, 2005). I refer to ethnography as a guiding lens in designing other research tools that allow for observation and analysis, not as a method of long-term objective observation. My case studies could be described as rapid ethnography—methods aimed at studying users in naturalistic environments within a shortened timeframe (Millen, 2000).

To study how a person is impacted, changed or affected by an object as unique as anthropomorphic VAs, it was crucial to align the research with a framework that validates the richness of diverse realities and experiences. Ethnography emphasises the "member's point of view", seeking to understand not just the actions performed by participants, but their subjective experiences in performing those actions (Dourish, 1999). It seamlessly supports a social constructivist approach, as it aims to document the subjective realities of diverse people aligned in a shared culture. That culture, on a macro scale, is the experience of VA technology in Western domestic settings, and on a micro scale, the multiple cultures of interaction defined by the contexts of individual households.

Cognitive ethnography

While traditional ethnography investigates the meaning created by the cultures of participants, cognitive ethnography investigates how this meaning is created. As Williams (2006, p. 838) puts it, "traditional ethnography describes knowledge; cognitive ethnography describes how knowledge is constructed and used".

Cognitive ethnography has previously been used to analyse how users learn to play video games via an after-school game club; researchers were interested in gaming literacy (Dubbels, 2011). Participants were asked to reflect on their experience when rewatching footage of their gameplay. "What were you thinking here?" was a common prompt to encourage participants to interpret their reasoning and decisions. A key instrument in this methodology is to record what happens, to pause the action and use this artefact for participant reflection. Adding cognitive ethnography to this research shaped how I performed fieldwork, ensuring I prompted participants to reflect on *why* they acted in a specific manner, not just describe *what* they did.

In deploying cognitive ethnography, I used voice history documentation and live interactions as prompts to elicit reflective responses from participants. This helped shed light on their perceptions, motivations, and barriers when using VAs. Object interviews proved a useful tool to elicit deep, reflexive responses regarding experience with an artefact (Nordstrom, 2013). In Case Study 1 (Interviews), I asked participants to perform interactions in real time where I could prompt them to reflect on their decisions and outcomes. Interviews concluded with participants reflecting on their voice history log through a computer or phone. Case Study 2 (Autoethnography) was rich with cognitive observations and conversations with household members to determine the reasoning behind VA interactions, as well as reflections on my use.

CASE STUDY 1: SEMI-STRUCTURED AFFECTIVE OBJECT INTERVIEWS WITH 12 LONG-TERM USERS OF VAS.

Semi-structured affective interviews including interaction demonstrations and voice history review with adult participants (between the ages of 18–60) in proximity to a VA device used in their home. All participants had used a VA standalone device for more than six months.

CASE STUDY 2: AUTOETHNOGRAPHY OF THE RESEARCHER'S EXPERIENCES WITH ALEXA AND OTHER VAS.

I built this case study throughout the research project, making notes of my reflections on Alexa's interactions with myself and my immediate community, such as my family, friends, and co-workers over the past five years (2019–2024). As well as documenting observations of VAs in my household, I included desktop research using Amazon and Google developer documentation available online to the public. This helped compare the culture of interaction from the developers' viewpoint with the long-term domestic culture observed in fieldwork.

Experience over time was a factor shared across both case studies. Studying users' long-term use was vital to capture experiences from households that had time to engage with their VAs. User experience shifts over time as interactions with products evolve, necessitating an understanding of temporal changes (Kujala et al., 2019). For ease of recruitment, I determined that more than six months constituted the minimum long-term use for interview participants. While Case Study 1 (Interviews) did not operate in a linear manner like Case Study 2 (Autoethnography), it represented a point in time and asked participants to reflect on their experiences over a period before the interview.

Case study design provided a way to present and study deep and long-term experiences with VAs within their unique contexts from the perspective of participants and the researcher's reflexive experiences. Amazon's Alexa AI and its associated devices (Echo Spot, Echo Dot, Echo Hub, or Echo Show) were chosen for my autoethnography, mainly on account of their availability and affordability in Australia. Other VA choices at the time of autoethnography collection in 2019 included Google and Apple's home VA devices. Alexa resonated with me partly due to its human-sounding name, which I found compelling, influenced by the sensationalism surrounding its portrayal in media and academic discourse—particularly Gina Chen's (2013) critique of digital domesticity, which examines how artificial agents are scripted and perceived to embody femininity. However, during fieldwork, other forms of conversational AI emerged as they were used by my participants, especially Google's VA (named Google Assistant, with home devices referred to as Google Assistant Hub, Nest or Mini) and Apple's VA Siri (with home devices referred to as HomePod or HomePod Mini).

Technology and ethnography

Ethnography was initially integrated into HCI methodologies to investigate how individuals use technology in naturalistic environments, departing from controlled laboratory conditions that seemed artificial and inadequate for addressing designs to meet users' contextual requirements (Rapp, 2018). Keeping a human-centred perspective was crucial to exploring new technologies and AI solutions. My research agenda was greatly influenced by the work of Sherry Turkle. Although her academic background in sociology and clinical psychology informs her style of enquiry, ethnography is the primary approach through which Turkle has produced an intriguing and rich body of work on HCI. The following words resonated with me, inspiring the questions posed in my investigation:

> My primary concern is with how its [a community's] relationship with an artifact provides a metaphor for what is important in life as this is expressed in the group's mythology and dominant ideas about human relationships.
>
> *(Turkle, 2005, p. 307)*

While this research revolved around describing people's interactions with an internet-enabled technology, VA interaction occurs in real environments, not digital or online spaces. Digital ethnography, as described by Varis (2016), is the study of people's practices and communications online. VA interaction is analogue: users' voices are projected into physical space and are not transmitted to an online user in an online space; it is a one-way human-to-computer interaction with artificial intelligence in a physical environment. Physical ethnography was deployed to understand people's offline movements, practices and communications with VAs in the home (Murthy, 2008). Yet digital infrastructures shape every interaction—the cloud processing, the brand ecosystems, and the invisible APIs. The basics of storytelling through ethnography were deployed in this research to follow participants' journeys, taking ownership of artificial intelligence in their domestic spheres.

I also drew on ideas of technology ethnography from Paul Dourish, where he explores the intersection of research, ethnography, design, and culture:

> What ethnography problematizes is not the setting of everyday practice, but the practice of design. Certainly, though, what it does is to refigure "users" not as passive recipients of predefined technologies but as actors who collectively create the circumstances, contexts, and consequences of technology use.
>
> *(Dourish, 2006, p. 546)*

While my research retains the word "users" to describe participants in their interactions with VAs, the research uncovered a multitude of novel and unexpected perceptions and uses. Participants were not passive recipients of the technology as defined by developers, but active agents who engaged with, disengaged from, or adapted their VAs based on the circumstances of their households and the cultures of interaction that emerged between co-users.

RESEARCH DESIGN: TWO CASE STUDIES

Case studies were selected to understand how users perceive and use VAs in their natural domestic environments over time, in collaboration with household members. A case study approach is suitable when: (a) the focus of the study is to answer "how" and "why" questions; (b) the researcher cannot manipulate the behaviour of those involved in the study; (c) the researcher wants to cover contextual conditions because they believe they are relevant to the phenomenon under study; or (d) the boundaries are not clear between the phenomenon and context (Yin, 2003 in Baxter & Jack, 2008, p. 545). I found these points highly related to the research problem proposed, in that I asked a "how" question, wished to document and analyse situational behaviours in context, and the boundaries between context and VA use were the focal point of investigation. Using the methodological approaches of ethnography, social constructivism and embodied interaction theory, I designed two case studies to answer the research question: how do users perceive and use VAs in domestic contexts?

Capturing the "How" Through Research Tools

Connecting with 12 families

For the first case study, I interviewed 12 long-term adult users of VAs to learn how they perceived and used their VA, their experiences over time of owning a VA, and their observations of the perceptions and use of VAs by other household members. These participants ranged between the ages of 24–54 at the time of interviews and were required to have owned and regularly used VA devices for more than six months. The reference to "regularly" was open to interpretation (something to be explored in the data), but loosely defined to participants during recruitment as at least a few interactions a week.

The interviews were semi-structured, focusing on affective interaction prompts for live interaction with their VAs and voice history transcripts (a text-based archive of their interactions accessible to review on a phone, tablet, or personal computer). These semi-structured interviews focused on an anthropomorphised object (the VA) and how interactions with this object were experienced by the participants and their households. Interviews lasted between 60 and 120 minutes and were conducted over Zoom video conferencing due to the severe Covid restrictions that intermittently lasted in Australia between 2020 and 2022. Pre-Covid, the interviews were planned to occur in person, with the interviewer visiting the participant's home to gain a holistic experience of observing interactions in the contextual spaces of their domestic worlds. Instead, participants were asked to be at home, near a VA in their home, or move a VA to an area where they felt comfortable performing the interview. This meant some participants were in their kitchen, living room, or study, and during the interview were invited to explain the layout of their homes and placement of VAs in their spaces. One study showed that physical placement of the VA in one's home had a significant impact on how they were used (Pradhan et al., 2019).

One limitation of this study was capturing collaborative experiences based on the recollection of a single family member through one-on-one interviews. VAs are ubiquitous devices that can be publicly used in private spaces; they are a technology more easily shared than other personal devices like mobile phones, tablets or laptops. Both case studies used in this book harnessed individuals as the point of truth for the experiences of their households. I acknowledge this limitation and the perception of the reporting individual and their recount of their perception and use, which may have been in conflict or misaligned with others' viewpoints. For example, I described the experience of the majority of my participants who identified as the user responsible for introducing

VAs into their household, managed the partner's VA phone application and expressed the most confidence in using VA devices (as well as other complex behaviours stemming from this identity). Capturing the viewpoints from other family members of the same household may have yielded interesting findings to compare different perceptions of VAs and VA users in a household. However, this may have introduced a complex web of perspectives that would have gone beyond the aim of this exploratory study to understand the user within collaborative settings. The perspective of the individual participant in this research was used as the bridge to all aspects of the VA embodied interaction experience, as explored in the findings; this included the user and their relationship to the hardware and software of the VA device, the spaces and places in which they interacted with the device and other users, and the relationship to information, developers and brands through interactions with skills, digital and material ecosystems.

There may be potential for a follow-up study that could investigate the alternative perspectives of multiple household members of the same household and build on the findings of this book. As well, it might have been difficult to come to the same framework and findings of this book if the concentration was purely between co-users from multiple perspectives and a greater focus on digital literacy and device confidence. Participants who volunteered for the study recognised that their confidence and digital literacy were sufficient to self-identify as long-term VA users. Other household members might not even consider themselves VA users and rarely interact with a home device in comparison; they may even be considered passively collaborative users.

What are semi-structured affective object interviews?

Semi-structured interviews

Semi-structured interviews allow participants to openly respond to questions and the interviewer to probe into these responses (McIntosh & Morse, 2015). Semi-structured interviews follow a protocol but are open for the researcher to create follow-up questions to further explore and understand responses. The researcher can retain relevance to the research objectives while clueing into the participants' responses and attitudes (Bartholomew et al., 2000). An interview protocol was also designed to be effective in eliciting memories and interactions based on emotional stimulation. However, some basic demographic and general use questions were included to obtain consistent information for later analysis and comparison:

On the other end of the interview research method spectrum, structured interviews are often used to diagnose an issue, where the objective is to uncover information related to a specified and un-exploratory viewpoint (Mueller & Segal, 2014). Semi-structured interviews gave me and the participant mental space to process and communicate responses that portrayed their authentic everyday experience.

The design of this study followed an emic perspective (Fetterman, 2008) as I was an active user of VAs and belonged to the same demographic as my interview participants, who were long-term users of VAs in a modern Australian domestic setting. The emic and etic dichotomy describes the two perspectives that situate the researcher in their topic. Fetterman (2008) defines an emic perspective as reality as viewed by an insider. In contrast, the etic perspective validates reality based on external "logical scientific analysis" pertinent to rules of consistency and replicability (Fetterman, 2008, p. 249).

TABLE 2.1 Interview questions

QUESTION	*INTENTION FOR DATA COLLECTION*
How many devices do you own?	To connect the number of VAs to other emerging data
Where are the VA devices situated in your house?	To map the environmental, spatial, and social contexts of points of VA interaction in the home
How did you come to own your VA devices?	To understand the preconceptions, expectations, and intentions of VAs before use and at the point of acquisition
Who else lives with you in your house?	To map the potential collaborators in VA interaction and understand pre-existing relationship dynamics that would affect co-interaction, such as a parent, child, sibling, housemate, or partner
What does a day in your life look like, including interactions with your VA?	To document the use of VAs in the context of the performance of daily routines, including those unrelated to VA use
Has there been a time when you deliberately chose not to use your VA for something?	To observe any perceptions leading to non-use
What do your family/house members think of the VA?	To document participants' perception of other users' attitudes, perception and use of VAs
Do you think other people in your household treat [VA name] differently from how you do?	Asks the participant to differentiate between the different subjective realities within their household. I used the word "treat" to infer different perceptions of interaction in a non-jargon way and acknowledge the anthropomorphism of VAs

The two terms demonstrate the contrasting nature of the different standpoints, critical to theorising on lived experiences in qualitative research. Due to the flexibility of the semi-structured interviews and my emic experience with the research topic, I sometimes shared my experiences with participants to elicit or cue their memories. I was mindful not to introduce bias through my subjective experience, but objectively mentioned a task or incident.

Affective Interaction

Affective interaction refers to an interaction that is influenced by emotional experiences (Lottridge et al., 2011). Rather than using this concept to analyse the research data, as it does not provide the same holistic lens to understanding HCI as embodied interaction might, I employed the concept in the interview design. Other than demographic and general use questions, I included questions that would spark recollection of interactions outside what they might think they actually do with VAs, for emotional experiences are linked to points of stress, workload, and multitasking, and can be considered as factors that impact the user experiences of these devices (Lottridge et al., 2011). In his book *Emotional Design* (2005), Don Norman illustrated, using various examples, that emotions play a central role in individuals' evaluations of or connections with artefacts and systems. Specifically, Norman outlines three levels in emotional design: visceral (immediate perception and aesthetic appeal), behavioural (usability and functionality), and reflective (personal significance and impact on identity). These levels were considered in how they might emerge through emotion and interaction-based questions.

In this study, I used affective interaction-based questioning to elicit responses and related interaction demonstrations. The base interview protocol asked participants to describe interactions related to emotional reactions. For example, my question "show me an interaction that made you laugh" inferred an experience that had sentimentality attached to a positive experience with a VA. This type of questioning allowed participants to centre themselves in the interview, rather than trying to place the VA as the central character in their interview narrative. Keeping this in mind, I asked the participants emotion-provoking questions, inviting them to redo the interaction, often pre-empted, or followed by an explanation of the original interaction that evoked this affective memory:

- Can you demonstrate an interaction with [participant's VA brand name] that made you laugh?
- Can you show me an interaction with [participant's VA brand name] that creeped you out?
- Show me an interaction with [participant's VA brand name] that impressed you.
- Show me an interaction with [participant's VA brand name] that frustrated you.
- Show me an interaction with [participant's VA brand name] that you like to show to friends or family. Why do you like to show them? How do they react when you show them?

Incorporating affective interaction theory into the design of the interview protocol offered a novel approach to eliciting participants' experiences and emotions associated with their interactions with VAs. By prompting participants to recall and demonstrate interactions that evoked emotional responses, such as laughter, creepiness, impressiveness, frustration, and pride, the interview questions aimed to unearth experiences beyond routine VA interactions.

Object Interviews

In some of the questions, I asked participants to demonstrate an interaction with their VA; this often elicited some unplanned or serendipitous sharing of information. The involvement of objects in sociological fieldwork helps to stimulate the elicitation of memories and narratives from participants (Hoskins, 2013). The method known as "cultural probes" (Gaver et al., 2004) is particularly notable for its aim to elicit responses from participants by providing them with a selection of objects with which to interact in their daily lives, such as a camera, a map, or a specially designed item. In a way, my participants had been living with this cultural probe, their VA, for over six months and had not yet documented their interactions or reflections. Hence, I reflexively looked to understand their experience by eliciting memories to not skew the findings. If they had been asked by a researcher in advance to use the cultural probe over six months, it might have changed their interactions, perhaps forcing interactions that usually would not have taken place. Instead, by asking participants to recount verbal interactions, I gained an understanding of their choices and experiences from within their naturalistic setting.

It was important for the user to be near a device with which they were familiar and used regularly for familiarity; Zijlema et al. (2016) describe this as object companions. Object companions gain significance over time, often bearing the marks of the owner's personal experiences, and evoke feelings of comfort and contentment when interacted with. Marks in the instance of VAs might reflect personalisation or routines that bear resemblance to users' use in less physical ways, but digital organisations of use.

Because the study aimed to understand in-situ interactions through an embodied interaction perspective, I chose to focus on out-of-the-box product VAs that had been available to Australian consumers since 2018. Google Assistant Hubs have been available since October 2018, and Alexa Echo devices since February 2018. While these assistants may have been available on phones and other personal computers earlier than the standalone devices (Siri had been available on iPhones since October 2011), they provided a different experience regarding ubiquity and voice interaction due to their portability in space and place. Hence, recruitment of participants focused on long-term users of "smart speakers", as these devices were referred to colloquially in Australia. However, interactions with VAs through phones were mentioned by participants and relevant to the findings presented as they were interwoven into the multi-modal and multi-device presence of VAs.

The addition of the VA into the semi-structured interview, evolving beyond verbal recounts of interviews and into observations of live interaction demonstrations, helped to observe interaction in action. Narratives uncovered through object interviews can help researchers differentiate between what participants say they do with an object (verbal recounts) and what they actually do (tangible interactions) (Woodward, 2001). During the interviews, the general and affective-type questions generated verbal accounts, and then I asked the participants to replicate the interaction during the interview. This usually helped the participants to cue their memory and note any differences between what happened before and how the interaction played out in the interview. This allowed for greater detail to be extracted from verbal accounts and generated data on live interactions, in the context of being performed again based on a past experience.

Voice history as artefact

Amazon and Google acknowledge their retention of user data. In the case of Alexa, this is referred to as the VA's voice history. I intentionally referred to the voice history as belonging to the machine instead of a history of an individual's interactions, as many users may be recorded and their utterances stored within the one cloud account at the company. A study of the use of VAs by Lau et al. (2018, pp. 16–17) found that users had diverse uses for their VA's voice history. In their study, Lau et al. analysed empirical findings against themes relating to attitudes and behaviours towards the user's privacy. First, one participant was not aware that their audio was being captured, and only one other participant actively deleted their voice history. Most participants accessed their Alexa voice history only to see if they had said anything funny. Otherwise, the remaining participants commented that there was no reason to view their past interactions. However, some exploited the VA's function to spy on secondary or incidental users, such as their children or guests.

I incorporated voice history into my interviews to act as complementary stimuli for the participant to reflect on the interview events. Their reaction to their voice history, as well as their chosen utterances, was invaluable in informing how the participants perceived their anthropomorphic VAs. Participants were instructed at the end of the interview to access their Google Home or Amazon Alexa voice history. The participant was given some time to select a few responses they believed to be interesting, shocking or meaningful. Taking note of the recalled interactions, the user was asked to reflect on their voice history excerpts based on what was discussed in the interview.

Connecting with my own experiences

In the second case study, I observed the interactions, as well as the verbal and physical reactions, of myself and my family members regarding activity with Alexa, as part of my autoethnography method. I maintained a personal VA journal throughout the research project, making notes of my reflections on Alexa's interactions with myself and my immediate community, such as my family, friends and co-workers over the past five years from 2019 to 2024. I obtained consent from participants who may be identifiable due to their relationship to me being made known in the book. Autoethnography allows "authors [to] use their own experiences in the culture to bend back on self and look more deeply at self/other interactions" (Ellis & Bochner, 2000, p. 740). It can extend sociological understanding through highly personal accounts that draw on the experience of the author/researcher (Sparkes, 2000, p. 21).

I built this case study throughout the research project, making notes of my reflections on Alexa's interactions with my immediate community (such as my family, friends, and co-workers). As well as documenting observations of VAs in my household, I included desktop research using Amazon and Google developer documentation available online to the public. This helped compare the culture of interaction from the developers' viewpoint with the long-term domestic culture observed in fieldwork. In tandem, I posed questions to Alexa to observe how it was designed to respond to conceptions of its sociality, role and influence. I expected my conversations with Alexa not to be as ethnographically fruitful as with my human participants; however, these static responses informed the phenomenon being explored and contributed a unique perspective to the overall study.

Autoethnography as method

As an ethnographic piece, my self-observations and observations of participants and co-users drove the direction of this exploratory research, capturing the culture of VA use. The book adopted a perspective of interaction based on real-world use, rather than what is simulated or tested in a lab. This approach allowed the research to document and present problems or misaligned designs through small, everyday interactions that may often be overlooked in larger quantitative studies.

Autoethnography focuses on the auto- (self), -ethno- (the socio-cultural connection) and -graphy (the application of the research process) to uncover the connection of stories to the larger social context (Reed-Danahay, 1997; Wall, 2008). As a research tool, it allows "authors [to] use their own experiences in the culture to bend back on self and look more deeply at self-other interactions" (Ellis & Bochner 2000, p. 740). Autoethnography is a reflexive investigation method, where the researcher is a member of the social reality being studied (Adler & Adler, 1987; Anderson, 2006); it can extend sociological understanding through highly personal accounts that draw on the experience of the author/researcher (Sparkes, 2000, p. 21). Since my research focused on how users perceive and use VAs in domestic contexts, it would have been extremely difficult to situate myself within participants' homes and expect them to act naturally for the sake of my research observations. Autoethnography meant I could study the domestic context to which I already had access and understand the complex relationships within it, allowing for greater insight into aspects of embodied interaction with VAs and the environments we interact within, and bringing these insights to inform my interviews with participants.

Regarding technology research, Rapp (2018) identifies two aspects explaining the utility of autoethnography specifically in the study of HCI:

Autoethnography as a "quick" method: The adoption of autoethnography in technology research was driven by the need for less demanding techniques compared to traditional ethnographies. Traditional objective ethnographies involved extensive periods of observation and analysis, along with the challenges of accessing and building rapport with participants (Cunningham & Jones, 2005). Autoethnography can facilitate deeper empathic understanding of user experiences, providing quicker access to ethnographic data and enabling researchers to gain insights into users' experiences in difficult-to-access contexts, ultimately offering valuable insights for technology development and evaluation (Rapp, 2018).

Autoethnography as a "reflexive" method: Grounding autoethnography in practicality and cost-saving as a "quick" method invited criticism for a lack of sufficient engagement with others and scientific rigour. However, situating autoethnography within a reflexive framework highlights the importance of the ethnographer's subjective experience, as exemplified by Williams' (2015) multi-year study on self-tracking technologies. Sundén (2012) further supported the methodological value of autoethnography, showcasing its ability to produce knowledge through intimate disclosure and epistemological uncertainty.

There has been some criticism of the execution of reflexive ethnographies in social sciences literature. Swan (2008), in defending the methodology, describes existing critiques of this methodological practice, by saying its critics "argue [that], first, it leads to narcissistic obsession with the self; second, it imagines the self to be the source of social problems and solutions; and finally, it individualises social and collective problems" (p. 386). This kind of criticism describes my wariness in using such a methodology, but as my interest in this topic came about through self-reflection, it would have been impossible to dismiss my lived experience from my research. As Ellis and Bochner (2000) stress, autoethnographic writing is meant to "expose the writer to a vulnerable state, through the intersection of 'personal to the cultural'" and the writer may, "move through, refract, and resist cultural interpretations" (p. 739). Hence, my experience, just like my participants' experiences, was socially and culturally produced within a context and was not just my special knowledge, for "it is not individuals who have experience, but subjects who are constituted through experience" (Scott, 1991, pp. 779–80). This personal experience was ongoing within my study and enriched and better informed my understanding of my participants' experiences with VAs.

Journalling

Data in autoethnography can originate from interviews, observations of participants, analysis of documents and artefacts, and journalling in a diary kept by researchers (Mayan, 2001; Morse & Richards, 2002; Wall, 2008). Journalling was conducted sporadically over a four-year period, with entries typically recorded about once every fortnight. These entries varied in length and detail, often depending on the relevance or complexity of the interaction being documented. The reflections included notes on functionality, social dynamics, emotional responses, and situational factors such as time of day and household activities.

The autoethnographic process produced over 50 journal entries, representing a broad spectrum of VA use cases across different times, settings, and moods. By combining these autoethnographic insights with participant data, the research offered a multi-layered understanding of how VAs are integrated into everyday domestic life. I recorded my journal in an online document that was password-protected through UTS in an application called Microsoft OneNote. This allowed me to access the journal on any internet-enabled device to make notes as needed.

While journalling is argued to provide hard evidence of a situation, writing from memory is often discredited in research, as its validity and rigour are questioned by the subjectiveness of memory, including forgetting and selective remembering (Muncey, 2005). However, as Sparkes (2000) suggested and was illustrated by Wall (2008), data collected through a third party has more perceived legitimacy, even though it is based on their subjective memories. Sparkes related a story about the use of his published autoethnography in an undergraduate class, explaining that his students did not consider his autoethnography to be research. However, when asked whether it would be research if someone else had interviewed a man named Andrew Sparkes, collected his medical records, diary excerpts and newspaper stories, and analysed the collection and written it up, the class said yes. Likewise, Wall (2008, p. 45) states that,

> … if a researcher had interviewed me about my experiences as an adoptive mother and had recorded and transcribed it, it would have legitimacy as data even though both the interview transcript and my autoethnographic text would be based on the same set of memories.

I can directly compare this to my two case studies, as they represent the two sides of this conundrum. In Case Study 1 (Interviews), participants were asked to recall memories of interaction based on their demographic and my affective question protocol, drawing on their past couple of years of VA ownership. While I did not ask myself the same questions in Case Study 2 (Autoethnography), I recalled similar memories of frustration, elation and melancholy. I could have gone into more depth in autoethnography, compared to a point-in-time interview that was limited to the pressures of human conversation, speaking ideas into words and coherent sentences, sizing up the conversation and conversation partner, and condensed into less than two hours of potential data extraction.

Both case studies are not featured equally in the findings and discussion chapters. Not as equal halves as having two case studies might suggest; rather, my autoethnography was condensed as if I were another participant in Case Study 1 (Interviews), where my stories were just as valuable as theirs. I did not use my autoethnography to fill in the gaps of Case Study 1 (Interviews); some sections may only feature my experience, or were the catalyst for seeing the same behaviours of interaction in the interviews. Another study by Cecchinato et al. (2017) employed the same combination of semi-structured interviews and autoethnography to study early adopters' perceived value of using smartwatches. They reported that the self-observation of autoethnography helped the researchers to gain first-hand experience in using the novel technology and saved time in observation of users in private settings. The autoethnography was also helpful in informing their interview questions. So, autoethnography is a useful tool that leverages the scientist for being something more than one who performs science and considers oneself as an equal participant in this research that endeavours to bring context into the greater world of their research.

ANALYSING THE DATA THROUGH THEMATIC ANALYSIS

Thematic analysis focuses on identifying themes and patterns of behaviour or lived experience within qualitative data (Aronson, 1995). These themes are validated through connections to pre-existing literature and presented in a coherent narrative that contextualises the research findings within the researcher's objectives (Aronson, 1995). This method was particularly well-suited to the research as it allowed for the analysis of diverse data sources—interview transcripts, interaction observations, and journal entries—offering flexibility and depth. Braun and Clarke (2006) describe thematic analysis as "the searching across a dataset—be that a number of interviews or focus groups, or a range of texts—to find repeated patterns of meaning" (p. 15). This aligned with the scope and methodology of this study, which explored the evolving perceptions and uses of VAs over time. Moreover, Braun and Clarke's (2006) perspectives supported the theoretical foundation of this research by emphasising the socio-cultural contexts and structural conditions shaping individual accounts, which resonated with the social constructivist and ethnographic frameworks adopted in this study.

Thematic analysis conducted within a constructionist framework cannot and does not seek to focus on motivation or individual psychologies, but instead seeks to theorise the socio-cultural contexts and structural conditions that enable the individual accounts that are provided (Braun & Clarke, 2006, p. 12).

Thematic analysis underscores the contexts of situations, as does social constructivism, ethnography and embodied interaction theory; hence, it was chosen as the analysis method for this research.

MOVING FROM THEORY TO PRACTICE

This chapter has established the theoretical lens through which this research examines VA, including embodied interaction theory, with its dual focus on tangible and social computing. But theory alone cannot capture the nuanced, messy, creative ways that people actually live with these technologies. The remainder of this book turns from philosophical foundations to empirical practice. The next chapters present findings from 13 Australian households, revealing how the concepts explored here—space and place, attention and context, power and social dynamics—manifest in the everyday reality of domestic AI.

Space and Place 3

THE SMART HOME

The term *smart* was used to describe VAs, their homes, and other household members by many of the people I spoke to. The diversity in the definition, context, and use of the word *smart* struck me, especially from the perspective that it's become the accepted prefix for any device that has increased technological capabilities beyond its initial purpose. The common vernacular of smart home has many definitions but is often used to describe a domestic space that contains connected IoT devices that can be remotely controlled and automated (Schiefer, 2015). From a marketing perspective the term may be used to suggest a more advanced or useful product, but what does it mean to users?

In this book, you'll be reading direct excerpts from my interview participants: people who have lived with stationary VAs for a sustained time. I talk more about these special people who were participants in my PhD research while at the University of Technology, Sydney, later in this chapter. Meet Mark, who holds a degree in software engineering. His description of *smart* aligns with a traditional definition from the field of computer science of smart devices, which is described by Silverio-Fernández et al. (2018) as associating smart with qualities such as autonomy, connectivity, contextual awareness, and user interactivity.

> So why would I describe them as smart … I would put it down to the… mostly the **lack of physical interaction gives a really intelligent vibe…**
>
> Mark, 4 person, 4 device household

I interpreted this to mean the reduced physical effort required when using the device or the absence of a physical interface that allows for less physical exertion during interaction. Regardless, the absence of a physical, tangible, or graspable interface is acknowledged as a characteristic of smartness.

> … **it's a lot of the behind-the-scenes** like how does it know that I'm saying a particular word, where does it pull it that information from, how does it put those words together and form an instruction, and then how does it execute that properly. To me, that's just crazy. So I think on that level, it's quite intelligent.
>
> Mark, 4 person, 4 device household

DOI: 10.1201/9781003680840-3

Mark notes the autonomy of his VA devices, as his Google VA processes information without multiple commands, but puts together a set of actions based on fulfilling Mark's question or request. This is confirmed in Silverio-Fernández et al.'s (2018) definition of autonomous devices, where they perform tasks autonomously without the direct command of the user. Mark also uses the word "intelligence" to describe the process of connecting his spoken input to a relevant action. Sarker (2022) offers definitions to differentiate between smart and intelligence in the context of Human Computer Interaction (HCI)—smart being the capability to be self-aware in monitoring, analysing and reporting, and intelligence to be able to extract and present knowledge from usable data.

> … and they've made the devices quite universal**, they're really compatible with so many different things now**, so you could make almost a fully smart home by just using these plug-into Google devices, which **I think is also quite an intelligent thing**.
>
> Mark, 4 person, 4 device household

It is unclear if VA users use the words smart and intelligence interchangeably or if a clear difference is perceived. Mark comments on the compatibility of the VA devices, in that they can be used to create a smart home, using the word intelligent to refer to being able to connect to different IoT devices.

Living in the Future

Lien's desire to construct a home of the future echoes Mark's smart home potential. While Mark was driven by his existing relationship to use Google technology in achieving his smart home, Lien was driven to find a brand that offers a better array of *smart characteristics*.

> I've always been into these AI gadgets that I want to **make the house smart**. So I've been actually been tossing between the Google Home and the Amazon Echos for quite a while, and I did see some research saying the echo is more **compatible** with other devices, so they've got more skills as compared to Google Home, which is more **user friendly**.
>
> Lien, 4 person, 6 device household

A sense of living in the future was also a sentiment shared by participants in describing their experience with VAs.

There are the smart plugs, and we've got a robotic vacuum cleaner. I'd **like to try to make the house smart as if we are living in the future** and put anything into Alexa and ask it to control it...

Lien, 4 person, 6 device household

Or, by participating in VA interaction, they are mastering voice and conversational AI interfaces of the future.

I think my dad wanted it to be. He's like, all like, **"it's voice assistants in the future"**.

Joey, 2 person, 1 device household

Or that the reality of living in the future is correct for generations who never thought to experience the non-tangible intelligence that is depicted in science fiction. Sophie shares her parents' exclamation of the future as she shows them how to control their television through Alexa. Sophie describes the "jump in technology" experienced by her parents. By not being early adopters or following the lifecycle of a technology, their initial interactions with a VA came with no experience with VUI.

Sophie: They don't really use any of the new technology stuff so for them it's jumped so far into the future. They don't use Siri or anything else like that. **So, the jump in technology is just mind-blowing that the TV is voice-controlled and it is all off the internet**.

Indra: Interesting. Have they kind of struggled with phones and apps and stuff—and didn't really understand how to do that? Do you think it's because it's [VAs] easy to use and why they are blown away by it?

Sophie: I think it's more because there is nothing like that around—it's all in the movies and sci-fi stuff—it's far in the future but then now things in your house can have this capability ... Even five years ago it was unheard of. Like only the movies with robots or millionaires.

But unlike other smart technologies where some sense of automation, compatibility or user experience, characteristics of smart technology are added to existing technological products, VAs are complex intelligences that transcend a personal and social context.

> When they first came out with the Google speaker, I was really intrigued about the **smart technology** aspect of them, and the fact that they were meant to be this really—well I think they still are, but this really technologically advanced device that was really responsive to you, and there was a… Kind of **on a personal level**, but not so much that it was intrusive, so I thought that aspect of it was really cool. So that's why I bought it.
>
> Mark, 4 person, 4 device household

A Device Tethered in Place

In embodied interaction, the focus is on the role computers have and how they are embedded in our lives from virtual and physical perspectives. Dourish (2001) points out the connection between personal computers and their physicality in our environments and how this dictates the context in which users relate to them and the environment:

Interaction with the keyboards requires both of our hands. The computer sits by the desk and ties us to the desk too. So, it is not simply the form of the computer that has changed remarkably little over the last thirty years; it is also the forms of computer-based activity and the roles that we imagine computers playing in our everyday lives (Dourish, 2001, p. 27).

Ubiquitous technologies that blend into our environments, like the VA, use other mediums of interaction to limit the need for human input and attention. Gripping the handle of a wooden spoon and stirring the contents of a pot, manipulating our dexterous fingers and wrists on a video game controller, or performing other activities where users can be productive and through voice-controlled interaction connecting to or augmenting the virtual world through VAs into everyday life. My conversations with interview participant Jen reflected this established preference of interaction with VAs over other attention-holding and physically occupying technologies:

> Yes, I like the idea that **I can just speak without touching it** [Google]. I really like that. I do; I think it's because **I don't have to stop and sit down or stop and hold my phone and do something**… Right. I can be anywhere in the house and ask what I want to ask, and I'm gonna get an answer.
>
> Jen, 1 person, 3 device household

Mobile phones have a similar effect to attention-holding personal computers in that they occupy hands and eyes, and to the extreme, wearing a VR headset completely removes the user's other senses and therefore attention from the physical world into the virtual world. Mobile phones have introduced the ability to interact anywhere and anytime that personal computers do not enable. People are not physically tethered to the technology; rather, the mobile phone is tethered to the person, following wherever their day takes them (and in many instances, people are tethered to their mobile phones, especially when they need to be charged). However, metaphorically, one's attention can still be tethered to one's smartphones.

In the case of VAs, devices are tethered to a place where they must be connected to a constant power source. This means the user must move towards the device in their environment, and to overcome this limitation, many participants describe buying multiple devices and placing them throughout the house to extend the ubiquity of VA interaction to the extent where participants like Jen perceive they can access a VA from anywhere in their house.

> I've been doing tons of packing, I can be silly on the floor, wrapping something up with sticky tape and scissors and all that sort of stuff, **and I can just talk... I'm not stopping and picking up my phone** and doing something.
> 👤 Jen, 1 person, 3 device household

VAs are an almost "interact anywhere anytime technology" within a defined area without much attention needed from the eyes or hands (note the *almost*—this book describes physical and social factors that inhibit VA technology from true seamless ubiquity). However, less attention from eyes and hands is an assumption; I find that more cognitive attention is needed to interact with VAs concerning positioning, orientation, cultural expectations and translating human intention into "natural" language commands. This form of computer-based activity and the role VAs play in everyday lives is unique from the experiences of desktop computers, mobile phones and other computing interfaces that mediate the connection to information and communication with other people.

A **desktop computer** is tethered to a space, so users are tethered to the device and space.

A **mobile phone, laptop or tablet** is not tethered to a space but to the user (until it needs to be charged, then it is experienced like a desktop computer).

A **VA** is tethered to a space; users are not tethered to it, yet users are tethered to the VA's space to interact.

Because VAs are tethered to a location, easily accessible, and the interface of voice is projected into space, the experience of VA computing is closely associated with the surrounding environment.

Location Matters

Now, in considering a VA device that has no mobility functions, space or physical interaction is not always the first consideration for researchers studying conversational AI devices, although VAs may imperceptibly control a person's mobility within a space when they want to interact. As of now, VAs do not need to move around the space to perform any of their functions as they harness IoT connectivity. Many participants considered VAs as an inconsequential but utilitarian device that, instead of moving throughout the house, was a centralised control mechanism that could perform functions throughout the house by connecting to other IoT devices. This was supported by participants who talked about its imaginary centrality and omnipresence, where interaction with one device could be experienced from multiple points in the home.

> … I can actually just cast to all the speakers around the house and have the music playing **everywhere**.
>
> 👤 Phoebe, 2 person, 3 device household

However, some users preferred keeping their number of devices to a minimum (usually due to cost) and strongly considered where a physical centralised device should be set up (although they might own one VA device, they might have many other IoT devices that use the VA as a centralised intelligence), forcing them to consider space, place and fields and selecting a "central" location for VA interaction.

It is important to consider the context of what activities are performed and where, the location of places within the space, and the distance between the fields of the VA's reach in constructing a centralised intelligence.

Sophie justifies the purchase of another VA device to extend her VA reach to two places she often thinks of using her Alexa—in her bedroom and her workspace in the living room. She moves her one VA device between the two spots regularly, unable to decide the most "centralised" location in her apartment based on her daily routines. In her interview she considers the variety of her day—will she spend more time sitting in her workspace or lying in her bed?

> [Alexa] used to be on my desk in my old bedroom. I would like to **put her in a spot that is between the living room and the bedroom**, but I don't want to buy another one.
>
> 👤 Sophie, 1 person, 1 device household

As I demonstrate throughout this chapter, participants consider the organisation of space, the visibility of technology and the frequency of being in those spaces, as well as the purpose of an occupied environment that brings humans to different places in their homes. So, how might space and place affect conversational VA interaction?

There is "a distinction between those interactive phenomena that are derived from the nature of the **space** in which they unfold and those that are instead predicated on an understanding of the **place** that is occupied" (Harrison & Dourish, 1996 in Dourish, 2001, p. 89, emphasis added). I explore different manifestations of how space, the way the environment is organised, and how this affects VA perception and use. Regarding *space* and VA interaction, I discuss observations on the distance between users and objects, openness and being overheard, and visibility of objects. Then I look at *place* and how the meanings people associate with specific organisations of space also affect VA use.

SPACE

I begin with space because it is the description of an environment with the absence of human meaning; it is how objects and structures are organised (Dourish, 2001). One aspect of space is the containment of it and the boundaries that mark the end of one functional space and the beginning of another. People refer to these as rooms, and they are usually demarcated by walls, floors and doors. Borders of spatial boundaries are significant in VA perception and use, as how people perceive borders of walls, floors and doors affects potential VA interactions. It is significant in the fact that VA interaction takes place in open space and, unlike other information-communication technology, is not contained to screens that are demarcated by aspects of virtual space, such as windows, webpages, apps, wallpaper, or the fold of a website—the visible part of a webpage before the user scrolls down. In the study, the organisation of homes, the walls where sound cannot travel through, and the points where people can access a VA affected how participants constructed a mental model of their space and used their VAs.

Domestic Divisions and Ontologies of Space

One consideration is populating a house with VAs based on the division of rooms. Take my conversation with Lien; he has the most VA devices in his home, with six standalone Amazon Alexa VA devices.

> It's not a very big house… It has two living rooms and four bedrooms, so I got one Echo dot in each room, then the Spot in the master bedroom.
>
> 👤 Lien, 4 person, 6 device household

He speaks about ease of use, especially in reducing the strain of shouting to interact with a device. He continues to reason that he employs a shout test. If he shouts and fails to connect to a device, it is an indication to buy a new device. Here, he talks about rooms, and in the case of his shout test, he gives the example of the pantry. He tests the boundaries of the interaction field of his VAs' microphone and speaker range, but ontologically refers to a room in reference to the distance capability of his VA devices. This is a fine expectation; by talking about spaces instead of fields, users can map the tangible boundaries of space. If users could visualise fields of interactions in their real environments, what potential aspects of VA or other voice-based technology interactions could that enable?

Lien: They are separated, I've put them in different rooms so it's easier, you don't have to shout loudly to access the main device. They are all connected, so I don't see any difference.

Indra: It's funny, like the other people I've spoken to, I ask them where it is, and they say, oh, it's in my bedroom, but I'd like one in the living room, but I don't want to get another one. But if I talked to you, you'd say—okay! I'll get another one.

Lien: I don't mind, as long as... Say I'm working in the pantry, and I have to shout to get Alexa there, I'll think, ah, I have to install one in the pantry because they can't hear me.

In more mobile robotics, researchers could take a "space" lens to dictate HRI. For example, Pacchierotti et al. (2005) tested HRI in a hallway, where they needed to specify interaction parameters based on the space—moderately long and narrow rooms, and the place of the hallway—to move between other rooms without many opportunities for stopping. Pacchierotti et al. tested "robot speed, the signalling distance at which the robot starts the maneuver and the lateral distance from the person for safe passage" (p. 164). Their robot is equipped with many sensors that provide it with more data for greater informed interactions, modules that map the local environment using sonar and laser, track people using laser, navigate in narrow spaces and dynamically change targets.

Perhaps more data points are needed for better VA–human interactions that help the VA understand the environment's context in terms of space as well as the cultural practices of the place the VA inhabits. Context-aware computing is an area of research that refers to autonomous sensing of the environment by the technology, which directly impacts its immediate operation (Sezer et al., 2017). An example of a simple measure to sense is volume. The volume of the users' audio input could indicate distance or if a participant is conducting a *shout test* to test distance.

Users' architectural layouts and visibility of VA devices influenced their interaction patterns. Visibility was dissected from the perspective of seeing the device as a reminder to interact, with different preferences for visibility of features like time on virtual screens and the attention focused on other devices already used for tasks such as laptops for work or study. I found and described the role of spatial boundaries, such as doors, in mitigating VA mis-interactions as well as the whisper function, permitting lower likelihoods of mis-interaction by intentional users; however, these strategies may not be enough to defer non-intentional interactions. The drop-in function, which transcends traditional spatial constraints, enables users to communicate across different locations within a household. Overall, the participants and their interactions with VAs are dictated by the space in which they organise their homes; walls, doors, and distance are important barriers to hearing, seeing and using VAs.

Another aspect of context-aware computing could be sensing the space of the environment—what walls, floors and ceilings limit the VA interaction field? Are there doorways that could be mapped to ensure noise does not escape the room? I found that a *lack of spatial boundaries cause VA mis-interactions* leading to user dissatisfaction. The spatial composition of the home, such as open space living compared to a home with many rooms, impacted how VAs were used. Open space environments have been considered in VA–human interaction in terms of open space offices that consider noise pollution as a detrimental factor when testing VA interactions (Bogdan et al., 2021) or the vulnerability to intentional electromagnetic interference (Xu et al., 2021) or laser-based attacks (Sugawara et al., 2020) on VAs due to the lack of barriers. Open spaces or walled-off rooms may provide another layer of challenges for engineers working on user localisation technology for VAs. User localisation may use algorithms to interpret echoes bouncing off walls to determine the angle of arrival of sound to detect where the user is, as was used in Shen et al.'s work (2020). While these are important factors in improving the VA user experience, my findings suggest that users with open living spaces had few devices in centralised locations because they were able to interact from multiple places within their house. Overall, there is a need for greater contextual awareness in VA technology, advocating for integration of data points related to spatial and cultural dimensions to enhance VA–human interactions.

Spatial Ontologies

Countering the hyper-division of spaces into rooms and walls as barriers to voice interaction, Joey provides a comparative experience where his one Google Home device is used across a three-level split home. Joey employs a shout test over time, day by day, to test the boundaries of his VA's microphone capabilities. He refers to his position in relation to the VA device instead of the room in which he is, a more spatial-orientation-focused map of his position in relation to his VA. Joey says "up here" instead of "study", but accounts for the lack of walls between himself and the VA device, inferring he is in the same room as the device, so perhaps this is why he says his distance and direction in less room-bound terms. But the "room" extends vertically across the three levels. The open space means that Joey has only needed one device instead of Lien's six.

Joey: Oh, that's okay. It can hear me from up here though.
Indra: Yeah? And you can hear what it says.
Joey: Yeah. So, it's on our middle level, in our dining room. So, there are stairs there.
Indra: Ah, where…?
Joey: And down those stairs are pretty much where it's sitting. So, because it's all open from here to there. It can hear me pretty easily.

I refer to this as spatial-orientation-focused (e.g. up, down, close, far, here, and there) or architecturally focused (e.g. living room, bedroom, kitchen, and bathroom) ontologies in communicating space. Another example of the use of spatial orientation-focused and architecturally focused ontologies to describe VA interaction came from Mark:

> I've got Google and Google Home, Google Assistant yeah, I've got a smart clock **there** as well, which has Google Assistant, and then we've got two mini speakers and one in the **kitchen**, one in the **loungeroom** as well, and then I've got my speaker just **here** as well.
>
> Mark, 4 person, 4 device household

Returning to Lien and Joey, a few factors must be considered when comparing their experiences with VAs and space. Lien will consider purchasing another VA device if the room he is in does not have a VA device. He still tries his shout test and eventually moves towards another space within a VA's interaction field. Joey is inclined not to buy another device, as there are fewer walls and rooms between himself and the primary device. Yet Joey tells me of strategic behaviours he deploys to delay interactions due to the distance between himself and the interactions he wants to play out while he is in a room far away. Although it seems Lien is more inclined to purchase more devices due to the fact that he has more walls that muffle voice interactions with his VAs, there must be another factor as to why Lien will choose to purchase five more devices. Potentially, factors such as attitudes towards spending money, amount of disposable income and frustration with the process of setting up new or adding more devices mean more cognitive load when considering the steps in VA interaction from an embodied perspective.

Also, in the context of VAs, a conversation with the user could identify so many more data points for context-aware computing, such as the *ontological vocabularies of describing space: spatial orientation-focused and architecturally focused.* Participants spoke in different discourses of space, from a spatial orientation or architectural ontology. Murtazina and Avdeenko (2020) define three common ontologies to describe orientation from a cognitive sciences perspective: "orientation is a cognitive function through which a person is aware of [themself] and [their] environment. There are three types of orientation: personal orientation, temporal orientation, spatial orientation" (para. 7). Spatial orientation refers to an individual's awareness of physical space and their ability to navigate and understand their environment. It involves perceiving and interpreting the spatial relationships of objects and locations (Jander, 1975). In thinking about architectural ontologies of space, Flury et al. (2004) infer different possibilities for talking about space from a data perspective for ubiquitous technologies. Lastly, Flury et al. affirm that "from the very simple architect map, an entire taxonomy of indoor space can be formalized in this way" (p. 56). So, it is essential to consider the ontologies of space, spatial orientation and architecture when considering voice and conversation-based technologies like VAs.

PLACE

> "Place" refers to the way that social understandings convey an appropriate behavioral framing for an environment. It's not for nothing that we use the term "out of place", but not "out of space"; the idea of "place" often plays a much more central role in determining behavior.
>
> *(Dourish, 2001, p. 90)*

Following space, I examine the theme of place and how VA interaction is affected by the mutual or conflicting shared understanding of domestic places within the home. While place is demarcated by the familiar arrangements of objects and people in fulfilling standard human needs—to eat, sleep, and socialise—as well as other tasks such as maintaining hygiene, storing personal objects, and enjoying hobbies in a safe and stable location. To support human life, outside searching for information and controlling IoT objects, VA interaction is designed to enable some domestic needs and tasks through voice interaction. I explore these tasks and VA integration through two headings: how the context of a place defines interaction and VA affordances, and then the emergence of non-conventional VA use shaped by the characteristics of places. I describe instances of opposing relationships with different places in the home and how these affect VA placement and use.

Context, Ritual and Place Defining Interactions

In the interviews, participants were asked to talk through a common day and their interactions. Commonly, participants would describe starting their day in their bedroom, then how they would move throughout the house and interact with the different VAs in each space. Rather, they interact with the VA as they move through their spaces to perform activities within a place. This is illustrated in the following quote, where Avish makes connections between his VA activity and morning ritual in the kitchen.

> So, interaction during the day is mainly with the display [Google Nest Hub], you know downstairs, and I guess **it starts coming downstairs for breakfast and looking at the time, sometimes putting on breakfast radio**, usually the news, listening to the news, and sometimes putting on music.
>
> Avish, 3 person, 3 device household

I also observed further place-tied interactions as well as non-place-tied interactions that were performed from non-specified locations, such as asking about the weather, time or controlling IoT lighting. Activity-inspired interactions occurred in the same location in a space, meaning it was tied to the social significance of a space. I call these place-tied interactions, such as turning on the TV in the living room or setting a timer in the kitchen.

> **"Turn on the TV". "Open YouTube". "Open Netflix"**. I think would be the commands I usually use the most if I'm in the **living room**, say. And that's... Alongside turning on the lights and turning off the lights [...] and sometimes [Vincent's partner], when **she's cooking, she would set a timer**.
>
> 👤 Vincent, 2 person, 4 device household

Not only does the meaning of a place define the interactions of users with their VAs, but also the type of VA device they will have in a particular place. For example, Hugo prefers to have the VA device with a screen in the living room to act as a digital photo frame.

> The reason is the **living room is the display one**. So, I had the photo digital frame, you know, all of the Google pictures passing on the Google Max. So that looks nice.
>
> 👤 Hugo, 4 person, 8 device household

Hao takes a similar approach, placing the device with a screen where others are more likely to use it.

> We use the **Google Nest Hub downstairs [with a screen]**, and so she [Hao's wife] uses the Hub more than I do and **uses it for cooking** or listening to music and so on, because **I tend to use the little one here [his bedroom VA Google Mini]**, just for in the morning when I wake up and try and work out what the weather is like or I listen to the news.
>
> 👤 Hao, 4 person, 2 device household

Hao's reasoning is based on his wife's preference for activity-inspired interaction in the kitchen. Her place-tied interactions require the use of a screen to support the use of the recipe skill—the VA will speak and/or show the steps at the user's pace. Users can start the interaction and speak "next step" to advance the recipe interaction. Due to the visual components of this VA interaction, Hao's wife requires the use of a VA with a screen in the kitchen more than Hao would in their bedroom. Not that his wife would need the screen to listen to music, but the recipe skill is popular and mentioned in many of my interviews with long-term users. A continuing theme of larger, screen-enabled devices in more public and frequented areas of the house was observed, defining what interactions occur and what kind of devices are positioned in what space in the home.

Just as the need for extending the reach of VAs throughout a space, place also had some effect in encouraging the purchase of more devices. The desire to support activities that occur in particular places inspired Mark to buy another VA device to be specifically used in the kitchen to enable the interactive VA recipe interaction, especially new device formats that support exciting interactive VA interactions like the recipe interaction.

> I was excited about when they brought out the Hub, 'cause I just thought that'd be a good opportunity to put it somewhere else, like the kitchen, so you could use it for recipes and things like that, so that's the only time I've been interested in buying another one.
>
> Mark, 4 person, 4 device household

Participants' interactions with VAs are influenced by the spatial layout of their homes and the significance of places within those spaces. Users were driven to buy more devices based on emphasis on either space or place, for example, space-informed adoption of VAs, like Hao, who needed a device if he was forced to shout to the closest device, or place-informed purchase, like Mark, considering purchasing another VA device to support an activity he performs in a place, such as supporting cooking in the kitchen. Additionally, the type of VA device present in a place is determined by the meaning of that place and the activities performed there.

Interaction being in specific spaces means there is an opportunity to specialise in the intersecting places' context. This could include a higher bias to action common tasks known in that human place when NLP accuracy has a low match rate or greater conversation repair, suggesting actions commonly performed in that place. For example, the VA in the kitchen could have a higher bias towards recipe-based or timer commands and could proactively suggest actions or information around recipe suggestions. User localisation is one area of research looking to improve the contextual awareness of VAs through greater information on the users' location within the house. I refer to Shen et al.'s (2020) exposition on the potential benefits of greater user localisation awareness:

> (1) Knowing the user's location could help determining which light the user is referring to, when she says, "turn on the light". Naming and remembering every light (or fans, thermostats, TVs, and other IoT devices) is known to become a memory overload for the users. Similarly, Alexa could help energy saving in smart buildings if it understands where the user is when she says, "increase the temperature". (2) More broadly, location could aid speech recognition by narrowing down the set of possible commands. If Alexa localizes Jane to the laundry machine, then a poorly decoded command like

> "add urgent to groceries" could be correctly resolved to "detergent". In fact, Google is working on "generating kitchen-specific speech recognition models", when its VA detects "utterances made in or near kitchens" from the user. (3) Lastly, localizing sounds other than voice—say footsteps or running water—could further enrich context-awareness. Alexa could perhaps remind an independently living grandmother to take her medicine when she is walking by the medicine cabinet or nudge a child when he runs out of the washroom without turning off the faucet.
>
> *(p. 1)*

User localisation could also consider if users rely on few singular devices as a *centralised device* or many devices throughout the house, treating the VA as a *centralised intelligence*. Is there only one VA on each level of the house? Could designers build a model with greater sensing capabilities to accommodate this? The Google Hub or Echo Show with a screen and Google Mini or Echo Dot hockey puck versions of VAs are examples of this design consideration, where they have different microphone, speaker and screen capacities.

Familiar Organisations of Space within Different Places

Macro and micro conceptions

Expanding on the notion of place, the home is identified as a macro level of place, compared to other areas such as an office building. I use the term macro, in comparison to micro, which might better describe a room or organisation of furniture in a small area. Macro conceptualisations of space may holistically describe the attitudes towards a whole building. Avish recounts trying to use a VA at work and feeling uncomfortable doing so.

> I only use the VA at home or on my phone sometimes … so it's more home-based. I guess **I still feel slightly odd if I'm in the workplace, or if I'm out and about using the voice assistant**, it doesn't feel comfortable.
>
> Avish, 3 person, 3 device household

Through his assessment of the shared office environment as being a place of concentration and focus, he is deterred from using VA to not disrupt his colleagues. Work offices are intended as places to perform work and not deal with personal information loudly. Avish speculates that he would be less inclined to ask his VA anything private or confidential.

Avish: Well, at work, it's an open-plan office. So, unless I've got headphones on, people can hear what Google would say back to me. But also at the same time, unless I'm on an actual phone call, I try and minimise vocal interactions just because it's an open-plan office, **it's not like a call centre or anything. It's like an office office…**

Indra: Yeah, that's a thing. Hey, all these open-plan offices these days are such a weird dynamic, even if I have a phone call with work-related calls, I feel weird taking them.

Avish: Yeah, it does feel weird **because you're aware of causing noise that may interrupt other people**, but you're also aware that it's not private, so whatever you're saying, everyone else can hear. **It's two issues**, I guess **I've tried to be a good colleague in terms of making sure everyone can work properly, but… And the second thing is the issue of confidentiality and privacy…**

Avish even highlights the different types of "offices", places that define culture and behaviour in spaces. These two spaces might likely be organised similarly, with offices usually featuring open-plan desks, cubicle walls, a water cooler, a coffee station and a whiteboard hanging on a wall. He describes a call centre as a place to talk loudly on the phone, as opposed to where quiet is required, like his office, which is a place for people performing high-focus work.

I identified *macro and micro conceptualisations of space and place*, where domestic and work settings are examples of macro places. Domestic places of meaning are complicated and personalised to the composition of the home, the relationships between the human occupants, and the layout and space of the house. In comparison, VAs deployed in more standardised places like the office have institutional cultural expectations to follow, and the relationships between people and their preferences do not matter as much. As in Bogdan et al.'s (2021) implementation of an office VA, the tasks for which it may be used were part of its rollout, especially as these features require bespoke skill programming to other systems like JIRA or IoT devices in the office. Their office VA and surrounding technological architecture allowed employees to interface "ambient control, attendance system and reporting, but also interact with project management services used for planning, issue tracking, and reporting" (Bogdan et al., 2021, p. 1). This study also supports VA integration in preference to the cultural expectations of a place, and more so, the importance of setting up bespoke skills and IoT integration for seamless interaction. This also supports my finding that users were inclined to use their VA devices so as not to interrupt the IoT setup of their home systems. Once an IoT ecosystem is established, users are more inclined to operate it through voice to not switch off devices manually—that may disrupt or sever an IoT device connection.

Phantom interactions

Conceptualisations of space and place were also evident in causing another VA mis-interaction for Hao, Lien, and I. Phantom interactions are described in the HCI literature, originating from the idea of phantom limb syndrome, where amputees sense the limb is still there after removal. I use this term to describe the behaviour of phantom interactions with VAs and explain how the ubiquity of the device and familiarity of place trigger these habitual interactions. While these interactions have no impact on a person's VA interactions, they demonstrate the habitual tie of certain voice commands to repeated actions and the familiar organisations of space that might confuse users' actuality of place.

> I was staying at my sister's house, ready to fall asleep, I had been watching YouTube on my phone with the lamp on. I check my alarms on my phone, reach over and plug my phone in to charge. I roll over and pull the blankets up to my chin. "Alexa, light off", I say, shutting my eyes as I give the command. Nothing happens. In my interaction pause, waiting for a response, either Alexa's voice telling me the device cannot be reached or the sound of the power board switching off the socket that connects to the plug for my lamp, and my room turns into darkness, followed by the hypnotic "OK" from Alexa, that sounds the same every time. None of these things happen. I open my eyes, I'm not in my room, this is not my bed. There is no Alexa here. My eyes widen and I laugh in shock that this just happened. This has happened to me perhaps a few times over the last five years.
>
> 👤 Indra

In performing my bedtime routine in a space that is like mine, my sister's couch became the place where I go to sleep. However, in my bedroom, the place I usually go to sleep and follow a bedtime routine—Alexa is part of that routine. Yet I am not in my bedroom and cannot interact with her. This mistaken conceptualisation of space and place did not have any negative effects on my VA use, but for Hao, it often disrupts their VA interactions as they recall the incorrect VA brand in different spaces.

> **Hao:** … although it does get frustrating at times because when I'm in the car… when I'm in the car, my car interacts through Apple Car Play. There's no Google there, and I've got to remember that it's Siri and not Google.
>
> **Indra:** And you've accidentally pushed it [voice activation button in a car] and said, Hey Google?
>
> **Hao:** Yeah, I've sent that off until I've done Hey, Google. Hey, Siri.

For Hao, his car is the place to interact with Siri, and at home, he interacts with Google. Similarly, Lien also uses two brands of VAs due to VA use in a vehicle.

> Because I drive about 45 minutes to work and then spend a half hour every day on the road, **I use Google Home when I'm driving. But at home, I'm using Alexa**.
> Lien, 4 person, 6 device household

Hao and Lien use different phone brands with their respective VAs (Siri for iPhone and Google Assistant on Pixels and other Android devices) than brands used within their home VA ecosystem. This suggests that VA usage in their vehicles is of lower priority compared to organising their home VA devices, as evidenced by their resourceful tendency to use the VA available on their phones instead of installing a vehicle-specific version of their home brand. However, this inclination may stem from the limited availability of VA devices designed for automobiles, leading to reliance on mounting smartphones on car dashboards. For instance, while no Google Home is designed for cars, an Alexa device, the Echo Auto, is available for purchase in some countries.

> I did try to play the trivia games on Google Home with the kids when we got long driving as I had to keep them occupied when we did that. But yeah, **I think I know Alexa more than Google**.
> Lien, 4 person, 6 device household

Because Lien uses a VA in the car less frequently compared to his home devices, he has accumulated more interactions with one VA brand compared to the other. This means he needs to learn skills and interactions for two VA brands, which might limit or expand his use of VAs. Either he uses VAs more often because he knows a few interactions for both, or his use of one VA is limited in comparison to the other, so he might use that VA less often.

An affordances framework can help conceptualise *place-tied interactions*, where activity-inspired interactions occurred in the same location, meaning the interaction was tied to the social significance of a space.

A single technology can result in multiple action possibilities because individuals have agency in how they use it. These possibilities are finite and relatively stable, framing possibilities for action that are triggered in situ. An "affordances framework" in communication is therefore partly about how affordances "set limits on what it is possible to do with, around, or via the artefact" (Hutchby, 2001, p. 453).

VA interactions are limited to possible options that challenge the agency of individuals in what actions can be triggered in situ. However, the affordances of VA interaction are so complex and invisible that there are limited points of inspiration for human agency in interacting based on the device alone before users attempt to interact and learn the device's limitations through trial and error. The surrounding environment, either perceived as space or place, acts as a point of inspiration for a VA interaction. The affordances of the space or place inspire in situ VA interaction. While VA interaction happens in real environments, space and place have been applied to create pleasant virtual environments. In Champion's *Space and Place in Cyberspace* (2023), they infer recreating aspects of human place in virtual reality through five factors: (1) uniqueness of atmosphere, selection of artefacts, etc., (2) some places in nature have the ability to shock or overawe the spectator, (3) memorable places have the power to evoke memories and associations, (4) some places act as a stage or framework on which communal and individual activity can "take place", and (5) communal places have the ability to identify and reflect individual participants. As VAs augment digital information and communication onto physical environments as an auditory mixed reality interface (McGill et al., 2020), how can designers infuse VAs with a greater role in facilitating place characteristics?

CONFLICTING PERCEPTIONS OF SPACE AND PLACE AFFECTING VA USE

Augmenting Social Presence

This section highlights how users' conflicted understanding of the dichotomy of space/place directly affects their usage of VA devices. I provide the below quote to exemplify two perspectives on technology within a household related to space and place, and how this conflict limits and presents opportunities for the use of VAs in Hugo's home. This situation stems from Hugo's belief that his family should be conservative with water, as bills are expensive. Hugo and his wife would shout through the closed door of the bathroom, only to be ignored by their daughters in the shower. Hugo infers that his daughters do not stop their showers even after his wife has yelled at them to stop; he looks to take this burden from his wife and automate a solution. However, in automating his solution, he needs to respect his wife's perceptions of technology, space, place, and automation in the process.

> I have sensors as well in **windows**, **doors**, you know, even for water. But again, I have like a water sensor that could potentially start the timer by itself… but my wife doesn't understand that it is not dangerous, and **she said, "I don't want electricity in the bathroom"**. It's a battery anyway… So, I didn't implement the full automation. So, **I need to use Alexa when they [their daughters] start [to shower] instead of automatically starting**.
>
> Hugo, 4 person, 8 device household

Hugo takes a space perspective on the bathroom and technology. He speaks about the physical aspects of the bathroom, windows and doors, using those aspects of containment and functionality to hang things on the wall, taking advantage of vertical instead of floor space. Hugo describes the water sensors he planned to hang, to keep them away from water and up high to sense moisture.

In comparison, Hugo's wife takes a place perspective on the bathroom and technology, projecting her beliefs about technology onto the use of the sensors. Historic messaging about electrical cords and water has limited what she has allowed Hugo to set up in the bathroom. Hugo counters this belief by explaining that the sensors are battery-operated, so there is no risk of accidental electrocution, but this is not enough to convince his wife otherwise. So, no matter how much Hugo has spent on devices, how many he has, or how technologically advanced they are, culture, beliefs, and attitudes have stopped him from being able to use them.

There is no Alexa in the bathroom, but Hugo regularly locates an Alexa as soon as he hears the shower starting in his house to initiate the routine he has set up to flicker the bathroom lights ten minutes after the shower has started. Place defines the situation again, as the expectation of extreme privacy and showering means that other people should not enter the room. This means that Hugo and his wife are limited by how they can interact in this situation—by yelling through walls and doors, unable to guarantee action or a response from the other persons or automating communication through their VA and other IoT devices, which also does not guarantee any response, but saves the initial person's physical effort in communicating throughout the home.

It also augments Hugo's presence, affecting the compositions of space and place. Hugo bypasses the barriers of walls, doors and windows to remotely be present in the room. He changes the restraints of space via ubiquitous computing. In doing so, he redefines the context of the bathroom as a place; now, the bathroom transforms from a private place to shower and relax, into a place to be policed by controlling and frugal parents. These changes to the space and place of the bathroom have occurred with VA assistance to flicker the bathroom lights after 10 minutes, although there is no VA device in the bathroom. However, the parents use VA to control the activities in the bathroom, from elsewhere inside the home, listening for the sound of running water. In this scenario, the VA is a supporting tool in this ecosystem of smart technology that transforms the definition of places in the home.

This conflict of space and place causes Hugo to use his VA, and his use of his VA ignores the boundaries of space and can impact the contexts of places—what people do there and believe they should do there. Hugo's story is an extreme example of the manipulation of space, place and the people that occupy them through VA use and an exemplar for the capabilities of VA. This is reminiscent of extended-self theory, where "external objects become viewed as part of self when wearable to exercise power or control over them, just as we might control an arm or leg" (Lin et al., 2022, p. 26357). However, because VAs are not wearable (except for VAs in phones and watches), they do not become an extra body part but instead a body part that can be controlled remotely. In considering the extended mind theory, Atkinson and Barker (2021) describe the importance of information and communication interfacing technologies like VAs to support, rather than replace, human memory in conscious decision-making.

There is also Hutchins' (2020) distributed cognition theory, which describes all cognitive processes as distributed in some way. This could describe how VAs support the cognitive processes of its users, supporting memory, action and sensemaking. However, neither of these theories encapsulates the finding of the effect of *users' non-consensual presence in spaces they are not physically in*. Perhaps a better theory to describe this phenomenon would be the social presence theory. Social presence theory emphasises how the message sender is perceived as a "real person" in a mediated communication setting (Gunawardena, 1995; Gunawardena & Zittle, 1997; Shao & Kwon, 2021). However, this has been applied in describing the overarching anthropomorphic identity of a social prescient AI persona in VAs (Shao & Kwon, 2021), rather than the concept of extending human social presence via VAs throughout different spaces of the home. So, while extended-self, extended mind, distributed cognition and social presence theories infer a similar experience to extending human capabilities and presence through technology, VA interaction offers the unique affordances of controlling other spaces and mediating human presence in those spaces without their consent.

As well, designers could develop new data points for context-aware computing to capture common cultural beliefs that overlay different spaces, such as no technology in the bathroom or no loud noises after sundown. Conflicting understandings of space/place led to contention from two or more users, where their perspective of analysing the location of the VA's interaction field applied a space or place discourse. Organisation of space conflicted with shared cultural understandings of a particular place. Similarly, this has been observed in larger-scale disputes of space and place; for example, Hopkins and Dixon's (2006) discussion on understanding space and place in political psychology, where they discuss conflicts between larger communities of nations and towns. They highlight the disputes of ideas of space and place, where some parties do not have the power to act on their understanding.

To observe that different groups may construe the same space in different ways does not mean that all are equally placed to act on the basis of their understandings. Often, particular constructions predominate and are so effective in shaping people's spatial behaviour that we are blind to their operation. Indeed, it is only when we are faced with people or practices that appear strangely "out of place" that we become aware of the degree to which spatial behaviour is controlled by particular conceptions of place (Hopkins & Dixon, 2006, p. 177).

While political psychology explores space and place on a wider scale, researchers could refer to political psychology research to learn more about disputes on which places or spaces VAs are welcomed and used. I extend the sentiment of Hopkins and Dixon (2006) that not all users are "equally placed" to enact their desired purpose of a space.

Transient and Intentional Places

However, other instances of space/place intersections are benign in how people organise their smart homes. Another example of space and place is where the VA takes centrality. Avish lives with his partner and roommate, James. He tells me where the Google Home devices are placed within the house.

So that's the device and we sit it in the **kitchen area**, which is **open plan**, so that it is **accessible from the kitchen dining area and the living area** ... It's got a good screen, so when we come downstairs from the bedroom upstairs, we can see the time and we can see the screen if we've got other stuff on.
Avish, 3 person, 3 device household

Avish talks about the different places that make up the open living space: kitchen, dining room, and living room. He speaks about the stairs and division of space, where different landmarks throughout the house are marked by seeing a VA device. From leaving a bedroom upstairs, one is instantly met with the downstairs VA device opposite the staircase. Avish tells me about the activities the household performs with their kitchen VA, and their experience together is elevated by the ability to select music freely, set timers, and follow recipes by everyone in the same open living space.

It starts coming downstairs for breakfast and looking at the time, sometimes putting on breakfast radio, usually the news ... And then during the day, we would hardly use it [Google Nest Hub VA], and towards the end of the day, it would be like putting on **music while we prepare dinner**, it would be using the timer function to time stuff that's cooking or an activity.
Avish, 3 person, 3 device household

The VA invites community and collaboration—it is remarkable how the presence of a VA device invokes shared experiences within a space. I compare my own experience.

There are plenty of times in my own house where community is absent. When I'm cooking, I cook alone and I follow a recipe I can see on my phone, that no one can "glance" at to join in on, I play my music from my phone because I am occupying this space for a short time, I don't plan to dwell here. It's my place to cook for this moment in time. In other moments, it's my stepdad's place, or my sister's. Occasionally, the room becomes a communal place, in that we happen to all be in the kitchen at the same time as a byproduct of an activity (My sister grabbing a glass of water, my stepdad washing his hands after gardening, and I'm there washing the dishes). It's unlikely we're there to interact with each other; instead, we are trying to achieve our individual tasks and move back to a place where we feel more comfortable. For me this is mine or my sister's bedroom with our respective VAs (and my mum's room when she was still with us). When my mum was alive, the kitchen was always her place, with her sewing project scattered across the dining table, her cooking simmering on the stove, her music playing through the speakers or her favourite cooking channel on the TV. After her, at this point of the story, my sister, stepdad and I sit at the dinner table together, the place to eat a meal someone has prepared to be shared. My sister and I sit there more because we'd be faced with a stern disagreement from our stepdad if we ever took our dinner plate to our room and ate there. Sometimes, being forced to sit there turns out to be a pleasant experience, in that sometimes the company is nice.

Indra

Notable in comparing Avish's and my experience is the communal aspect of the kitchen space as the shared and celebrated understanding of place by Avish's household, signified by the intentional collaborative use of their VA.

Differing perceptions of space and place impact the use and placement of VAs. VAs contribute to the reshaping and definition of spaces within the home, despite not being physically present in every room. The clash of place and space perspectives illustrates how cultural beliefs shape technological adoption within the home, affecting VA perception and use. In contrast, Avish's household demonstrates a more harmonious integration of VA devices within their living space and celebrates the communal understanding of place facilitated by VA technology. My description of a place demonstrated the concept of transient places and, over time, how places change depending on the interpersonal relationships of people within the home. Comparing these experiences underscores the nuanced relationships between space, place, and VA use.

In considering space and place, one can consider VA interaction through the paradigm that,

> knowledge is shared by a particular set of people based on their common experiences over time. Practice emerges over time in the space; but at the same time, the space is also turned toward the particular needs of the moment.
>
> *(Dourish, 2001, p. 90)*

Place infers a sense of community and shared social understanding. Building on the capability and opportunities of user localisation, VAs could also learn the non-conventional place practices of the family; for example, homework at the dinner table, dog washing in the laundry, dance practice in the living room and so on, by matching the voice history to different devices in allocated places in the home.

Domestic spaces are also organised by intention: eating, sleeping, learning, entertaining, or relaxing. However, spaces only become places for these activities when humans agree to enact that context, which may agree or conflict with the space's organisation (until it is reorganised). To illustrate this, think of sleeping on the living room couch instead of in the bedroom, and the bedroom becoming a place to store folded laundry, changing the designation of a place to sleep to an unconventional location.

Human appropriation of different living spaces comes with balancing social expectations with personal needs and the affordances of the space. An extreme example of this appropriation of space into a unique place of meaning is a displaced person, who could have made a raised step with a small alcove in front of a large glass window into their place to sleep for a night. It is possible to imagine that VA use can be improved by considering elements of place in user localisation in the design of future VAs. I referred to these as place-tied interactions, where the place's context influenced the reason for VA interaction in certain spaces. However, as highlighted, designers should consider the unconventional activities performed where humans may reappropriate spaces.

As I found, *places are transient*, depending on the interpersonal relationships and presence of people in the home. How might the presence of a VA in a humanoid form affect transient places? In my conversation with Mark, we speculated on how a humanoid embodied VA would pass the time and where it would wait for commands. Might the spare room become the charging room for the device, or the kitchen where the robot sits and waits for its next command, in the busiest and most communal place in some homes? I talk more about this in the final chapter, when robots eventually walk in and occupy greater space than the current VA forms.

FINDINGS FEATURED IN THIS CHAPTER

TABLE 3.1 Chapter findings

User–device or device–user tethering	Distinguishes if the user is isolated to the space of interaction or if interaction occurs where the user is. Examples of user–device tethering: mobile phones, laptops, tablets Examples of device–user tethering: desktop computer, VA, television.
User–device or device–user tethering	Distinguishes if the user is isolated to the space of interaction or if interaction occurs where the user is. Examples of user–device tethering: mobile phones, laptops, tablets Examples of device–user tethering: desktop computer, VA, television.
Centralised intelligence and centralised device	Centralised intelligence: a system that is used across multiple devices, perceived as a centralised intelligence. Centralised device: a device in a central location for optimal interaction field engagement.
Spatial-orientation-focused and architecture-focused ontological descriptions of space	Different vocabulary describes location, including spatial orientation-focused (e.g. up, down, close, far, here, and there) or architecturally focused (e.g. living room, bedroom, kitchen, and bathroom) ontologies.

(*Continued*)

TABLE 3.1 (Continued)

Consideration of space and place by users may lead to purchasing more VA devices	Space inspired users to buy more devices to spread the reach of VAs across distances and spatial organisations. Place inspired users to buy specific devices for actions performed based on the associated meaning and activity (e.g. placing screens in areas where visual-based interactions were desired, such as the recipe interaction in the kitchen). As well, interactions based on place inspired users to buy a VA for place-tied interactions (e.g. buying a VA for the kitchen was driven by the desire to perform the recipe interaction).
Shout test	Participants engage in a "shout test" to measure the effectiveness of their VA device placements throughout their homes.
Place-tied interactions and non-place-tied interactions	Activity-inspired interactions occurred in the same location in a space, meaning the interaction was tied to the social significance of a space. I call these place-tied interactions, such as turning on the TV in the living room or setting a timer in the kitchen. Non-place-tied interactions were more centralised intelligence-type requests.
Macro and micro conceptualisations of space and place	In comparison to other environments (the office and car were discussed), the home is distinct in affecting expectations and the type of VA interactions performed there. Macro conceptualisations of space may holistically describe the attitudes towards a whole building. For example, an office is a place to work. Micro conceptualisations of space better describe a room or organisation of furniture in a small area. For example, a reading nook (an armchair in the corner of a room next to a bookcase) is a place to relax.
Phantom VA interactions	This phenomenon demonstrates the habitual tie of certain voice commands to repeated actions and the familiar organisations of space that might confuse users' actuality of place.
Place perspective may override spatial perspectives on VA placement and use	My findings showed that culture, beliefs and attitudes associated with place can inhibit the use of VAs in certain spaces. For example, the avoidance of electrical equipment in the bathroom.
Redefining place by transcending space through VA and IoT	Extending human presence into rooms in which they are not can change the context of the behaviour within a space. For example, the bathroom transformed from a private place to shower and relax into a place to be policed by controlling and frugal parents.
Places are transient	Places may change depending on the interpersonal relationships and presence of people within the home.

Time, Fields, and Audible-Conversational Space

4

INTERACTION FIELDS

Giusti et al. (2022) proposed the terms interaction field and potential interest to describe the overlap of the proximity of the user and the artefact, and the potential opportunities and behaviours within defined boundaries of space. The authors define an interaction field as "the region of space surrounding an actor, either a user or a device, that carries particular significance for interaction" (p. 6) and potential interest "tracks the overlap between interaction fields to continuously estimate the level of engagement between people and devices" (p. 3). The interaction field includes the area around human users as well as devices.

Giusti et al. (2022) use these ideas to inform interaction design based on exploiting the distance proximities of object and user interaction fields. For instance, the design of a Google Nest Hub interaction, where the closer the participant was to the device and the action and pose performed with the potential interest zone informed the play/pause of a recipe reading interaction. When "a video plays while the user is engaged with the recipe. The video pauses while the user turns away from the device and is no longer engaged with the screen" (p. 13). Interaction field and potential interest can be applied to a diversity of connected artefacts, regardless of their spectrum of ubiquity or virtuality. Giusti et al. recognise that the study of "fields" emerged from definitions of *peripersonal space* in the context of computing, which refers to the space surrounding a body (human or machine) where they or it can be reached by external entities, including other individuals or objects (Giusti et al., 2022; Rizzolatti et al., 1997), based on Brain's (1941) "grasping distance" in neuroscience literature.

Importantly, Giusti et al. (2022) discuss the implications of their interaction fields in defining socially intelligent spatial computing. These characteristics of interaction fields and potential interest manifest throughout the research data from this study; in particular, a focus on "social spaces", "social construct", and "individual spaces", as the research dissects social embodied interactions of long-term users with VAs. These terms infer closer examination of the social aspects of ubiquitous technologies and how they

DOI: 10.1201/9781003680840-4

physically manifest within HCI environments and imagined perceptions of those environments. In turn, it affects the perception, understanding and use of ubiquitous technologies like VAs.

Focused Fields

Proposed by Giusti et al. (2022), they define two types of fields around objects that support directional or non-directional sensing:

> The non-directional orientation defines an interaction field that surrounds the device; while a directional orientation extends forward from one side of the device. Non-directional orientation can be used when the angle of approach is not relevant for the interaction; directional orientation can be used to respond to users when they are in front of the device, rather than behind or to the sides.
>
> *(p. 7)*

Try to visualise a non-directional orientation, where the interaction field surrounds the device like a circle of potential, while a directional orientation extends forward from one side of the device (Giusti et al., 2022). Giusti et al. (2022) also consider the directionality and skew of the human interaction field, which changes from a circle to an ellipsis, as "when a user is in motion, contains valuable information about the actor's intent and level of interest in their surrounding space" (p. 6).

Giusti et al. (2022) developed an algorithm to measure the area of potential interest, based on the intersection of user and object interaction fields. As the actor begins to move, the field transforms into an ellipse, with its eccentricity growing proportionally to the actor's speed. Despite the field's total area remaining unchanged, the major axis of the ellipses expands with increasing speed, while the minor axis contracts, pushing the interaction field ahead. Interaction fields can intersect, measuring an area of potential interest in interaction. In their study, Giusti et al. predict this to a mathematical amount that can inform different types of interaction based on the proximity of intersecting user and device interaction fields.

The interaction fields theory encourages novel ways of understanding how proxemics can be quantitatively calculated by machines to inform interactions. Their case study experiments prove there are many design implications in being able to calculate the potential interest of human–VA interactions. However, from a user perspective—the boundaries of interaction, an interaction field—does this have any influence on user perception and use? How are interaction fields perceived by users? How do other factors in embodied interaction, like space and place, affect conceptualisation of interaction fields? For example, do the affordances of rooms within a home project a larger or smaller field of interaction space?

This is illustrated by participant Phoebe explaining the placement of her Google Minis in rooms, but also speaking of them as a whole, where room separation, in an architecturally informed ontology, is used to describe edges of interaction instead of a field of interaction. By measuring room size instead of field interaction capability, this may infer that the interaction field is smaller or larger than it is. For example, the interaction field may take up an entire smaller room but only parts of a larger room (especially considering split-level or open living designed homes).

> We've got the **fan in the living room**, and we've also got a smart bedside lamp that can be turned on for that as well, **in the bedroom** [...] because then **it'll spread through the house**, or I can just leave it and just playing in **one room**.
> Phoebe, 2 person, 3 device household

Users were shown to have perceived other spatial boundaries like walls and floors, instead of the VA's interaction field, to distinguish between different areas of interaction, and, as discussed before, place more devices throughout the home to create a layer of seamless interaction.

The Robot's Point of View

Boundaries of interaction are viewed in robotics often from the perspective of boundaries of the safety of a human (how close should the robot get to the human user?) and is often tied to proxemics—the study of appropriate fields of distance centred on the human experience (Patompak et al., 2020). When boundaries are described from the robot's point of view, constructs such as field of vision (FOV) are used. FOV defines the region in which a robot's sensors or cameras can perceive and interact with its surroundings, humans or other objects and auditory range (Patompak et al., 2020). FOV then defines a robot's ability to detect and process sounds or speech in its environment and interaction range. Thus, FOV dictates the physical distance at which a robot can engage and affect its surroundings or human users.

My findings support the need for amplified sensing systems for VAs to take advantage of the interaction field theory and consider the contexts of space and place dynamics. VA hardware infrastructure could benefit from richer sensory inputs as tested by Miksik et al. (2020), who included cameras and more microphones to support proactive VA interactions, or better leveraging of just auditory ranges and capabilities, like Huang and Wang's (2020) work on developing algorithms to detect walking sounds by VAs for improved context awareness. In this study, they elevated what sounds are detected from audio captured by VAs (after the wake word was spoken). Just as VAs are coded to interpret other auditory cues or listening features like whispering and loud invasive (Simonite, 2018), VA designers could create better sound recognition algorithms for other auditory cues.

TIME

> Time perception is an integral aspect of human experience and has numerous implications for the communication between humans and computers. When interacting with computers, user experience is often compromised by non-optimal latency and temporal misperception.
>
> *(Riemer et al., 2023, p. 1)*

In this section, I explore time-related behaviours in VA interaction, focusing on real-world environments. I highlight instances of interaction pauses, disruptions and latency, drawing from personal experiences and interviews. Common computing complications related to time, such as pauses, losing time by restarting the interaction and lag, are experienced in real environments in VA interactions. As well, I discuss future interaction planning, where users pre-emptively request actions to accommodate spatial and temporal constraints. Lastly, I speculate on the physical embodiment of VAs and its implications for time and space in interaction. These instances are also informed by the space, place and field epistemology of understanding VA embodied interaction. Understanding the interplay between time and embodied interaction sheds light on the nuances of user experiences with VAs in real-world settings.

Interaction Pauses

I tell below my experience of a phenomenon in my daily life with Alexa and my family of what I term as human–interaction–pauses in VA interaction.

I often found myself walking out of my mum's room after chatting to her, making sure she was okay (she was perhaps three rounds into chemotherapy at this point), tuck her in, as she prepares to fall asleep. Then as I go to leave the room, I have the sudden thought that mum might enjoy some music to fall asleep to. So, I stop in the middle of the doorway, turn around, turn back towards the room, and ask her Alexa to play some music. I stop and think about what song I want to play, how to phrase it and consider what mum would enjoy.

I follow the VA embodied interaction process but steps regarding VA location identification are shortened as I quickly identify the VA in mum's room near the door. I realise I stop to interact, blocking the doorway, people need to squeeze past me to get into the room, my mum has to wait till I'm done speaking to Alexa to say something to me. Staying in the same spot, I barely move a muscle and I interact by speaking my request to my VA.

After my interaction, I still find myself physically paused as I wait for the light to come on and the response from my VA. There's been other times that I've tried moving and talking to Alexa. Usually the interaction fails, I assume the microphone does not pick me up or movement distorts the audio recording of my voice. If I really want to complete a goal through VA means I've learnt to keep relatively still. Once I was rushing off to work and said "Alexa, light off", while walking out my door, with no effect. Now I slow down to check if it's been done. If there's an error (which happens very often and will miraculously fix itself days later), I'll have to stand there, try again or decide to act and physically turn the lamp switch off myself (or if I'm feeling especially lazy, leave it on).

Indra

In this autoethnography, I was drawn to how much my physical body is still and often the success of the interaction is reliant on this stillness, where I can pause and think through, and perform the action to the best of my ability. While users may experience a similar process when using other technologies, these pauses before interaction might be more obvious before, during and after interaction. Because VAs are ubiquitous, users might often be interrupted in action and freeze in strange positions to spontaneously interact.

This is similar to how a person might suddenly stop walking to type a text message on their phone, and the person behind bumps into their back. Users interrupt their actions and those of other people through spontaneous VA use. This becomes a more salient phenomenon when users interact with VAs in front of or with other people. These pauses break the natural conversational flow of human conversations, where: (1) I am unable to process any other interactions while I am in my interaction pause, waiting for the VA to process my request. I could not process what another person was saying to me; my ability to listen and comprehend was minimal, similar to how users are sucked into their phones and computer screens, and users might struggle to process conversations or actions around them. Because the auditory affordances of a VA interaction are public, (2) other people are drawn into my pause as they also wait to see how the VA responds, and (3) other people may need to wait for my pause to complete to resume or begin a conversation with me. In this way, it is like a human conversation where one pauses one conversation to process a quick task on the side that involves talking to another person.

Participants experience pauses before performing a VA interaction, especially an interaction with which they are unfamiliar or in an unfamiliar environment. Interaction pauses are a form of hesitation phenomenon. In human–human communication, pausing is a natural component of the rhythms of conversation (Pennington & Doi, 1989; Jaffe & Anderson, 1979). Pauses in communication have been categorised as either speaker-relevant (aid in information-processing and planning) or communication (listener-oriented signals) pauses (Ballmer, 1980). I would consider the VA interaction pause I described as speaker-relevant, as the user plans their interaction. My findings suggest that VA interaction pauses are a type of speech-relevant pause that may affect VA interaction, especially as users interact in real environments with anthropomorphic devices, and pauses may even allow for disruptions by other people sharing that environment.

This was also observed in the pause in a human–human conversation to react to a *VA disruption*, as participant Hao and I paused when deciding how to interact with the device. However, what makes a VA interaction pause significant to understanding perception and the use of VAs is the disruption of activity and space in the real world in interaction with an invisible interface.

Disruptive and Unsolicited VA Interruptions

Hao and I experienced a VA phenomenon live during our interviews. It is an example of a common occurrence where a VA might give an unsolicited response, perhaps mistakenly identifying its wake word and a command.

Hao: I do like to text, because if I'm in a somewhat noisy environment, I normally like the text and look at the text, it's [VAs are] not gonna work in an environment where it's a bit noisy, I think, in like a home.

[Hao's Google turns on unexpectedly and resumes with the news update we were listening to. We stop our conversation; Hao takes charge and tells his Google to stop, silencing his device and the unwarranted interaction. I sit and wait for him to command his VA. I don't make the initiative to silence the device.]

Indra: … Okay. What were we talking about?

Hao: **Um, I don't remember**… being human? Ah, yes, being at home and in a quiet environment…

Our conversation was interrupted, and we instantly forgot what we were talking about. We both stopped talking and turned our attention to the device. We were forced to listen, as we were unsure why this occurred, and it spoke over both of us, meaning we could not hear each other. The digital presence of information through a sudden loud voice significantly disrupted our physical and cognitive processes. Hao hypothesised that it was the age of his VA device that caused it to malfunction and act out of turn. It was the oldest model he owned and preferred to give the newer models to his wife and children's room, as they would benefit most from better features and top functionalities. Most noticeable was the identification of ownership and location of the device that interrupted us. It was Hao's device and I felt almost rude to direct his device to be quiet. I have felt a similar feeling while walking my dog and bumping into another dog owner and having no say in or direct control over the other person's dog. So, from this small interaction in our interview, I was able to infer that (1) users are physically and cognitively disrupted by unsolicited VA interruptions, (2) users are left to hypothesise how the interruption occurred, and (3) users may feel uncomfortable or out of line when manipulating another person's VA device.

In other information and communication devices, such as smartphones and personal devices, interruptions in interactions describe the constant disruption of notifications from the multitude of apps and programmes that require human attention and are a distraction from intended tasks. The concept of attention management has been studied and implemented on smartphones to have better control over interruptive notifications (Anderson et al., 2018; Aranda et al., 2016). Anderson et al. (2018) describe these notifications as actionable information in situ, useful points of communication that can help the user, and are received at a critical point, such as a low battery warning to charge their phone. When dealing with physically and cognitively disabling effects on users, my findings suggest that VA disruptions may provoke different reactions than those of other devices.

Lag in Real-time Interaction

I describe an instance where lag in VA interaction caused Mark to partially stop engaging with his devices. He describes the process of waiting for his VA and other digital IoT systems to implement an action in his real environment.

> … once or twice with the lights in my old room, I just found that process just took too long, like you'd say, "Okay, turn on the lights", and **then you'd be waiting five seconds for the lights to turn on**. It's like you could just flick the light switch and the lights will turn on. That's the only time where **I did stop using a specific instruction, but I didn't stop using the speakers…**
>
> Mark, 4 person, 4 device household

I describe this phenomenon as VA latency, where the processing time to complete a request is not instantaneous and takes longer than the user's perceived processing time. Mark describes this in an answer to my question, "Has there ever been a time you stopped using your VA?" Mark expresses dissatisfaction with the action, opts to discontinue using the problematic interaction, and continues to use his VA for other activities.

> **Indra:** Did you take the light out or…?
>
> **Mark:** I left them in because I could turn them off and on with the wall switch, and I still use them with the Google speaker … So, it was kind of more of like a partial withdrawal from using the speaker with them, so I still use them but not to their full extent.

He suggests that VA latency discouraged him from engaging in this action, but not enough that he was driven to remove the smart lightbulbs. The opportunity to engage with a computational over a physical solution is still an option, but Mark decides not to use that command. It is only from interviewing long-term users that I can uncover instances like these. This also highlights the interplay of time and space in the perception and use of VAs during VA latency.

In HCI, pauses from a system or device may indicate a fault or latency (I found *lag to be a deterrent* in VA interaction). Designers of a system or device may deliberately or non-intentionally design pauses to mimic human–human speaker-relevant or communication pauses (Ballmer, 1980; Moon et al., 2021). For instance, designers may intentionally design speaker-relevant pauses, as described by Jiang et al. (2022), including visual cues such as loading graphics into their chatbots to avoid user disengagement. A common cue is using an animated ellipsis in a GUI chatbot message bubble to infer the system is thinking about and typing its response, like a human would. Also, deliberate speaker-relevant pauses by the chatbot mask the loading time of processing or the instantaneous retrieval of information that might not feel personable. This provides anthropomorphic hesitation, as UI characteristics of human hesitation in the context of instant messaging platforms are replicated. As well as speaker-relevant pauses, communication pauses have been intentionally designed into anthropomorphic conversational devices. In Koller et al.'s (2019) experimentation with gaze aversion, the time of non-action (pauses) by robot Peppa was measured to study the comfort of HRIs. Koller et al.'s findings suggested that longer pauses were more favourable for human–robot communication.

Planning Future Interactions

An interaction from Joey demonstrates the consideration of time as well as space and place in using VAs. As I detailed earlier, Joey travels through his three-storey home, where his VA device is on the second level, and his bedroom is on the third level. Joey will usually ask his VA to turn off the light in his bedroom, but needs to delay the request due to the distance between places and the rituals he wishes to perform before the request is actioned.

> But most of the time, I'll say like, turn off the bedroom light in 10 minutes when I'm going to bed.
>
> Joey, 2 person, 1 device household

Joey knows the interaction he wants to perform in the future will be outside Google's interaction field. Instead of making himself and other people in the house uncomfortable by yelling from the bedroom and being unable to gauge whether Google is processing his request, Joey has formed a practice of pre-empting a future goal and making a request that delays the action by the VA.

Indra: Oh okay, so you have to like pre-empt your actions because your Google is kind of far away. If you don't want to yell?

Joey: [laughs] But I would say a raised voice. The other option that we sometimes do if we're feeling lazy—just as easily, uh just with your phone going into Google Home and turning it off. **But if I'm like, on it, and smart, and walking past it before I go to bed, because our bathrooms downstairs, I'll be like turn it off in 10 minutes**. Because yeah, normally just jump right into bed. Do something and like **be on my phone for 10 minutes and then go to sleep**.

Joey understands the limitations of the VAs' interaction field, where the staircase and open area between levels create a transitory space to request interactions ahead of time. In this section, Joey's interaction with his VA illustrates the consideration of time, space and place in VA usage. This practice also reflects an understanding of the VA's interaction field limitations and the transitional spaces where interaction can occur but is experienced elsewhere.

VIRTUAL SPACE

Dourish's view on conversational interface systems (written in 2001, before VAs were released) encapsulates the difference in computers that exploit patterns of everyday human action but are still far from achieving true conversations that are embodied in social human behaviour.

Similarly, "conversational" computational systems, which use natural language-processing techniques and attempt to incorporate the rules of conversational interaction, may well make it easier and more natural to interact with computer systems inasmuch as they can exploit familiar patterns of everyday human action. However, encoding conversational rules about turn-taking and anaphoric reference is a world away from responding to the way in which those conversational rules arise out of a world of human social action, conducted through the coordinated media of spoken language, gaze, and posture. We inhabit conversations as embodied phenomena in the everyday world (Dourish, 2001, p. 102).

In the previous chapter, I referred to three definitions of context-defining aspects of embodied interaction: field, space and place. I used these definitions to explore the physical space in which VA interaction occurs, the organisation of the house and places in the home. As stated by Dourish (2001), space can be virtual or physical. In this section, I use embodied interaction theory to explore the capacities of the VA virtual space and how this affects interaction. VA virtual space is broken down into the different capacities for modes of communication, visual and auditory, bringing in excerpts from my participants that connect to the desire for visual experiences and the limitations of audible

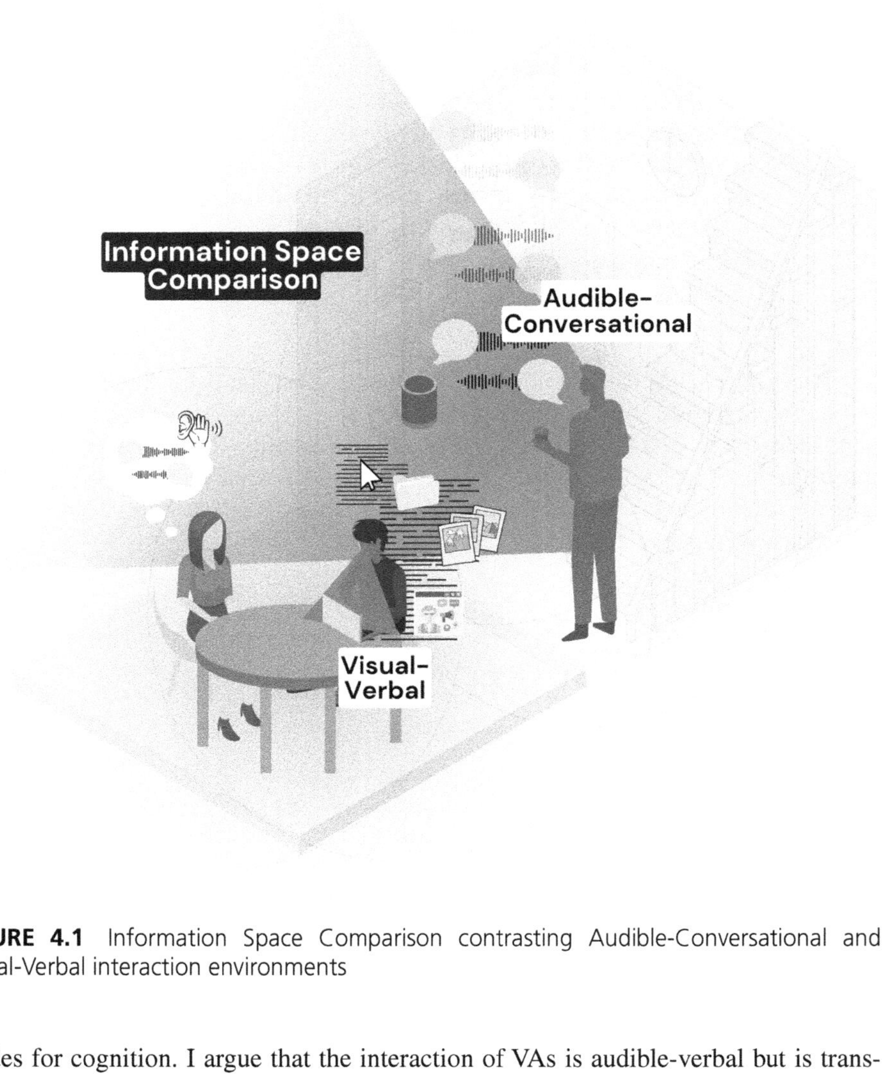

FIGURE 4.1 Information Space Comparison contrasting Audible-Conversational and Visual-Verbal interaction environments

modes for cognition. I argue that the interaction of VAs is audible-verbal but is transformed into audible-conversational as interactions are always expected to be two-way and engage the user as a listener and speaker. Space in audible-conversational interaction is used to describe the limitations of expressing and consuming information, and this affected the quality of action and information-based interactions. Examples from more advanced chatbots are given to highlight the differences in visual-conversational and voice-conversational interactions. I also make connections to the ephemeral nature of audible in situ communication and how Google and Amazon attempt to accurately record and present these secondary records of audible-conversational interaction through a voice history. Lastly, I explore strategies users engage in to navigate the challenges of the audible-conversational virtual space.

Visual Space, Verbal Space, Audible Space, and Conversational Space

I state differences in the amount of information that is portrayed through visual and auditory information-seeking and retrieval systems. In particular, the internet search engine interface has multiple touchpoints of periphery visual information. So, the illusion of choice from visual retrieval systems is replaced with the illusion of tacit knowledge in audible retrieval systems like VAs.

The experience of condensed audible space in comparison to visual space enables more anthropomorphism as users cannot see into the VA's processes, in what may be equivalent to being unable to view another human's mind, including how they may evaluate a situation, the emotions tied to a situation or the experiences that inform logic and emotion. Using a visual-based internet browser allows the user to see what the computer presents, not necessarily how the internet browser came to those results; those processes are still invisible, but users can view the result of how the system of algorithms and data has interpreted the command. Users can abstract informational cues from the search results that may help them rephrase their search query. Because there is more space available in visual computing, more visual information is available to abstract meaning and action. In voice interaction, space is experienced differently from visual space and is experienced audibly rather than visually. I draw on the concept of audible space, a term often used in music-based literature. As described by Young (2021, p. 355):

> Sound brings forth space. In contrast to visible space, audible space is kinetic and mutable, materializing, and dematerialising. It is perhaps the mobility that accounts for our feel for sounds as evanescent, and hallucinatory, as if objects heard belong to a less dense reality than objects seen.

Some participants described audible space in interaction as more of a deterrent to VA interaction. For example, my conversation with Jen about her experience trying internet banking through her Google Home VA.

Indra: Do you imagine yourself doing anything private on there, like checking your bank, buying stuff?

Jen: … You might say, "Can you log into my bank account?" I don't know if you ever do that, you know, **'cause you wanna see the results immediately in front of you… So I can't imagine doing that**. Shopping-wise, I use my phone for shopping all the time, and again, it's because it's in front of you.

Indra: Yeah, you need to look at it. Yeah, you're able to get you a… Yes, I was thinking of the banking… **Imagine it trying to read out the numbers. And how long that would take?**

Repeatedly, she talks about the lack of seeing as the main reason for not performing a highly private task or other tasks that include making decisions, such as shopping. In this excerpt, I refer to another form of communicable space—verbal space. When I refer to how long it would take the VA to read out the numbers relating to internet banking, I refer to not just seeing results but communicating these through vocabulary. Verbal space is another adjacent term to visual space but refers to the representation of language through written or spoken modes (Dai & Zhu, 2018). The difference in *seeing* and *reading* differentiates the modes of communication experienced by VA users. I experienced the sensation of reading and an overload of verbal information first-hand with Phoebe in our co-interaction with her Google Mini. Google joins our conversation as we invite it in, but quickly confuses us with its reply, and Phoebe asks it to leave our conversation.

Phoebe: Hey Google, what else has Anya Taylor-Joy been in?

Google: I found 13 on the website screen write dot com. All of Anya Taylor-Joy movies, ranked worst to best by IMDB. Here are the first five. One, here are the young man, seven point nine, ten. Two, split, seven point three, ten. Three, the witch, six point nine, ten. Four, Emma six point seven, ten…

Phoebe: [speaking over Google] Very confusing when you put the ratings on there…

Google: Want to hear some more?

Phoebe: No thank you.

Phoebe explains to me her perception of the issue with Google's confusing answer.

> Yeah, 'cause she's obviously reading from something that's got the number next to the thing and then the name of the thing and then like a rating of the thing … she'll literally just read the text from the website as it's written and that can turn out to be not very conversational and therefore hard to listen to…
>
> Phoebe, 2 person, 3 device household

Phoebe highlights the act of reading and a verbally overloaded response from Google, which compares conversational communication to that being written on a website. So, the medium of audible-conversational is mixed with text written for visual-verbal formats. The draw away from being conversational is pointed out as difficult to listen to. Phoebe continues to dissect the conversational programming of VAs.

So, if it was able to take the information from a webpage and **format it into a conversational way of presenting that detail**, so she was able to go like, "These are the titles of the films", "I will now put those into a script that I'll then read out in a way that is a bit easier to hear". That would probably be a better way for it to be programmed.
Phoebe, 2 person, 3 device household

Phoebe talks about programming and scripts, describing the process of how Google should organise and present information. Other than presenting ranked search results, Google has a process for formatting visual-verbal information called Knowledge Graphs, where the user's question is answered by Google compiling various sources for the correct and relevant information (How Google's Knowledge Graph works, n.d.), using interpretation of search queries to uncover their intended meaning (Iliadis & Ford, 2023). VA interaction uses the configuration of the audible-verbal space to conduct interaction. It builds on the verbal aspect in that interaction, which is always a two-speaker exchange between dynamic listener and speaker roles, otherwise referred to as conversation. So, I define VA interaction as audible-conversational interaction, in that it is different to conversation experienced visually and verbally in an instant messaging style interface, or even the exchange of letters over time. I refer to this as conversational space. It is this inherent mix of verbal, conversational and audio that confuses users in forming utterances or processing long responses from their VAs.

... you can absolutely include all that **fluff of conversational questioning** with the Google Home Mini, but if you actually type into Google quite often ... it won't always come through as an efficient way to ask that compared to if you just type in the keywords and it brings up the information you need ... **but with the Google home Mini, it works better if you actually are asking a question**.
Phoebe, 2 person, 3 device household

The condensed audible space of VAs significantly influenced user information-seeking and retrieval behaviours compared to the expansive visual space of internet browsers. The audible modality may promote greater anthropomorphism, as users attribute human-like qualities to the conversational interface, but it also introduces challenges in VA interaction due to the linear and limited nature of auditory information presentation.

Voice Histories Recording Ephemeral Interactions

Another factor in conversational interaction is time; often, visual interfaces are non-ephemeral, or if they are dynamic, like a video, users can navigate the virtual space to replay a video by using control buttons. If unavailable, they can refresh the internet page to see the fixed dynamic video or image again. In voice interaction, space is limited, and interaction is ephemeral in situ, but voice histories turn moments in time into a physical record that can be reviewed post-interaction.

Indra: That's it for the questions, but there is another component. Just for you to just look at your own voice history, and if there's anything that you find interesting, just to share it with me and your thoughts on it, it could be anything…
Mark: In the physical… logs?

Since these physical records only document metadata like time and content, other contextual information is missing. I observe Hugo trying to fill in the context, and while looking at the transcripts, Hugo is prompted to associate the entries with the individuals who initiated them and their reasons for doing so.

I see many… From… Maybe from my daughter … Yeah, my daughter uses it a lot, the… Well, every night, basically, she got lots of ear wax in and she had to put some wax in her ear, and she had to set a timer on every night, and that's what she used every night, and she said, "How many more minutes in my timer".
Hugo, 4 person, 8 device household

From the transcripts, he recounts a story about his daughter, what she was doing and why she would use a VA in that interaction. The single lines of the objective transcript turn into a story that Hugo can recall about the activities occurring in different places in his home. However, he is also left to guess who and why some utterances are said, but it does not seem to concern him.

I don't know who said, I love you, Alexa. Okay, could be my daughter.
Hugo, 4 person, 8 device household

In visual interfaces, users can navigate non-ephemeral content and replay dynamic media, while VA interactions are fleeting and create physical records that can be reviewed post-interaction. Users like Hugo associate voice interactions with individuals and their reasons for initiating them, transforming objective transcripts into meaningful narratives.

Phoebe was also perplexed by the notion of fixed personalities and constrained scripted interactions. I delve into how these aspects contribute to the perception of VA personality in the following chapters.

FINDINGS FEATURED IN THIS CHAPTER

TABLE 4.1 Chapter findings

Spatial boundaries > interaction fields	Participants like Phoebe discussed placing devices based on room boundaries rather than interaction fields, suggesting that users perceive spatial boundaries over interaction fields.
Audible and conversational space	Interaction is limited by the affordances of spoken words and exchanges between two consenting conversational partners. VA content was not optimised for this format, as it spoke information that was written to be read (visual space).
VA interaction pauses	Interaction pauses describe the physical and mental stillness before, during and after VA interaction. As the user is engaged with a digital voice interface, they are physically paused in the real environment and may become an obstacle in spaces. These pauses highlight the reliance on stillness for successful interaction, as movement can disrupt sound and audio recording, and consequently the VA's ability to process commands. These pauses are experienced in real environments and interrupt natural conversations, affecting communication and social interactions with other people.
VA interruptions affected users negatively	Unsolicited VA interruptions affected users physically and cognitively. Users ceased conversations to listen to the interruption, then struggled to recall the topic of the conversation.
VA latency	VA latency was experienced and discouraged the use of slow interactions.
Planning future interaction	Users planned future interactions based on their proximity to a VA, space/place during a routine, e.g. asking Google to turn off the light in 10 minutes.

Ownership, Custodianship, and Negotiating Control 5

INSIDE OUR ROOMS

Visibility, Manipulating Space, and Barriers

In earlier chapters, I discussed space regarding the division of areas in the home and ontologies of space in VA use, whether it is spatial-orientation-focused—near, above, up—or architecture-focused—rooms, pantry, kitchen. I have discussed them in the context of audio and voice interaction, particularly the distance between the microphone and speaker capabilities. Another factor to consider in VA interaction in the context of space is device visibility. Visual cues for interaction have been studied in VA use from the perspective of communication, such as visual listening cues (Moon et al., 2019), but it is often overlooked in the context of VAs, considering the main modality of interaction is sonic. However, speaking to Sophie, she highlighted the importance of visually seeing her VA as a cue to use her device, similar to personal objects and their role in cueing memories (Van den Hoven et al., 2021).

> And because she's in my bedroom … when I'm at my desk or in the living room, I'm not near Alexa, so I can't see her and think about it as well. **I think if she was on my desk and I could visually see her**, I would probably use her a bit more, I don't think it is worth getting another one, though.
>
> Sophie, 1 person, 1 device household

Sophie lives in a small apartment by herself; her open-plan living room contains her kitchen, workspace, and TV area, and the room connects to her bedroom and balcony. Since Covid, she has been working from home at her desk facing the balcony in a corner of her open living space. She is drawn to her desk to work for seven to eight hours; similarly, she spends the same number of hours in her bedroom to sleep each night. Sophie's space is small and open; she is happy to walk the short distance between rooms to

 DOI: 10.1201/9781003680840-5

interact with one device. One question to consider is: would seeing more devices in one's environment trigger more instances of interaction? But as evidenced here, Sophie blames the lack of visibility as a reason she does not use her VA devices as much as she would like. In the next quote, Sophie uses the word "looking" not to describe visibility, but the attention that is directed to her laptop, where the time is always visible in the virtual space of the laptop screen.

Sophie: No, I've never asked her the time because I prefer to check my phone.
Indra: You haven't been lazy enough?
Sophie: No, I'm always looking at a laptop, so the time is there. So, I'm either on my phone or on my laptop.

Next, in considering space, I discuss controlling divided space through doors. On a normal day, Anavi tells me she can hear her aunt interacting with the VA in the next room.

My aunt uses the one in her room pretty frequently [...] and I can hear her [Alexa] reading out the news [...] and sometimes it sounds like a **muffle if my door is closed** but I can hear her [Alexa] most of the time.
Anavi, 3 person, 3 device household

Anavi's experience suggests the organisation of one's space to ensure privacy and minimise others' access to their VA device, or closing the door to enclose their interaction space to block mis-interactions from noisy co-habitants. Anavi speaks of shutting her bedroom door to block the sound coming from her aunt in the next room. She refers to the doors as transient partitions of space, while she uses them to block off her room, she does not trust that they are reliable at blocking external noise from penetrating her VA's interaction field.

Once my aunt was having a meeting or something, and **my door was shut, and her door was shut**. But she talks very loud, so I could hear her say, "Alexa, Alexa, Alexa", and I was very scared that Alexa was going to... pop up.
Anavi, 3 person, 3 device household

Echoing Anavi's experience, I've also been experiencing some mis-interactions with VAs due to the layout of my home, combined with my preference to keep my bedroom door open when writing on my computer.

> My sister's bedroom is right across the hallway, her doorway opens right across from my bedroom. She installed an Alexa Echo Dot a year ago, and it sits on her dresser, while my Echo Spot sits on a bookshelf right next to my desk.
>
> When I'm at my desk, I can read the time and weather with a glance at my Echo Spot, the time displayed on the Echo Spot is in a larger font and it hurts my eyes less looking at the time on the Echo Spot rather than the tiny font size of the time displayed in the bottom right corner of the monitor of my Windows desktop PC. Moving my eyes away from the bright screen and into the depth perception of the real environment is refreshing for my eyes.
>
> I digress, I've been trying to play music as I write, speaking at my normal volume, and I turn on my sister's Alexa most of the time! It starts playing her "liked music" playlist on Spotify when I ask my Alexa to play mine. Both Alexas start blasting music and I need to physically walk into my sister's room to focus my voice towards her device and remove myself from my VA's interaction field, to stop her music, without turning off mine. I am surprised every time this happens, as I'm not even conscious of potentially activating her Alexa when thinking of performing an interaction. I am so focused on my device and what I want to do.
>
> When my door is closed, I don't wake her device and am saved from mis-interactions with unintended interaction recipients. I also find myself whispering to target-activate my device and not the devices in other people's rooms—but I find myself balancing the level of volume correctly to trigger my device but not too loud as to wake others as I stifle around at 2 am.
>
> 👤 Indra

From my and Anavi's experiences, the organisation of space leads to mis-interactions, yet users have some agency in manipulating space through doors to limit these unwanted interactions, as well as using the whisper function to limit the dispersion of voice during interaction. While both options allow the active user to limit mis-interaction, only blocking off space may limit the mis-interactions of non-intended interactions by surrounding household members.

Revisiting an interaction by Hugo, where he transcends barriers of space by using the "drop-in" feature on his Alexa VA network to broadcast to multiple locations in the house. Hugo uses the language of the drop-in feature by Alexa to describe dropping into the spaces his children occupy. The drop-in feature allows the user to project their voice from one Alexa VA speaker to another under the same account. Google's VA equivalent of this is called "Broadcast"—for example, "Hey Google, broadcast to the living room, it's time for homework". The user can direct a message to a specific VA device—in my example the VA device is named "living room". This is a common naming convention that is encouraged by the setup process of Amazon and Google. Hugo uses the drop-in function to transcend conventions of space and communicate within other spaces without the need for consent, overcoming obstructions and physical movement.

> I do use that **drop-in function a lot** and announce function 'cause the kids could be not with us, and I just say, "Announce dinner is ready". And then they can come over or **I drop into them**, "Hey, can you turn down the volume?" Things like that.
>
> Hugo, 4 person, 8 device household

Compared to a phone, which allows communication with others in faraway spaces, the receiver must accept or decline the call. With the VA drop-in, participants have the power to infiltrate spaces without consent, and from Hugo's experience, he uses this feature to extend the reach of his power and dominance over other people in the household. So, the drop-in feature is linked to power in relationships when one party can intercept the peace and privacy of another without consent.

Ownership of Spaces and Claiming Place

Another behaviour observed is the ownership of spaces that dissect homes into different domains of personal place. It became apparent that some participants spoke about shared spaces that were communal and some that belonged to others, for example, my daughter's room or my aunt's office.

> I have a third, third-generation Echo Dot in **my daughters' rooms**.
>
> Hugo, 4 person, 8 device household

Other participants, particularly those who lived alone or as a couple, spoke about the entire home as belonging to them, with no external prefix of to whom different spaces belonged. These participants and their smaller households were reported to have perceived shared ownership over all spaces in the home. Occasionally, some areas were more inclined to belong to one person, which may have been determined from negotiation or signalled by storing personal possessions or frequency of occupying a space. Such as Phoebe, who refers to her partner and herself as "we".

> **We** have one in **the** lounge room, one in the kitchen. One in **the** office and in one of **the** bedrooms.
>
> Phoebe, 2 person, 3 device household

Not only do the occupants of the home in collaborative experiences affect the perception and use of VAs, but occupancy and presence by others in a space contribute to the confidence and ownership of place in the home. I am drawn to recount my experience of living independently with my ex-partner, where we rented a house and shared a bedroom. I describe the change in my perceived ownership of space, as I broke up with my ex, moved back to my parents' house and experienced living with three other people again. Two of them were parental figures and had explicit monetary ownership of the space that I did not.

For a year and a half, my ex and I rented a three-bedroom, two-storey house. We had claimed the front room as the office, where both our computers sat. I had my Alexa there to play music, or to test my Alexa Developers experiments that I would code from my computer. Another Alexa, with a small screen, sat upstairs in our bedroom on my bedside table. So, between the front office room and my bedroom was the staircase and landing.

Over time, I had learnt it was okay to speak loudly to Alexa while walking up the stairs, as I was confident that either Alexa device would capture my voice. Usually, it was to turn the bedroom light on, as I switched off the downstairs lights before making my way to the bedroom upstairs. It was normal and comfortable to shout to Alexa in this house and I was confident to complete these interactions in front of my ex, as he would use the same commands I would, or I would regularly be home alone.

Moving back to my parents' house… I find myself now whispering to my Alexa. I set up my Alexa in my bedroom and helped my mum and sister set one up in their bedrooms. One reason I whisper is the pang of embarrassment, to not interact too loudly when my parents are potentially nearby or watching, especially my stepfather, who I'm sure would have something "funny" to say about talking to an object.

👤 Indra

I believe my ownership of the space and place, combined with the absence of others, allowed for a different style of VA interaction compared to my parents' home, where the boundaries of ownership of different spaces intersected with the personal places of other people. Living in a home where I "owned" each room, where I controlled and created every place, I could truly interact from everywhere and anywhere at any time. Our relationships with the people we live with are consequential to the co-creation and cohabitation of places. Like Avish, who shared how his partner and roommate had consciously decided to co-use their VA devices, demarcated by their exchange of ownership of devices through simultaneous gift giving.

Avish: We gave them [Google Minis] to each other as Christmas presents and I think it was all part of trying to make this house that we are living together as tech-savvy as possible.

👤 Avish, 3 person, 3 device household

Their collaborative intentions shone throughout their collaborative acts. Alternatively, even without VA gift giving, being one of the perceived owners of the home and the parent in a parent–child relationship grants greater power to delineate a shared place. Like Lien in his home, where he and his wife dictate which areas are "open" or for "family".

> We let them use the devices because **they [VA devices] are there in open areas** and I try to setup the devices not just for myself but as **a family device**. Like some people would put the to-do lists, reminders or a purchase list on the Alexa. Because this is an **account shared by all the family members**, so I don't put all those on it. And yeah, we got Spotify connected to it, so they got their playlists, they got my playlist, but there's **nothing personal on Alexa**.
>
> 👤 Lien, 4 person, 6 device household

Lien's story highlights that the ownership of places comes with careful consideration of how others will use the device. A different perspective comes from my experience, where my concerns were based on my lack of confidence in interacting in front of others and my embarrassment in interacting loudly. Lien is instead concerned about the misuse of record-keeping interactions, like the high-stakes interaction of adding to an Amazon purchase list. What Lien also considers is that each potential shared user has some opportunity for personalisation even on a family device, in that household members can access their personal playlists due to Spotify's customisation features. Personalisation is organised through another system, as collaboration-enabling features like split customisation based on user voice recognition were not brought up. This highlights Lien's mindfulness towards ensuring that each user feels a sense of ownership and individuality when interacting with the family device, an aspect of consideration beyond technical functionalities. Lien's perspective on VA usage underscores the importance of considering how others will use the device, particularly VAs in nominated shared spaces.

RELATIONSHIP TYPES STEMMING FROM COLLABORATIVE INTERACTION

Novel social identities and relationships stemming from VA co-interaction do not always occur in tandem, but it could be considered that smaller behaviours derived from these identities could be observable in most VA households. The VA device custodian, VA parents and general automation of domestic relationships stem from intention to use, perception of technology and confidence in use.

Device Custodians

I use the term "device owner" to imply all participants and their household members who perceive some ownership over a VA device. Ownership infers having control over something in one's possessions, where an owner has been defined as "a person who owns something: one who has the legal or rightful title to something: one to whom property belongs" (Merriam-Webster, n.d.b, para. 1). While in a home, one person may have purchased or acquired the VA devices, but often these are used collectively. The lines between ownership of individual devices become blurred when the ownership of the places where the devices are located may take precedence over who paid for the device. Therefore, if anyone can assume ownership, I use the word custodian to refer to a separate identity, as it refers to "one that guards and protects or maintains" (Merriam-Webster, n.d.a, para. 1). The custodian identity extends to other relationships associated with parenting and dependent users. In this section, I outline three responsibilities of custodians: gatekeeping and VA setup, monitoring household co-use to enhance interactions and managing codependent interactions from other household members.

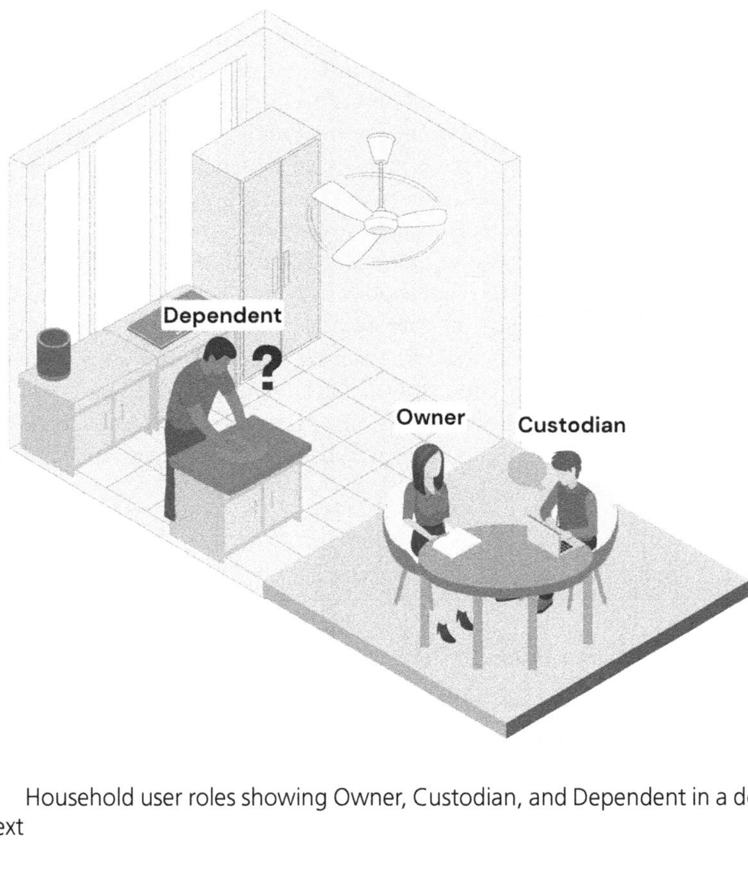

FIGURE 5.1 Household user roles showing Owner, Custodian, and Dependent in a domestic VA context

Gatekeeping set-up and interactions

Custodians are usually involved in the setup of devices, managing the associated VA application on their smartphones, and are usually called on when a technical issue arises for other VA users in the home. To illustrate how custodians manage the setup of VA devices, I draw from my experience as the main VA custodian in my household.

> I had bought the smart plug a few weeks ago in between work and I finally got around to setting up the lamp in mum's room, so she'd be able to turn it off without getting out of bed. It took me three days to set up the Alexa Echo Dot and the smart lamp smart switch in my mum's room. After downloading two apps, going through the installation process about 12–15 times for unknown technical issues, taking a break and starting again the next night, finally my mum could turn her lamp off from her bed when she nodded off to sleep. I needed breaks in between attempts as I was getting extremely frustrated as the lamp didn't want to connect to Alexa. Between work, study and my social life, I was motivated to help mum, but only when I was in a positive mindset to work on the problem. So, my mum's use of Alexa and this interaction was dependent on my ability, availability and energy in setting up the device and its connections. Mum wasn't upset that I couldn't get it to work; she was very grateful that I wanted to help her. I did eventually get it to work; finally mum could turn her lamp off from her bed when she nodded off to sleep. There's a quiet contentment of the mask of darkness when you've finally fallen into that deep state of sleepiness after a restless night. She no longer needed to keep an ear out, listening for the fateful footsteps of someone walking down the corridor. I used to hear her call out my name, "Indi". I would pop my head in her door, it was always slightly ajar in case she needed us. "Yeah? What's up?", I would say. "Turn my light off please". "Ok lady, goodnight, I love you". "I love you too". After I set up the smart lamp, I would hear her softly say, "Alexa, lamp off" and know that she was about to drift off to sleep. Even though she didn't need me to turn off her lamp anymore, I would still pop my head through her door every hour or so, or when I haven't heard her move around the house in a while.
>
> Indra

Custodians will tailor the VA and IoT setup, and other users, like my mother, rely on these customisations to enhance their interaction with the device. Thus, the custodian role extends beyond technical setup to encompass the facilitation of personalising VA usage for household members. As well as being dependent on the time and effort of the custodian, other users were also dependent on the skill availability of the custodian. In a few cases, I observed the gatekeeping of skills to the rest of the household.

Well, 'cause **most of the skills you have to activate on your phone before you have to enable it on your phone before you can use them**. They're [Lien's children] pretty familiar with all the settings in the current things they know. All the devices that are linked to Alexa, they know how to play a song, look at the photos with all those new skills, **they got no idea, unless I add it and ask them to try it**.

Lien, 4 person, 6 device household

In the case of Alexa, users must enable skills from the app before they can use them. This means the experiences of others depend on the custodian's perception and preferences. Compared to other visual interfaces where users are offered visual previews, perhaps a recommendation of what to watch next on YouTube or suggested apps in the App Store, users may have an idea of what other digital services are available to them. In comparison, users of VAs may have limited awareness of available digital services. Hugo echoes this sentiment, surprising his family with new routines he has put together for their smart home ecosystem.

Indra: So, when you come up with the new routine, say, this one about the showers.
Hugo: Yeah.
Indra: How do you communicate this to your family? That it's something.
Hugo: Yes, I surprise them!

Hugo takes his role as custodian seriously, even developing a business case for different routines he will create for the home. When I enquire about his process for devising these routines, he explains that they stem from the various issues his family members bring to him.

That's the tricky part, is to come up with a routine. That gives some value. You know what I mean? Some advantage. It's not for fun. So, I have really routines that help... my wife says, "Oh, at night I want to have this light, that light, that night, that night" or whatever she wants to. So I say, "Alexa normal or night or..." And that configures different setting of lights. You know, when they go to sleep my daughters, might say, "Okay, I want to have some kind of light or, 10% that light, or 20% the other one" or whatever. So I have different routines and I'm trying to make with kind of like a, like a business scenario...

Hugo, 4 person, 8 device household

It is unclear if Hugo's family members know that VAs and other smart technology will be part of the solution or if the problems of his family are coincidentally addressable through VAs and IoT smart lights. This contradicts the narrative presented later by Hugo, where he is concerned that his daughters cannot keep up with his technological fixes involving complex VA interactions and IoT connections.

My research suggests a broader understanding of power dynamics emerging through VA custodians. They often function as protectors, enablers and managers of smart technology, particularly in the context of VAs. In the literature, terms like "owner" and "ownership" are frequently used to distinguish between users who cannot access the full functionality of a device, as highlighted by Cecchinato and Harrison (2017). This lack of access can stem from factors such as tangible limitations, such as not having a mobile phone to use the Alexa app, or intangible barriers, such as being unable to access a password-protected account. In cases of full access, there tends to be a perception of singular ownership, which may discourage co-users from using the device out of respect for the primary owner (Jacobs et al., 2016).

While the studies mentioned focus on multi-user interactions primarily from the owner's perspective, there is a notable gap in research regarding how owners and their influence are perceived from the standpoint of co-users (Shavitt et al., 2021). Once more, my findings predominantly reflect the perspective of the perceived owner. However, I advocate for a nuanced shift in discourse by using "custodian" instead of "owner". This recommendation is informed by my research on space and place in VA interaction, highlighting how partial ownership of VA devices is influenced by their location within the home. While one individual may have complete access to the VA account, they might not have unrestricted access to the physical spaces where VA devices are located, such as someone's bedroom. Consequently, the allocation of ownership over each device becomes blurred when ownership of the spaces where devices are situated may take precedence over financial ownership. Thus, although anyone can assume the role of an owner, I use the term "custodian" as an identity, as it encompasses the responsibilities associated with caretaking and management—"one that guards and protects or maintains" (Merriam-Webster, n.d.a, para. 1).

Monitoring co-use by household to optimise interactions

Hugo explains that he devises business scenarios to address problems that might necessitate the use of VAs and IoT technology in a solution. In business, planning for a scenario helps "decision-makers identify ranges of potential outcomes and impacts, evaluate responses and manage for both positive and negative possibilities" (Luther & Ali, 2022, para. 1). As a VA custodian, Hugo not only creates business cases for routines to optimise his life but also goes through this process to encourage the use of VAs by the household.

Indra: You mentioned **you create like a business case for each routine**. Is this because you like taking requests from your whole family? You try to work out what they want?

Hugo: 90% of request is just for myself. **However, many of them I'm thinking are orientated to them to enjoy this and see the advantage of having** [the VAs]. Like, normally they are getting them and now from time to time I've seen my wife starting to use it in real scenarios.

Hugo has seen his efforts to empathise with his family transform from a scenario into a VA function that is actively used and appreciated by other co-users. He speaks about understanding the way *his* wife cooks, the individual behaviours unique to his wife's personality. He recognises her cooking style in that she uses multiple timers at once. In domestic environments, users can observe their co-users' daily behaviours to plan and create custom empathy-driven VA experiences.

Hugo measures the success of his business scenarios through independent use and feedback from other users. He appears genuinely satisfied with his wife's use of the VA IoT setup he created for her. She uses it independently without requiring his presence and gives him positive feedback.

> My wife now, when she's cooking, she need like a four or five timers at the same time. You know, different times or whatever. So, she is asking now Alexa for different timers of the clock on the wall is putting on the timers and **she is using even when I am not here**. And she also told me… **She also told me that she reckon that this is a good purpose to have an Alexa there and she's kinda happy with that part of the ecosystem, so she's using a lot for cooking**.
>
> Hugo, 4 person, 8 device household

In another household, Mark monitors the uptake of usage by other household members. However, he has been disappointed by the lack of VA uptake by his parents. His disappointment is implicit as he describes the limited variety of VA interaction by his parents and his sister's preference for playing music with conventional non-VA speakers over the Google VA devices.

> I was really excited about them [Mark's family], and I was like, "So cool, you know you guys could join the family [referring to the system of VAs] and train your voice to it" … **But they're just not interested in the technology**, I guess my sister has her own Bluetooth speaker and she used that before she goes … Dad will only use the Chrome cast to turn on Netflix, but he won't dictate anything to it. And yeah, mum, she literally just used the speaker to play Spotify music pretty much.
>
> Mark, 4 person, 4 device household

His disappointment may stem from the effort he has invested as the custodian in teaching his co-users how to communicate with the VA. Mark goes as far as creating personalised scripts tailored to everyone's preferences, drawing from his knowledge about the person and successful phrases he has learnt from his VA interaction experience.

Indra: How did your mum come to do the things she does with them, did you…
Mark: I showed her, so like the first few times I was like, "Oh. And so, you have to say, Okay Google or Hey"—the whole room just lit up… **You have to say the words and then just ask it what you wanted to do, either say, "Play Elvis on Spotify or listen to country radio"** or something like that. And yeah, that could be that she just doesn't know how to give it instructions as well, maybe.

Mark concludes that his mother's inability to give clear instructions is why she does not perform many VA interactions without his help. But Mark also has a few more hypotheses based on his observations of her use.

She's [mum] made some discoveries. I didn't teach her about the radio stations and things like that, that sounds… that's something she learnt. She also… 'cause you can broadcast to the home… She learnt how to do that … Yeah, but not many discoveries, what she has experimented with it most of the time, **yeah, she might get a response that's not what she's asking, so she just reverts back to her standard… Go-to instructions**.
Mark, 4 person, 4 device household

Mark realises that his mother has made discoveries but believes she is easily discouraged and reverts to the knowledge he has bestowed on her as a custodian. He notices that his prompts, derived from his VA-prompted language, work more effectively, indicating that his mother may not have mastered this method. Instead, she resorts to a communication style similar to one she might use when speaking to someone who has difficulty listening or hearing, such as someone who is deaf or has English as their second language, by drawing out the sounds of her words.

But I think it's because Google is anticipating that you talk like you would to a normal person, **they're not anticipating that you draw out your words and your syllables, so maybe that confuses the speaker maybe**, 'cause she talks quite slowly.
Mark, 4 person, 4 device household

The reasons behind the specific behaviours of Mark's mother remain ambiguous due to the limited number of non-custodial users I interviewed. Furthermore, potential participants may not self-identify as VA users, believing their proficiency inadequate, which could deter them from volunteering for research interviews. As a custodian, Mark observes his co-users and actively identifies VA-appropriate utterances personalised for the individual. He attempts to teach them these terms by suggesting them in conversation and monitors their usage over time. Mark notes interactions that the co-users discover on their own and forms hypotheses about their discoveries and lack of use. The role of a device custodian implies a distinct relationship with the VA compared to other users in the home and those without a custodian in the household.

My research revealed that custodians play a significant role in shaping household VA usage patterns. As custodians, participants were observed to closely monitor co-users and proactively identify VA commands tailored to their needs. They often attempted to teach these commands by incorporating them into everyday conversations. Custodians passively monitored VA usage patterns of co-users over time, observing interactions that co-users discovered independently. They also formulated hypotheses regarding these discoveries and the reasons behind the lack of usage in certain instances. The existing literature has explored the influence of multi-user interactions and shared accounts on non-adopters in VA usage (Gebhart, 2017; Janes et al., 2020; LeFebvre, 2017). However, there is a gap in research regarding the coercion of passive co-users into becoming active users and the strategies employed to achieve this. Research has examined the reasons why passive co-users may not engage with a smart product, from low self-autonomy, self-efficacy or responsibility (Shavitt et al., 2021), or navigating ownership and assuming specific rules and patterns of behaviour with an object based on a perceived owner (Garg & Moreno, 2019). For example, breaking the rules of shared use by co-users led to revoking access to IoT devices (Garg & Moreno, 2019).

Another strategy employed by custodians to encourage the adoption of VA usage by passive co-users involved solving the problems of these co-users through VA solutions. My research discovered VA custodians creating business cases to help clarify problems that may require the use of VAs and IoT technology in the solution for their family. There appears to be no related experience documented in the literature where users articulated strategic planning not only for their VA routines but also for those of other household members. Comparably, research has pointed towards upcoming prediction-based automation that leverages IoT and VA interaction data to automate smart technology routines based on past user behaviour (Rafferty et al., 2017; Lunardi et al., 2018). Chiang et al. (2020) tested their prediction-based VA and IoT ecosystem; however, their testing focused on the experience of individuals, overlooking the dynamics of multi-user interaction and shared living experiences within smart home environments. Without prediction-based automation in current VA technology, participants are compelled to be thoughtful and considerate, evaluating the effort and adoption of routines by household members in their role as custodians.

Discussion on smart homes also takes a gendered scope in the literature regarding power and inequality, such as Chambers' (2020) discussion on gender, asking if men and women are invited to participate equally or unequally in smart home technology. Alternatively, the continuation of the archetypal male technologist, who is often characterised through their concerns with energy, efficiency, and reducing household labour, achieving these goals through the lens of principles from economics, engineering, and computer science (Strengers, 2013; Ehrenberg & Keinonen, 2021), instead of more emotional or socially based principles of creating change. Some participants exhibited characteristics like those described in the depiction of the male technologist.

Smart technology reshapes the power balance of the home by introducing new tools to control our environment and handing control to the home itself. In the process of extending control over the home, smart technologies change the way that power is constituted through overt and discreet observation, constraining interactions, and predefining practices in the home, thereby re-aligning the network of relations within the home (Ehrenberg & Keinonen, 2021, p. 7).

Custodians thus occupy a unique position of power within smart home ecosystems—not through explicit authority, but through their technical knowledge, their capacity to define household routines, and their ability to shape which family members engage with VA technology and how. This role, whether assumed voluntarily or assigned by default, transforms them into mediators between the promises of smart home automation and the lived realities of their households.

Interaction codependency

During my interview with Avish, he revealed details about the setup and cost of their home VAs, which he shares with his partner and housemate. However, despite the devices being registered to his Google account and having full access to the partner app and voice history, Avish's dependency on James for certain interactions raised questions about his role as a custodian. Avish began to describe a common interaction the household has in the kitchen with their Google Nest Hub (a VA with a large screen) during our interview.

Indra: Could you maybe give me a demonstration of…
Avish: Oh… James is the one who mainly does that… Hang on.
Indra: Have you tried it yourself?
Avish: No, I've not used the screen for recipe, I've used it for videos and music, but… James will be home soon, so I can ask him how he does recipes on it. Yeah.
Indra: Okay, does he speak more to it or does he touch and type…
Avish: Touch, I've seen him touch and type the screen or scroll the screen.

After this our conversation shifts, but I redirected the discussion back to the recipe skill, as I was curious to know what prevented Avish from trying it himself or attempting it now.

> Yeah, **I've seen him do it, but I've helped done it**, so… Yeah, as I said, he should be home from his work and a minute now, so **I'll ask him** when he arrives.
> Avish, 3 person, 3 device household

Thirty minutes later in the interview, James arrives home.

Avish: One second, James' here, so I'm just going to ask him that question.
Indra: Okay.
Avish: Um, when you look up the recipe for whatever it was you made the other day, you had it on the screen. It wasn't YouTube was it? No?

[Some soft talking from James I can't make out.]

Avish: Yeah.

[More soft talking.]

Avish: Did you Google it on here? How did you do that? We're just going to watch what he does.

One could consider James as a custodian for the recipe action in Avish's household. James is perceived by Avish as the performer and knowledge keeper of this skill. It is possible that his reluctance stems from his limited experience in using the skill, lacking the precise conversational commands to initiate it. However, the lack of interest or experience in performing a skill does not necessarily mean he should not attempt to demonstrate it. Instead, he acknowledged his unfamiliarity with the interaction, but Avish consistently refers to John as the individual who "does it". This story suggests that custodianship may vary in scope, from managing the entire VA ecosystem to concentrated scenarios such as managing specific skills or actions.

When considering who manages the VA, an "othered" identity arises in the form of other co-users in more passive roles. I have not formally identified other identities besides custodians and parents, as I collected most of my data from conversations with custodians. On reflection, it became apparent that most of my participants were device custodians, with Anavi being the only exception, as she did not have access to the Alexa VA app. The device in her room was registered and managed by her aunt, who purchased and introduced the device into the household. Being a custodian was not screened for during participant recruitment. The primary criterion was individuals who had used a VA for more than six months. However, this observation raises another consideration: custodians were more likely to volunteer for interviews about VAs. This could indicate that custodians are more confident in discussing their VA experiences, thereby highlighting the disparity in perception between custodians and other household co-users. Future research could explore how non-custodians interact with the VA app, use skills and perceive general control of the VA without having access to or the same perspectives as custodians.

Parenting in Smart Households

As custodians of their children, individuals must balance these responsibilities with the presence of interactive technology in the household. Without passwords to initiate interaction (users can set a pin to protect specific skills or actions), Alexa and Google will respond to all users who can pronounce the wake words followed by a command (I have witnessed adorable three-year-olds stumble over the word Alexa, unable to wake her up). This means children have access to the internet as well as controlling other IoT devices just by using their voice. What I present here is the connection between children's actions and the role of parents and parents as general VA custodians. Among my participants, I have three parents of young children: Hao, Lien, and Hugo.

Compromising VA interaction for children

The last observation noted was in Hugo's household, where the integration of more smart objects controlled by voice instead of physical touch was a concern for the younger people in the home.

> ... especially I have a lot of issues at the beginning with the switches for the lights because they're not like a normal switch like this one ... **To remember all of this stuff—It's a lot of things. It's a little bit overwhelming for my daughters sometimes**.
>
> 👤 Hugo, 4 person, 8 device household

Children may find it overwhelming to navigate these highly computerised controls, particularly if they encounter issues with the devices that restrict basic functionalities, such as turning on lights or accessing temperature controls.

In the case of children, decisions about their access to VA devices often require communication and negotiation among the parents. Often, the VA custodian needs to negotiate with the other parent on the functionalities of VAs when children might be involved. This manifested in discussion and compromise for Hugo and his wife.

> **Indra:** Interesting. So, are you kind of balancing your wife's interests?
>
> **Hugo:** Yeah, I need to balance. Of course, I'm doing the same because she liked the traditional photo printing and put it in [Alexa], and I don't like that. **So we negotiate, this is marriage, you know, normal stuff and family and I give something, and yeah**.

Limiting children's interactions and monitoring techniques

The first observation concerns the concept of restricting VA capabilities for children to avoid outsourcing learning opportunities. This became apparent during my conversation with Lien when he described his daughter using Google to help her with homework. Lien caught his daughter using the VA as a voice interface calculator. The advantage of using a voice calculator over traditional physical calculators or calculator apps on phones or tablets is the invisibility of a voice interface. Lien's daughter does not need to hide or conceal an object to avoid getting caught. The voice interface allows Lien's daughter to sneakily access the VA from a distance when her parents are not watching or listening in.

Lien: When my daughter, she was doing her homework, she basically asked Alexa to do the math for her... **Yeah, which I asked her not to do**. But yeah, initially when I heard it, that's smart.
Indra: Tell me more about that. Was she being sneaky about it or anything?
Lien: She knows that she can't do it and doesn't do it in front of us and tested a little bit.
Indra: Okay. Was it a hard question? Do you remember?
Lien: Like 282 plus 100 something? Yeah, yeah, she can do it by herself... it's a quicker way.

It was in Lien's interest as a parent to monitor the use of the inconspicuous interface for automating opportunities for children to learn. As well, Lien monitors access to content that is restricted on other media technologies, such as phones, televisions, laptops, or tablets. In their house, Lien has placed an Alexa Echo Show in the main living area. It has a large screen that can be voice controlled. For example, the command "Alexa, play Baby Shark on YouTube" would open the YouTube application and begin playing the video and music instantly on the small screen.

There's some days when the kids discovered that they can actually use the Echo Show to go on YouTube, which is the point when I got a little bit mad about that, **'cause they're not supposed to watch TV, but they trying to be sneaky and watch it on Alexa...** I did think about what I should implement like as a parent, parent restriction, and I found it ... **either it recognises your voice, or you put in a pin. We basically rely on it quite a lot, so I didn't do it**.
Lien, 4 person, 6 device household

Parents are required to rethink how their children can access VAs and how to manage parents' and children's access with the restrictions available. Lien describes the two features he discovered for restricting access: voice recognition and authorisation (referred to as VoiceID by Amazon) or a voice PIN (a 4-digit number to be spoken to unlock specific interactions), both of which he decided were not useful, since they are disruptive to his vision of the living room VA as a shared family device.

Indra: Did she stop doing it after you told her? What happened?
Lien: Yeah, yeah, she stopped. But basically, we let them use the devices because they are there in open areas.

Lien references space and place in reasoning why he forgoes parental controls in favour of a smooth collaborative experience for the family. It is not clear if he refers to open space, like a floor plan with little walls, or an open place, where everyone is welcome to congregate. Regardless, Lien expresses his awareness of the children being able to overhear his interactions, which in this case discourages him from using the voice purchasing feature with Alexa.

Indra: Have you bought stuff talking to Alexa, like just voice, or is it on your phone and computer…
Lien: Mainly on the computer, I haven't bought anything over the device, as in the Echo device, like I mentioned, sometimes I have to be careful with the kids, try not to copy and get me lots of stuff when they know that they can do it.

Because of Lien's desires for his family to embrace VAs as a collaborative family technology, he chooses to post-monitor—instead of pre-monitor his children's use of Alexa. Pre-monitor activities referring to actions such as preventing his children from inappropriate VA use. Instead, post-monitoring includes the review and analysis of VA and other smart home data to assess if his children have broken any rules. Lien post-monitors his children's VA use by accessing the Alexa voice history and their YouTube history.

I just trust that they [Lien's children] won't do it again, and I told them not to, and basically, **I can track later histories of what they did and YouTube history as well**. So, I just told them not to use it or not to watch the TV on the Echo Show.
Lien, 4 person, 6 device household

As I described above with custodians and gatekeeping, Lien is selective about what Alexa skills he enables and which ones he communicates to his children to use. Not only does he monitor what inappropriate content his children may be accessing, but he also monitors what they enjoy, removing what he observes is not popular.

> I think I just activated the fart game and then just ask them to go to Alexa and ask her to do the fart test. And that's when they started laughing and that wasn't a very interactive game, **so I had it removed after that**, yeah. Okay, 'cause well… **it's like a one-off thing**.
>
> Lien, 4 person, 6 device household

I continue to probe Lien about the descriptor of "friend" he used to describe his children's relationship to Alexa.

> **Indra:** Do your kids talk differently with Alexa? Do they talk to her like it's their friend?
>
> **Lien:** They are **pretty consistent with what they talk to Alexa, 'cause there are only limited commands that they know** or they would navigate on the [Echo] Show. Yeah, so when they talk, they will be the repetitive commands that they're using.

Lien benefits from his children's inability to browse Alexa's skills and functions. In combination with his other post-monitoring activities and trusting his children to listen to his instructions, Lien perceives this as enough countermeasures to opt out of using the parental controls offered by Amazon, such as VoiceID and voice PINs.

In my research, I identified patterns of interaction and management among parents in households with VAs. Participants in my study acted as VA custodians and parents, extending and adapting their custodial behaviours to their children. From the literature on parenting with VAs, studies have observed augmentation through VA mediation (Beneteau et al. 2020) and active monitoring of VA use (Beneteau et al., 2020; Porcheron et al., 2018). Works such as Garg and Sengupta (2020) have systematically mapped the uses of VAs from the perspective of fathers, mothers and children over time, highlighting that children have different patterns of VA use in comparison to parents. Although my research did not exclusively focus on children–parent interactions with VAs, it contributes to understanding parental behaviours in monitoring audible-conversational digital spaces. This includes limiting interactions to prevent children from copying or automating learning opportunities. Additionally, my research explores how parents negotiate with other parents and adjust smart home ecosystems to ensure they are accessible and appropriate for children.

In my research, I found that parents use pre-monitoring and post-monitoring behaviours to regulate their children's VA use. Pre-monitoring interactions involve actions such as enabling and disabling third-party skills, strategically communicating available skills to children, and passively monitoring through physical presence. Past research has also identified parents strategically introducing VA functionalities to their children

(Beneteau et al., 2019; Druga et al., 2017). The inability to browse skills works in favour of parents who wish to monitor the usage of ubiquitous technologies relying on voice interaction. Parents can monitor usage from a distance as long as they can hear interactions, especially since children are likely to move into the space where the VA is located to interact with it, such as the case of Lien's living room VA speaker with a screen. I identified post-monitoring activities by parents/custodians that included asking children about their use, checking the voice history and reviewing application history on secondary APIs like YouTube. Also notable was the limited use or discussion of parental controls provided by Amazon or Google in their VA systems, such as VoiceID or voice PIN. Participants described these controls as distracting from the purpose of having a shared family device.

FINDINGS FEATURED IN THIS CHAPTER

TABLE 5.1 Chapter findings

Lack of spatial boundaries causes VA mis-interactions	Mis-interactions occurred when sound penetrated unwanted spaces unaligned with users' intended VA interaction. Manipulating spatial boundaries, such as doors can help users mitigate the risk of VA mis-interactions. Using the whisper feature also helped to curb mis-interactions due to spatial organisation. However, manipulating spatial boundaries can only deter non-intended interactions by passive users.
Lack of consent in transcending spatial boundaries	The VA drop-in (Amazon) or broadcast (Google) function allows users to transcend conventions and communicate within other spaces without the need for consent, limited obstructions and physical effort. This feature is linked to power in relationships when one party can intercept the privacy of another without consent.
Perceptions of home ownership	A user's perception of ownership of places in the home affected their use of VAs.
Personalisation of shared devices	Users expressed a desire for each household member to have a sense of ownership and individuality when interacting with a family device.
Voice histories as evoking storytelling	While revisiting their voice history, users transformed objective transcripts into meaningful narratives.
VA custodian	I introduce the term custodian, which refers to a person who guards and protects or maintains. This infers specific behaviours and perceptions of VAs. Custodians are usually involved in the setup of devices, managing the associated VA application on their smartphones, and are usually called on when a technical issue arises for other VA users in the home.

(*Continued*)

TABLE 5.1 (Continued)

VA owner	I discern VA owners to imply all participants and their household members who perceive some ownership over a VA device. There may be one person who purchased or acquired the VA devices, but often they are used collectively. The lines between ownership of individual devices become blurred when the ownership of the places where the devices are located may take precedence over who paid.
Custodians as facilitators of personalisation	The role of custodians extends beyond technical setup to encompass the facilitation of personalising VA usage for household members.
Custodians as gatekeepers of skills	Users must enable skills from the Alexa app before use. This means the experiences of others depend on the perception and preferences of the custodian user. VAs may have limited awareness of available digital services due to the lack of browsing ability.
Creating a home automation business case	Participants devised business scenarios to address problems that might necessitate the use of VAs and IoT technology in a solution. In domestic environments, users can observe their co-users' daily behaviours to plan and create custom empathy-driven VA experiences.
VA custodians monitor household VA use	Custodians monitor the use and sentiment of household co-users regarding VAs through observation, particularly focusing on individual interactions recommended by the custodian. Custodians were found to be disappointed with the limited variety in co-users' usage patterns and the use of other technologies for similar purposes. Custodians noted interactions that co-users discovered independently and formed hypotheses about co-users' discoveries and lack of use.
Utterance coaching	Participants actively identified and coached other household members on personalised, VA-appropriate utterances.
Interaction codependancy	Participants showed reluctance to perform certain VA interactions, preferring to wait for the perceived expert to handle the interaction.
Covert VA use by children	The voice interface enables children to covertly interact with the VA from a distance when parents are not observing or monitoring their activities.
Parents did not use inbuilt VA restriction features	Voice recognition and authorisation (referred to as VoiceID by Amazon) or a voice PIN (a 4-digit number spoken to unlock specific interactions) were not used, as they conflicted with the concept of the VA as a shared family device. Users opted to forgo parental controls to maintain a seamless collaborative experience for the family.
Pre-monitoring and post-monitoring VA use	Pre-monitoring activities involve measures to prevent inappropriate VA use by children, such as restricting access or establishing usage rules. Post-monitoring involves the review and analysis of VA and other smart home data to determine if children have violated any rules, including examining the Alexa voice history and YouTube watch history.

(Continued)

TABLE 5.1 (Continued)

Selective introduction of VA skills to children	Parents exercised discretion in enabling Alexa skills and selectively communicated to their children which skills to use. This process involved monitoring the skills that were enjoyed and removing those observed to be unpopular. Parents benefit from their children's inability to browse Alexa skills and functions.
Over-computerisation of the home	Parents expressed concern that their children might find it overwhelming to navigate highly computerised controls in the home, particularly when encountering issues that restrict basic functionalities such as turning on lights.
Negotiating VA use with other parents	Often VA custodians need to negotiate with other parents on the functionalities of VAs when children are involved.

Human-AI-Brands: The Relationship between Capital, Designer, and User

6

THE "VOICE" OF GLOBAL CORPORATIONS

Dourish (2001) discusses the relationship of the user and designer through technology in understanding social computing through embodied interaction theory, where "the communication between design and user takes place against a backdrop of commonly held social understandings" (p. 56). Metaphors around interfaces come from social expectations to be interpreted and used. The relationship between designers, users and co-users is defined within the constraints of social and cultural practices, and this is what the research focuses on by using embodied interaction theory, where "technological systems are themselves embedded in a set of social and cultural practices that give them meaning at the same time as being constrained and transformed by them" (Dourish, 2001, p. 97).

Reputation

Social reputation of VA brands

Throughout this book, the relationship between users and brands emerges as being shaped by factors such as reputation, personality, ecosystems, and partnerships. Third-party skills and actions within a brand's VA experience also play a critical role in shaping user perceptions and behaviours. Central to this is the role of brand reputation and its influence on how users engage with their VA devices. Reputation is defined as,

> A perceptual identity formed from the collective perceptions of others, which is reflective of the complex combination of salient personal characteristics and accomplishments, demonstrated behavior, and intended images presented over some period of time as observed directly and/or reported from secondary sources, which reduces ambiguity about expected future behavior.
>
> *(Zinko et al., 2007, p. 165)*

DOI: 10.1201/9781003680840-6

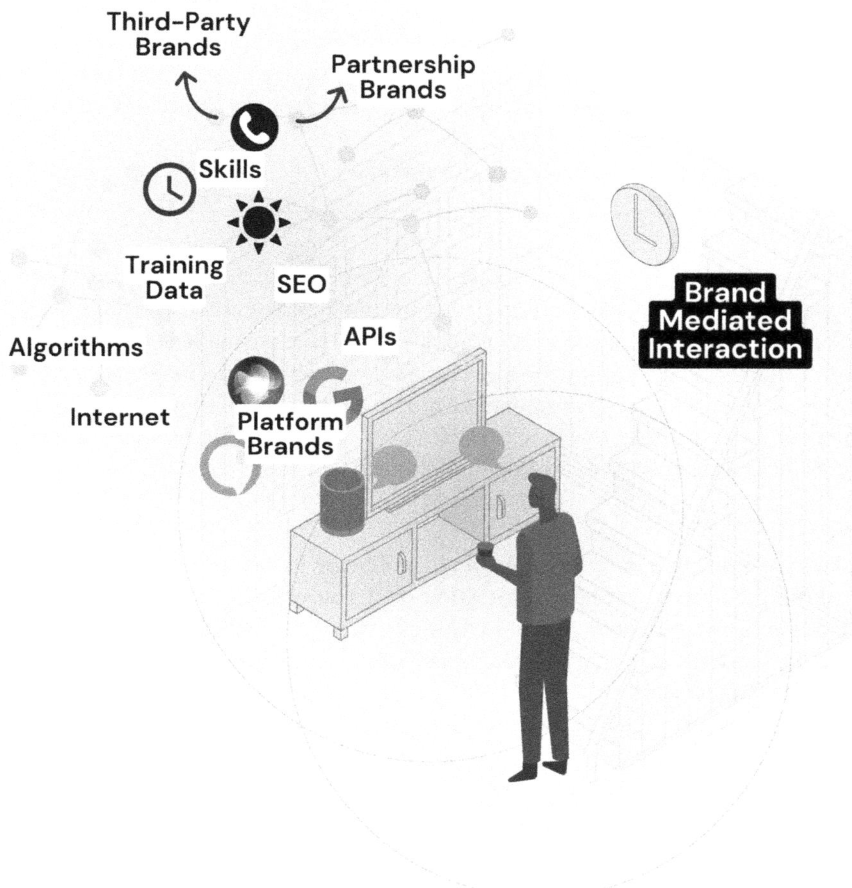

FIGURE 6.1 Brand-mediated interaction showing the commercial ecosystem underlying domestic VA use

My decision to explore the persistent reputation of companies as reflected in the user experience of their VA products was prompted by the association of specific traits with Google or Alexa, often making comparisons between the two brands during our interactions. I found that the reputation of brands Google and Amazon emerged as a factor in the interviews, with the Google VA being perceived as an authority for information and the Alexa VA as an automation device and marketing platform. Vincent, a Google Home Assistant user, relates his decision to purchase a Google-branded VA to his perception of Google's values.

> I just think that it's one of those things that Google has been around for the longest time. I think that it's always the whole... **I think the mission statement of Google is to help people find answers to things, if you need answers for anything, that Google's there for you**, and I think it's just natural that I think some **consumers would be more inclined to choose a Google Home device over all the other competitors out there**.
>
> Vincent, 2 person, 4 device household

From Vincent's perspective, Google's association with the VA device has enhanced its reputation for finding answers and as an information searching and retrieval service. For Vincent, Google's consistent and lengthy reputation encourages him to continue to select Google for his information needs. His perception of Google as a brand, he believes, would influence consumers like him to adopt a Google VA. It is not just that he compares Google's VAs to other brands; rather, he highlights his unfamiliarity with other brands associated with information retrieval and task execution.

> And I just feel like maybe with buying the Google Home devices, it's just a natural thing **where if you have a question or if you want things to be done, that Google is your answer**. Whereas I think Alexa, I'm not too familiar with the whole Amazon ecosystem. **I didn't even know that Alexa was part of Amazon for the longest time**.
>
> Vincent, 2 person, 4 device household

Vincent's lack of association between Amazon and its VA persona, Alexa, highlights the power of a brand's reputation in providing familiarity to the product. He is more familiar with Google than Amazon, thus choosing a Google VA and the tied perception of the use of a Google VA as a simple but reliable information search. Another observation is Vincent's familiarity with Amazon's CEO, Jeff Bezos, rather than a clear mission statement to align with potential VA use. This seemed common, as Jeff Bezos was mentioned in several participant interviews.

> I didn't know that they owned Twitch, I didn't know that they owned the cloud and it... Yeah, yeah, they're basically... **Yeah, it was only till I realised how rich Jeff Bezos was**, like, okay, he owns a lot of stuff...
>
> Vincent, 2 person, 4 device household

While Vincent remains unaffected by Jeff Bezos and uses a Google VA, Sophie mentions how his presence influences her interactions with her Alexa VA, deterring her from engaging in certain interactions. In particular, Sophie discusses her perception of suggestions from Alexa to use the Amazon default product for a service. For instance, users can link their Spotify account to their VA, accessing their premium account and existing personalised recommendations. However, when starting with Alexa to play music, the system defaults to Amazon Music as the streaming service, although users can change this in the Alexa app if they like.

Sophie specifically mentions the shopping list skill and its related reminders. There are a few aspects to what Amazon calls voice purchasing, which includes connecting to the shopping list skill. This skill allows the user to add items to a list, which can be read out loud by Alexa or viewed and shared with other people in the Alexa app (Shop with Alexa, n.d.). In America, users can order items through their Alexa shopping list from connected grocery stores like Whole Foods and Amazon Fresh; an online and physical grocery store connects to their Amazon account for purchases (Amazon Fresh Groceries, n.d.). However, in Australia, users can only add to their shopping list, using it as a reminder rather than purchasing through the Alexa device. As an Amazon core service, the shopping list and related reminders are experienced differently from other third-party skills, in that Amazon developers can make more use of the Alexa interface through follow-up comments and proactively reply to users during relevant shopping or list-related interactions.

> Yeah, **I can see when it's being transparent about trying to get you to use Amazon stuff**, and then you are like, "No I don't want that". Tries to get you to use more Amazon services like the shopping list—reminders—or reminders to buy this. **I've never said yes to anything because I don't want to make Jeff Bezos richer**.
>
> 👤 Sophie, 1 person, 1 device household

Nevertheless, Sophie's point underscores the perception that Jeff Bezos and Amazon are primarily associated with retail. She maintains her view of Alexa within the framework of a business marketing tool.

> **Indra:** Do you ever imagine Jeff Bezos when you interact with Alexa?
> **Sophie:** Do I think about him? No, I only think about him maybe when she's trying to upgrade me—so, I remember it's a business.

The reputation of Google and Amazon diverges: Google is renowned for providing access to information, whereas Amazon is recognised for selling products. Sophie elaborates on this by further framing her perception of Amazon VA devices as a marketing tool.

> Like that's why Alexa is so cheap. Alexa isn't just like you bought it and that's it, you bought it, and you are a continuing customer and Alexa is a marketing tool. And that's when it breaks the thing. Like it was $30 but now she's trying to sell me things and its advertising.
>
> Sophie, 1 person, 1 device household

Sophie remarks that the low price of her Alexa VA made it an accessible entry point for exposure to more Amazon marketing. Drawing from her marketing background, Sophie describes a campaign that used VAs to expand users' brand experience beyond traditional advertising methods.

> I remember when Burger King made an ad—where people would order burgers through Alexa. But **it went beyond advertising** and people found it creepy. So, people don't like to do a lot of Alexa marketing.
>
> Sophie, 1 person, 1 device household

Sophie refers to a 15-second television ad by Burger King in 2017 that hijacked thousands of Google Home Assistant devices as the actor triggered the devices from the TV audio, asking Google a question about the Whopper burger. The VAs proceeded to read out the ingredients of the burger until a user could command the VA to stop, effectively extending the commercial beyond television spots (Anderson, 2017). Overall, Sophie continues to use her Alexa device, dismissing interactions she deems as marketing. She uses the device more for home automation and some information retrieval, which sets the stage for the following section where participants discuss the reputation and reliability of VAs in home automation.

Material and tangible reputation

My discussion with Hugo echoes Google's reputation as an information provider, but over time, he has uncovered a different perspective on Amazon products. Through informal testing of both ecosystems over the past two to three years, Hugo has found Amazon's VA product to be quicker in automating and connecting to other IoT devices compared to Google's. This observation speaks more to the system's quality than the brand's social reputation. However, the reputational difference infers Hugo's use and placement of VA devices in his home.

> **I believe that Alexa is faster than Google** in that [he uses Alexa for more automation and IoT control], you know, I use Google for different purposes. **I use Google for more when I have a question**. A specific question with regard to general knowledge of Google is much better than Alexa.
>
> Hugo, 4 person, 8 device household

While he has a different opinion on Amazon than Sophie or Vincent, he continues to hold the same beliefs about Google. In contrast to other participants, Hugo owns multiple devices from both brands, which allows him to draw on his experiences interacting with Google and Amazon VAs to support these beliefs.

Indra: How did you come to find that? Was it just an observation or did you try to get Google to turn off some things in your house?

Hugo: No, no. **I have both ecosystem for a while now, probably a couple of years** umm. I have I configure basically everything in both, you know, when I try something. But then because I use it for a daily, daily basis and I need them to work fast or that type of things. **Alexa's more responsive in terms of the automatisation of stuff, but of course, Google is much better in their general knowledge**, and I usually ask both of them when one of them is not—it doesn't know the answer, I ask the other one and that is my observation.

What is unique about Hugo's perception is that he actively uses both brands in his home. His experience over time allows him to notice the subtle differences in speed, quality, and reliability of the information provided. Even though both smart speaker brands offer similar functionalities, the differences in the systems are enough for Hugo to use double the amount of VA devices as some of the other participants. Hugo has set up a Google and Amazon VA ecosystem in his smart home—multiple VAs plugged in, set up, placed around the home and connected to other smart home products. It would be like simultaneously owning Apple and Google phones, going through the extra effort to keep both charged and available to use the best features from each brand, aligning with personal goals. However, with both brand ecosystems in operation, Hugo feels better equipped to respond to the needs of his family according to the different places they interact in his home.

In the kitchen is where we have lunch and dinner with my daughters and they are the ones that ask a lot of questions, which I don't know. So, I need Google more than Alexa to answer their questions.

👤 Hugo, 4 person, 8 device household

Connecting to the findings from previous chapters, place not only influences where devices are placed in the home and what place-tied interactions are enacted. Hugo's story suggests that place-tied interactions may even influence which brand VA is used. Not only is the brand's reputation and consequent perception of software performance considered, but also the translation of this into the material hardware of the VA product. Intangible aspects like brand reputation and software performance, as well as tangible aspects like the hardware, are considered when assessing VA products. Just like Hugo compares his Google and Amazon VA ecosystems, others often use Apple's Siri as a comparison for VA interactions due to its availability on participants' smartphones. For instance, Hao provides an observation about the listening capabilities of Siri and Google.

> I find that the microphone is more sensitive on the Google products rather than Siri.
> 👤 Hao, 4 person, 2 device household

While he comments on tangible microphones, Hao does not consider the intangible algorithms that are used to enhance and understand input audio. Examples of these include Amazon Alexa's acoustic echo cancellation and beamforming algorithms. The acoustic echo cancellation algorithm is applied to the sound received to clean any distorted audio to improve the automatic speech recognition profile and natural language processing (NLP) of user utterances. Beamforming algorithms amplify the audio from one microphone and suppress audio interference from other microphones to improve the quality for improved automatic speech recognition and NLP processing (Audio Hardware Configurations, 2023). It seems these invisible algorithms are not considered in how participants perceive their VAs to work. So, when comparing VA brands, invisible influences of technical functionality, such as audio-enhancing algorithms, may be under-considered.

The reputation of the material hardware of VA products was considered in the reputation of small brand VA-related IoT devices. I use the term small brand to refer to smaller companies in the context of big brand experiences with Google, Amazon, and Apple. While big brands monopolise the reputation of their brand into VA personas, the marketplace for non-anthropomorphic smart technologies is open to developers who may offer VA-related IoT products for lower costs. Google, Amazon and Apple do not manufacture key IoT smart home accessories, such as power boards or lightbulbs. These are two popular components in my participants' smart homes. So, because VA brands Google, Amazon and Apple do not manufacture IoT accessories, VA users are forced to investigate a diversity of brands to complete their smart home setup. I found that participants considered purchasing from smaller overseas brands online due to their low prices, compared to purchasing from reputable electronic stores in Australia.

> … there are lots of other devices from China you can get, which you can replicate the same function similar to Garage opener [an IoT device that can be controlled via VA devices]. Often, people say **you can get it for 20 bucks if you buy it from China, but… I don't know** … **Even though most of them are made in China, I would still go for the brands that I trust**. It's mainly because **in case the house burns down** or because of the modification I'm doing now, I know it's something that meets Australian certification, the safety standard.
> 👤 Lien, 4 person, 6 device household

The reputation of "made in China" products is considered by Lien, but he makes the distinction between trusted and non-trusted Chinese-made products. While Chinese-branded IoT devices might be available for a lower price, participants preferred to stick with trusted brands sold in Australian retailers, even if all products are made in China. The safety standard of the material hardware is a selling point for what VA-related technology Lien buys and uses.

Similarly, Hugo deliberates that "othered" Chinese brands do not work as well with the big brand VAs. Hugo personifies the relationships between brands to represent the technical incompatibility and diversity of product quality. By personifying these relationships between brands, Hugo highlights the complex technical dynamics at play by portraying brand products as entities with distinct personalities and compatibility issues. The personification of brands in the way participants discuss their VA devices is a continuing theme in the following sections on personality, material and digital ecosystems.

> Philips with Siri works really well because they are the top of the market. But other I have Chinese brands where **Siri's not happy with Chinese brands** where Alexa is.
>
> Hugo, 4 person, 8 device household

My findings indicate that VA interaction intertwines users with various brands, partnerships and independent third-party developers. Therefore, it is important to examine VA interaction not only from the user–designer relationship perspective but also to consider the designer's position within a capitalistic network of partnerships with other designers. Understanding these dynamics may help researchers understand and shape everyday experiences with VAs in domestic settings. Spoken commands to material VA devices are not in isolation; rather, users are speaking to a symbolic persona of global conglomerates such as Alphabet (Google), Amazon and Apple, and their proprietary systems of protected algorithms and data. Vernuccio et al. (2023b) refer to this as *brand anthropomorphisation*, where technology like VAs becomes a "medium that enables direct dialogues between the user and the brand" (p. 303). In that work and others (Vernuccio et al., 2020; Vernuccio et al., 2023a; Patrizi et al., 2024), the authors advocate for distinguishing between the anthropomorphism of a VA device and anthropomorphism of a brand when exploring factors such as trust and engagement in human–VA relationships. My findings corroborate this idea by demonstrating that the brand permeated many facets of interaction with the devices. Users frequently reference the brand's values, associate better experiences with specific brands (such as Google for information retrieval or Alexa for automation) and are reminded of brand CEOs, which affect their interactions. Brand presence persists even when engaging with third-party skills. Brand was top of mind, rather than perceiving the VA as a generic intelligence.

As Patrizi et al. (2024) explain, brand anthropomorphism has existed in advertising for a long time. However, it has had a strong emphasis on studying visual and verbal codes in the literature, with limited scholarly work on vocal codes of brand anthropomorphism, such as what has emerged from this study. They note characteristics that define vocal codes as gender, pitch (Wiener & Chartrand, 2014), roughness and brightness (Zoghaib, 2017, 2019), which influence perceptions of competence and warmth of vocal experiences by brands (Wiener & Chartrand, 2014; Zoghaib, 2017, 2019). Notably, I also found a strong tie to the brand voices of VAs and unfamiliarity with foreign voices used in third-party skills. Users commented on the importance of speed, tone and type of questions, in association with the presentation of vocal codes of communicating a brand. The literature suggests parallels between VA voice and robot voice—the VA "voice is embedded within a physical object, may therefore trigger many of the same anthropomorphic tendencies that HRI studies have reported in response to embodied robots" (Cambre & Kulkarni, 2019, p. 9).

Personality

Personality can be defined as "the type of person you are, shown by the way you behave, feel, and think" (Cambridge Dictionary, n.d.b., para. 1). Personality in chatbots and VAs has been studied and proven to increase perceived consistency, trust and confidence (Alaieri & Vellino, 2016; André et al., 1999). Personality can influence whether users decide to converse with others and help adjust expectations on how these interactions may unfold (Cafaro et al., 2016). While personality in VAs has been shown to affect users, in this research, my participants commented more on how personality was performed by the personified system and how perceived performance affected their perception and use of VAs.

Testing personalities

Participants highlighted limitations on VA performance and capabilities in what inhibits them from believing and committing to the VA's illusion of personality. I refer to it as an illusion since the participants constantly talked about their attempts to curate a personality. For instance, Hao speaks about the transparency of establishing personality as an attempt to further the personification of the anthropomorphised machine. Hao talks about his attempt to discern the different personas of Google and Apple through their VA scripted responses. However, other aspects of the VA experience are perceived poorly by Hao, such as the mechanical voice of VAs, dismissing other humanising aspects like natural language and cultural references.

Hao: Yeah, I know, sometimes I go, is something like this, "Hey, Google. Hey, Google, I love you".
Google: Love is a beautiful thing. Thank you for sharing it with me.
Hao: And then I'll say the same to Siri. See, what Siri says. "Hey, Siri, I love you".
Siri: You are the wind beneath my wings.

Hao: It just said, you are the wind beneath my wings.
Indra: Yeah. How do you feel about those two responses?
Hao: I think what they're trying to do is distinguish themselves as two different personalities, and they're trying to make it feel as human as possible, but it's just... Still mechanical to me. Google still sounds mechanical. The Siri still sounds mechanical, it actually doesn't sound like a human...

Hao alludes to the speech quality of Siri and Google, suggesting they lack the naturalness of human speech. Unfortunately, we did not discuss the mechanical voice comment further. However, this experience suggests that users are instantly able to compare different brand VA responses in real-time against a constant variable. Therefore, users can critically assess personality, word for word, and the responses to the same question. While Hao does not discuss the impact of the subjective responses from VA brands, he later highlights inconsistencies in the accuracy of information while comparing Siri and Google, affecting his trust.

When engaging in scripted dialogue, VAs respond to subjective enquiries without accessing APIs to execute tasks or gather information. These VAs lack awareness that Hao is conducting a test, and they cannot adjust the script based on contextual factors (newer LLMs might respond differently). Consequently, the VAs' intelligence is constrained to manifest the personality as programmed by their designers. A year after the interview with Hao, I can confirm Siri still responds with "You are the wind beneath my wings" to the statement "Siri, I love you". Perhaps stagnant responses are an issue in VA user experience, something that further studies could explore.

Performing personality

Abercrombie et al.'s (2021) analysis suggests that "people tend to personify and gender the systems, irrespective of the efforts and claims of their designers. This seems to be, at least partly, a result of aspects of their design" (p. 6). The authors assess the subjective phrases that are products of brand decisions rather than transactional replies based on completing a task or information retrieval. Users were able to tell the difference between subjective and transactional type responses from their VAs.

The only time that the Minis would give a different answer to, if you just looked up and Google is **when you ask something that's personality-based. Like, "Do you like me", or things that are more subjective, it varies**. The answer that you'll get and then those things are also less likely to be an answer that you don't like, because it's like—Well, it's up to her how she answers, but then when you're asking for information, that's more something that... You're gonna get the straight answer.

Phoebe, 2 person, 3 device household

Abercrombie et al. (2021) refer to persona-related questions asked by human participants, which I term as subjective responses, to describe the biased answers to these persona-related questions, to contrast with transactional responses. In their research, Abercrombie et al. systematically tested 100 responses to persona-related questions using an adaptation of the Living Machines annotation scheme (Ardanuy et al., 2020). Researchers annotated responses as humanness or non-humanness, deciding if claims by the VAs were describing uniquely human activities. They found that "while Google Assistant, and to a lesser extent, Alexa, seem to blur the line between human and machine personas, Siri comes across as more practical and task-focused, evading the majority of personality-based questions" (Abercrombie et al., 2021, p. 7). My findings suggest that participants enjoyed these subjective responses, which added to their user experience using VAs, rather than the distinct switch between subjective and transactional responses, which disrupted the illusion of a personal interaction with their VAs.

In addition, Abercrombie et al. (2021) measured user perception of user emotionality towards their VAs through statistical analysis using the Linguistic Inquiry and Word Count tool on a dataset of Reddit posts about VAs. They tested the content of the Reddit threads for emotional tone, affect and positive emotion, where the tool scored text based on their prevalence in set categories (Pennebaker et al., 2015). The research found that users were most sentimental when describing Alexa (2.80) and Google (2.52) over Apple's Siri (2.24) (Abercrombie et al., 2021), noting that users described Alexa and Google affectively, while Siri's functionality was mostly commented on. The authors raised concerns about the mix of human and non-human suggestive responses that might confuse users, especially if VA personas claim not to be human in most subjective responses. However, Abercrombie et al. also acknowledge that an anti-anthropomorphism approach may conflict with Google and Amazon's commercial goals of enhancing high-level engagement with their VA products. Overall, their study strongly suggests that subjective responses from VAs highlight the intentional anthropomorphism designed by VA creators through scripting.

My findings indicate that users can discern when they ask persona-related questions to receive subjective responses, and they actively seek out these responses for entertainment and engagement. As well, the distinction between subjective and transactional responses was perceived and segregated by participants. To some it reminded them of how they might express their personality and humanness at work when providing a service.

> I always fall back on DND terminology when talking about the way that people interact, but people will come into the library and you'll just be an NPC who's there to serve a purpose. "How do I print this thing?" "Thank you", move on with your day. Will not interact with you as a person**, you are just there to serve the purpose of the job, and this doesn't have to be a person-to-person interaction**, this is a character to an NPC who I just need to get something from and on with my day and then **occasionally you'll get character interactions** where somebody actually goes like, Oh wow, I really love your broach when you get it… Oh, so cool. And **it actually can become something more…**
>
> 👤 Phoebe, 2 person, 3 device household

In the literature, this resembles *impression management*, which involves consciously enacting specific behaviours to influence how one is perceived by others (Bolino et al., 2016), particularly in the workplace. The distinction between personal and transactional interactions may reflect human interaction dynamics, as evidenced by Phoebe's perspective on these types of interactions mirroring her behaviour in her professional workplace. Phoebe highlights the potential for sharing less of her personality during transactional tasks for clients, akin to *front-stage* behaviour as described by Goffman (2002), where individuals present a more controlled and task-oriented self in public and formal interactions. Conversely, Phoebe mentions the ability to create more intimate interactions by being personable and discussing aspects unrelated to the task, akin to *backstage* behaviour, where individuals engage in more personal and informal interactions, revealing aspects of their personality beyond immediate tasks.

There were also similarities between subjective and transactional responses from VAs to relational and transactional psychological contracts from Chan's (2021) paper:

> A **relational** contract consists of exchanges, which are built on trust and implicit emotional attachment. This contract is often long-term and has some degree of flexibility between individuals and the organisation. Contrary to relational contract, a **transactional** contract consists of exchanges, which are built on direct and explicit expectations, focusing on tit-for-tat economic transactions. This contract is short-term and has a narrower focus between individuals and the organisation.
>
> *(p. 31, emphasis added)*

Relational contracts, which are linked to interpersonal factors such as trust and emotional attachment, align with the objective of subjective VA responses, as they foster emotional connections and trust between users and their VAs. On the other hand, transactional contracts involve exchanges based on clear and explicit expectations, similar to VA interactions that have a defined purpose, such as controlling IoT devices or retrieving information. There is potential for further exploration regarding subjective and transactional interactions to achieve a balanced approach in future voice AI interactions.

A comparison is also drawn between VAs and non-playable characters (NPCs) in video games. In the context of video games, authors Carvalho and Rodrigues (2023) recognise the similarities between VAs and NPCs,

> … when analyzing the roles of characters, their functions in the narrative, and the duality between playable and NPCs, it is possible to observe an analogy between the player and an AI voice assistant, which occurs when the voice assistant is compared to the role of an NPC, a conversational agent who participates in a dialogue to exchange information.
>
> *(Carvalho & Rodrigues, 2023, p. 1)*

Game design literature has been progressively exploring the role of voice interfaces in enhancing gameplay. Drawing insights from gamification and game design literature could greatly benefit designers of VAs and other socially embodied AI systems accessed through voice.

MATERIAL AND DIGITAL ECOSYSTEMS, PARTNERSHIPS, AND THIRD-PARTY SKILLS

After observing how global corporate brands are reflected in the anthropomorphic characteristics of VA interaction, particularly through reputation and personality, I now explain how these brands interact within interconnected physical and virtual ecosystems. Ecosystem in the context of computing is defined as, "any complicated system consisting of many different people, processes, activities, etc., especially relating to technology, and the way that they affect each other" (Cambridge Dictionary, n.d.a., para.1). I use this term to describe and ask about participants' use of the services and products of multiple brands in their homes. Users buy VA-related IoT products from other brands, linking the interconnectivity between devices to perform smart home interactions across different spaces in the house. Some participants who only had VAs and no other supplementary smart technology had a group of VAs spread across the home to extend VA coverage.

Material Ecosystems

In our interview, Hao describes himself as feeling locked in with a brand once he started to purchase their products. He makes connections to brands, products and compatibility. Because the VA serves as a centralised intelligence across various physical devices, users experience a feeling of being stuck in tangible and intangible ways.

> … the **worry of being locked into one environment say at Google, you're locked into Google completely**. Right, and so if you need to change anything, and if you wanna go to say Alexa, or if you wanna get to Siri, wanna go to anything else, you can't get on the Apple products or Apple Home products.
>
> 👤 Hao, 4 person, 2 device household

Hugo echoes this sentiment of the freedom to own and switch between VA brands as being difficult. However, unlike the other participants, Hugo has invested in two brand ecosystems, due to the differences in their system functionalities–using Google for information retrieval and Amazon for IoT connectivity. Reflecting on his experiences of a multi-brand VA household, Hugo highlights two factors that would alleviate the issue of feeling trapped within a brand ecosystem. First is the cost of being able to experiment with different VA brands, and second is the knowledge of how to set up a well-connected ecosystem.

> The problem again, the problem is… if you have **unlimited money** and you go from one brand and one thing, and **you know what you're doing**, it's much simpler.
>
> Hugo, 4 person, 8 device household

He expands on the difficulties of setting up a VA–IoT ecosystem, as different brands may not be compatible. Because of Hugo's budget, his experimental mindset and limitations in integration, he opts to purchase multiple products from smaller brands to equip his smart home with items like smart switches, garage door openers and other devices. These products are intended to be controlled and connected to his Google and Alexa VAs.

> The problem is it doesn't integrate with everything you know. And because I did my home like a low budget, I have like four of, say, four or five or maybe more different brands of devices, you know?
>
> Hugo, 4 person, 8 device household

Hugo realises that comparing both products was crucial for optimising his daily interactions with his VA and smart home products. However, he acknowledges the expense of acquiring physical products to support his experimentation with both VA brand environments, in the pursuit of creating the most optimal smart home ecosystem.

In our interview, Hugo refers to himself as an early adopter of this technology, suggesting it requires more experimentation to achieve the best experience. At the time of the interview, Hugo used a combination of second and third-generation Amazon Echo devices. While only material fixes are rolled out in new product versions, there is no change to the VA's intelligence between models, as software can be updated and rolled out at any time, usually unaffected by hardware changes. Hugo stands out as an enthusiastic experimenter with VA and smart home technology. Among the participants, he emerges as the most proactive user in setting up custom routines and connecting to a wide array of smart home devices, rivalled only by Lien. Notably, Hugo and Lien possess the highest number of VA devices in their respective homes.

> It's coming. It's coming. Not everyone will have it. But of course, **adopting the technology early has a price**, which I enjoy, but my wife doesn't.
>
> Hugo, 4 person, 8 device household

Users may find themselves constrained by the limitations of sticking to one brand for their VA devices, as they consider the value of purchasing another branded VA. As well, users might opt to purchase IoT products from other brands to broaden the scope and capabilities of their smart home setup.

Material manifestations of brands

The current research on experiencing VA and smart home technology finds that perceived compatibility between the same-brand smart home products influences brand choice concentration (Liang et al., 2021). This means that users are more likely to continue buying into one brand's technology ecosystem for perceived seamless compatibility. My findings support Liang et al.'s (2021) research that users are more likely to stay in brand product ecosystems for perceived compatibility. However, I also discovered that users deviate from this pattern when it comes to cheaper and less frequently interacted with items, such as smart switches and plugs. Participants are willing to explore non-name-brand products to expand their smart home capabilities. However, they felt constrained to stick to name-brand products for their VA devices.

Financial limitations further restrict users' ability to test multiple VAs, leading to a sense of being locked into their chosen VA ecosystem. While participants are free to trial cheaper and periphery IoT products, they may feel constrained to stay with one VA, one voice UI and one VA personality. This was reflected in the sentiment of my participants feeling stuck with their VA ecosystem due to the financial costs of buying the same-brand VAs. Financial constraints limit users from testing all available VAs in their home environment. While it is possible to download the phone app for Google Assistant and Amazon Alexa, accessing Siri requires a physical Apple product. Despite the difference in the embodied experience of interacting with a VA through a phone instead of ubiquitously, users can still assess the quality of information retrieval and personalised interactions. For example, Mark experimented with Bixby on his previous Samsung phone. Participants often engage with VAs through their phones and separate home systems to access different VA user interfaces—this was observed with Mark, Lien and Hugo. Hugo even compared the responses from Google and Siri word for word on the same question, which affected his perceived value of both brands. Further research exploring the lived experience of having multiple brands of VAs in one household would be valuable. Overall, this discussion highlights the complex interplay between perceived compatibility, brand loyalty and financial constraints in users' adoption of VA and smart home technology.

Digital Ecosystems and Brand Partnerships

The notion of being confined within a VA environment evolves into a more abstract experience, as users become comfortable with specific brand voice interfaces and services. Lien exemplifies the differences between experiencing limitations of material and digital ecosystems. He compares material and software compatibility in terms of sensors and signallers to other IoT devices, then he switches, describing the digital ecosystems and skills of Alexa, and the quality of the Google VA system as being more user-friendly and funnier.

I've been actually been tossing between the Google Home and the Amazon Echos for quite a while, and I did see some research saying the **Echo is more compatible** with other devices, so they've **got more skills** as compared to Google Home, which is more **user-friendly**. The only thing I heard is about the Google Home is that their **jokes are better**, but that's the only thing.

Lien, 4 person, 6 device household

In selecting a VA device, the experience and maintenance of a brand's digital services were a strong decision factor in selecting their VA brand. For instance, Avish describes his life as "Googlefied". He mentions that his ongoing use of Google services and decision to opt for a Google VA stemmed from his initial choice of Gmail years ago. Like Google's VA service, which can be accessed from a Google phone, laptop or VA, Gmail is a digital service that can be accessed from many interfaces.

Indra: Have you always been in that Google ecosystem for your…

Avish: Yeah, I personally have, I guess it all started with getting Gmail quite a few years ago. I sort of describe it as people sell their souls… **You sell your soul to Apple, or to Amazon, or to Google, and I chose Google. And my life is totally Googlefied now**. So, I run email off Google, all my other emails come into Google, I run my life through Google. And so, **it would seem logical when these kind of virtual assistants came on the market to go down the Google path** rather than other pathways.

Likewise, Mark's smart home setup predominantly revolves around Google products. He recounts experimenting with other brand VA systems, such as Samsung's Bixby, which he tried when he owned a Samsung Galaxy phone. His mention of owning a Samsung material product implies it was the sole reason for his ability to test Bixby's digital services. This connection between physical and digital products may play a significant role in the experience and selection of a VA.

Indra: I do see that you are in the Google ecosystem, do you think in selecting your voice assistant and have you tried other voice systems?

Mark: **I did use the Samsung one for a little bit** for… Absolutely terrible [Mark laughs]. Just **it struggled to interpret your commands**, I found whereas this [Google] one's quite fluent. I haven't used Alexa, I can't really compare to something [Alexa], which would probably be their biggest competitor…

Mark comments on the poor user experience of the VA Bixby on his Samsung phone, another point of comparison to strengthen his ties to Google.

Concerning digital ecosystems, where a brand encourages the use of its connected digital service suite, Hao highlights the imperative for brands to default to their digital products in maintaining their users in their ecosystem. Hao even extends the metaphor of ecosystem and environment to the metaphor of family, a loaded term that suggests high bonding.

Indra:	Do you think the two companies are civil with each other?
Hao:	When you look at the history, I think, **didn't Apple take away Google Maps at one stage? And use their own maps**. So, I think they understand that they're there in the market and they've got their own market space, and **once you lock into one environment, you're stuck in that environment**, and that's what they hope people would do and not... get different environments. So, if you buy a Google product, you're gonna continue to buy Google products, if you buy Apple products**, you're locked into the Apple family**, per se. You're not going anywhere else.

Another part of the digital ecosystem experience is the non-VA services to which VAs connect for information through an API. **These invisible connections of services heavily shape the construction of information and thus user knowledge**. This is exemplified in a live demonstration during my interview with Hao, where he noticed a difference between the answers we received from Google and Siri.

Hao:	And then they have their own... and **then they link off to their own services**. So, if I ask about the weather for each one of them, Google will have its own weather app, which it reads off that and it might not be as accurate. And then Apple have their own weather app and read off that, and so, it won't give you the exact thing. [Hao goes on to ask both VAs, Google and Siri, "What's the weather like today?"]
Google:	In [suburb name] today, it will be cloudy, with a forecast high of 27 and a **low of 17**. Currently, it is 22 degrees and mostly cloudy.
Siri:	It's currently partly cloudy, 22 degrees. Expect cloudy skies and rain starting in the afternoon. Today's high will be 27 degrees, and the **low will be 20**.

While both responses largely present the same meteorological data, Google provides a different number to Siri when describing the forecasted low temperature. Assuming they are both reading the temperature forecast for the same location (although

Siri specifies its geographical reference point), there is a difference in the minimum temperature reading by three degrees, and Siri expects it to rain in the afternoon, while Google does not. This suggests that Google and Siri may be connecting to different sources of information, or Siri is providing weather data for a different location. Of course, weather is not the most accurate phenomenon to predict, but this conversation highlights how VAs can present differing representations of information due to their connections to API sources. Investigating further, the first point of difference between Google and Alexa is the search engines to which they connect. Google uses Google Search, while Amazon uses Bing. These search engines have different SEO algorithms and algorithms to index and rank information. More investigation is needed to assess other representations of the truth and how they might affect VA usage and perception.

I observed a similar scenario when Hao suggested that VA brands have established partnerships with news organisations, implying a degree of selectivity in the presentation of news and facts during VA interactions. He refers to a partnership between VA brands, perceiving that they are aligned with different brands in an ecosystem of digital services that affect their responses and experience.

> See this is prerecorded by ABC, so **obviously they've got a deal with ABC**.
> [we sit in silence and listen to the newsflashes for a few minutes]
> Hao, 4 person, 2 device household

I also noticed how participants discussed encountering various brands through their chosen VA brand. Anavi points out the interconnectedness between brands that have affiliations with each other; once users align themselves with one brand, they become linked to a network of interconnected brands, some of which they may have less familiarity with or no desire to be associated with.

> **Anavi:** ... if you get Spotify premium, in the US, they send you a free Google Assistant.
> **Indra:** Really?
> **Anavi:** The cheapest one. So yeah, for Spotify Premium, you get Hulu and you also get a Google Assistant, but it's just the cheap small one.

Regarding an ecosystem of interconnected partnered brands, I want to emphasise the experiences of Mark, Vincent, and Phoebe, who received a complimentary VA device as part of their association with partnered brands under VA parent companies. This highlights how being integrated into digital ecosystems can tangibly expand the brand's material ecosystem within a user's lifestyle.

> Because I'm subscribed to YouTube premium. I opened up YouTube one day, and a prompt was just on screen saying, **'cause you subscribe to premium, we're gonna give you a free [Google] Nest Mini, so just click this link** and order it, and I thought it was like, obviously fake. So, I just clicked it and it took me to the Google website with the checkout cart, and I just had to select what colour I wanted, and it literally shipped to my house in two days, it was really absurd.
>
> Mark, 4 person, 4 device household

Changes to skills and apps during the research

One aspect of VA computing yet to be brought up is the integration of third-party skills and services in a voice marketplace similar to an app store to download apps. These VA applications are referred to as Skills by Amazon and need to be enabled on the Alexa app before use. Comparable to apps installed on a computer or phone, Amazon takes this route, and its effects roll on to relationships in VA collaborative usage. Amazon has an extensive skills marketplace, called the Alexa Skills Store, where skills must adhere to content guidelines and are reviewed for publication in 1–2 business days (Publish your skill to the Alexa Skills Store, n.d). To be listed on the Alexa Skill Store, creators only need to supply an Opening Phrase for users to summon the skill and a creator name that is reviewed to ensure they have the rights to use that name. Other details needed for the Alexa Skill Store are selecting a category, keywords to help customers find the skill in the store, an icon to visually represent the skill listing on the store, a short description that acts as an abstract for the skill, and a detailed description that lists every available feature of the skill. Creators are led through a short policy creation, or a link to the Terms of Use page can be provided. Once approved, it may take up to two hours to add skills to the store (Publish your skill to the Alexa Skills Store, n.d).

Instead of skills, Google refers to their equivalent as *actions*, and as of June 2023, is sunsetting third-party actions and only allowing actions that are linked to an Android app (Li, 2022). This means that third-party developers can no longer create actions exclusively for voice for Google VAs, like the Pikachu Talk action I discuss below. Since the interviews for this study were performed before the announcement of sunsetting voice-only Google Actions in 2022 and the actual discontinuation date in 2023, I cannot make any association from my interview data on Google Android App Actions, but have made inferences based on developer documentation and secondary commentary on how it would affect how my participants talked about their voice-only Google Actions available in 2021. Furthermore, it is notable that this change does not affect any voice experience for controlling IoT devices, as they use a corresponding Android app to install and set up the connection from VA to IoT devices (e.g. lightbulbs, heaters, and extension power points).

Third-party presence in VA use and perception

Based on the participant observations and interviews, I observed third-party skills featuring voices other than Google's or Alexa's default. Developers may use audio recordings or other digital voice generators throughout their voice skill, although some third-party experiences will use the default Google or Alexa voice to read out a custom script. From the interviews, there were a few charged moments when interacting with third-party skills. Since I did not ask directly of my participants to show me their favourite third-party skill or define what they believed they were, I do not have any clear findings on participants' perceptions of third-party skills and actions. However, users' emotive live interactions and reflections on third-party skills in the interviews highlighted the differences between interacting with third-party skills and default brand capabilities. The first third-party experience I highlight is the Pikachu skill. The Pikachu Talk skill and action by the official Pokémon Company, which has over 60,000 reviews on the US Alexa Skill Store, was the most frequently brought up third-party skill mentioned to me.

> The kids sort of like, they can ask **Alexa to talk like Pikachu** and yeah, they talk and whatever they talk Alexa will repeat as a Pikachu sound. It will also sing Happy Birthday as Pikachu. I find my kids are funny, I don't find Alexa funny.
>
> Lien, 4 person, 6 device household

What caught my attention is how the main brand, Google or Alexa, continues to influence third-party interactions even when their voice is not directly present. Despite the absence of the Google or Alexa voice, Lien and Vincent still feel connected to the personas even as they briefly embody Pikachu.

> ... the other day we tested the... I think, some sort of Pikachu thing... Oh yeah, yeah, it was like where you basically... You call for Pikachu, **GH [Google Home] just responds to you through the Pikachu voice**, but... It was pretty annoying anyway; we didn't know how to turn it off.
>
> Vincent, 2 person, 4 device household

Continuing the exploration of third-party skills and actions experienced through VA personas, a moment in my interview with Mark elicited a strong emotional reaction during a live demonstration of an interaction. When asking Mark about a time his VA made him laugh, he starts to tell me about the Movie Quiz Skill. The skill uses recorded audio of a booming male narrator's voice as the game show host, combining game show sound effects to mark game milestones. The unfamiliarity of the male voice evoked an emotional response from Mark during his interaction with this third-party skill.

> ... you can play a trivia game with it [Google Home], and I find the assistant quite funny because like **she transforms into this game show host, it is a different persona**, which makes me laugh for some reason.
>
> Mark, 4 person, 4 device household

Before demonstrating the interaction to me, Mark recalls the pleasant experience he had with this skill. He describes Google transforming into the game show host of the Movie Quiz Skill as a humorous experience. However, this perception changes as I witness the interaction again, live during our interview.

Mark: OK Google, let's play a game.

[Google Home replies in a muffled sound, that I can't make out over Zoom]

Mark: Wait, I might turn her up.

[More muffled sounds from Google]

Google: [in a louder volume] Alright, here is Movie Quiz.
Movie Quiz Skill: Welcome to Movie Quiz. How many people want to play Movie Quiz? You can say one to four.
Mark: One.
Movie Quiz Skill: What is your first name?
Mark: Mark.
Movie Quiz Skill: Where are you from?
Mark: Oh, okay. That's a bit personal. I'm going to stop that. [Mark laughs nervously] I've never done that one before.

Mark ends the interaction, and we do not play the Movie Quiz game. Mark and I look at each other through our computer screens with looks of shock, followed by remarks of surprise. I felt uneasy listening to the loud and urgent voice of the game show host. Mark remarks that this was not the same skill that he previously experienced, even though he suggests he used the same words to summon it, suggesting that spoken utterances are not reliable in retrieving consistent interactions. Or perhaps Mark did not use the exact same command, failing to remember a command he used in the past, and the inexact command produced an entirely different VA interaction.

I just thought about that **he was asking for personal information** and I was like, why is it so the **tone was so serious**?
Mark, 4 person, 4 device household

Mark is surprised by the type of information the skill asked for, interpreting his location as not relevant to playing a game (although this could be Mark's misinterpretation of the question, "Where are you from?"). He is also affected by the tone of speech of this unfamiliar voice rather than the usual voice of his VA. This experience points to not only the gender of the voice but also the association of the name brand putting on voices, familiarity and trust with voices, and the emotional ties to voices. Other items of note are the importance of speed, tone and type of questions in association with the presentation of voice. Despite this, users still feel a connection to their VA brand while using third-party skills or feel uncomfortable with unfamiliar voice experiences.

Another consideration of brand anthropomorphism in VAs is the way participants talk about their devices. Throughout all interviews, participants would switch between referring to the product name and the VA persona. For instance, Amazon Echo and Alexa were mentioned interchangeably. This interchangeability highlights the persistence of the VA brand reputation in influencing VA interaction. It suggests the importance of a brand's identity has grown, potentially becoming equally significant as the product (Klein, 2000). Such awareness of peripheral brand reputation outside VA interaction may deter users from performing certain VA interactions. For instance, Sophie's knowledge of Jeff Bezos' reputation deterred her from using Amazon's music streaming and shopping services available on her Alexa. I would describe this as a boycott of specific VA interactions, in comparison to conventional boycotts of a brand's complete range of services and products. Boycotts are often associated with consumer activism, where users in pursuit of social justice and social change engage in anti-brand activism (Denisova, 2023). While it has been proven that boycotting digital services has little impact on economic performance, it may affect non-financial factors such as brand love and perception (Koku, 2012, 2022). Delacote (2009) explains this is because activists, who are more likely to participate in a boycott, tend to have limited ability to damage a brand, whereas consumers with greater influence are less likely to engage in a consumer resistance movement. As a result, boycotts targeting specific VA interactions might not have a significant financial impact on VA brands. However, a negative brand reputation could discourage potential new VA users. Further research could investigate this aspect in more detail. Regardless of VA brand activism, my findings suggest that participants can separate the brand services that economically support Amazon, from unassociated skills that are free to use or associated with digital services they already pay for, such as Spotify, and choose to connect with these instead.

However, the reputation of global brands such as Google and Alexa continues to influence how VAs are perceived and used, even when using third-party app skills. This is evident in participants' consistent reference to Google or Alexa when describing their experiences with other third-party apps. In their study involving 52 participants, Sabir et al. (2022) found that most participants failed to identify between an Amazon and third-party developed skill based on Skill Library information (e.g. visual text metadata such as skill name, author, and description on the Alexa app). Major et al. (2021) similarly compared Alexa non-users with long-term users and identified that even long-term users misidentified third-party skills as Amazon native skills. In certain instances, participants seemed to be aware that they were interacting with a skill developed by a third-party developer. However, they still perceived the brand device to have some influence or mediation in their experience with that skill. Major et al.'s findings support this as they found a majority of their participants believed they interacted "directly with Amazon alone, and only Amazon possesses data from the exchange as a direct consequence" (p. 14). This is directly opposite to the reality of Alexa skills, where every user input in third-party skills can be directly accessed by third-party developers (Major et al., 2021). Amazon has a vetting process for its skills, but this has been shown to be ineffective as developers can bypass restrictions and publish changes post-deployment that may be malicious towards users in coaxing out private information (Lentzsch et al., 2021). Subsequently, the combination of low VA literacy and the ineffective governance of third-party skills by VA brands is potentially detrimental to users. However, the emergence of VA custodians, who actively monitor and regulate third-party skills before allowing them to be accessed by other household members, may serve as a protective barrier against potentially harmful or malicious third-party skills.

Additionally, users face the challenge of being unable to browse or search for third-party voice skills without access to a secondary GUI device, a phenomenon known as discoverability in HCI. Major et al. (2021) found through their survey that users often feel uncertain about the full range of functionalities available within the Alexa environment due to this lack of discoverability. Other research, such as that by Myers et al. (2018), has identified this lack of discoverability as a contributing factor to device abandonment, as users struggle to form an accurate understanding of available skills and functions. Work by Kocaballi et al. (2020) confirms the lack of discoverability of conversational systems and explores the concept of habitability to improve user experience. Through their systematic review of the literature on habitability, the authors define the concepts as "a habitable conversational system is the one in which system and interface capabilities and user expectations are aligned, and adequate accounts of system and interface behaviour are provided" (Kocaballi et al., 2020, p. 4). They list design implications for bridging the expectations of users and the lack of discoverability of VAs:

1. Habitability is not an instantaneous quality of user-system interaction.
2. Habitability requires establishing common ground.
3. Habitability required giving accounts of system and interface behaviour.
4. Habitability requirements may be different for task-oriented and non-task-oriented cases. (Kocaballi et al., 2020, p. 5–6)

My findings echo and support the implications for design suggested by Kocaballi et al. (2020) proving empirical evidence of habitability happening over time and the conceptualisations and behaviours of users on that journey, such as implementing shout tests and experimenting with audible-conversational space. My findings record the expectations of users and the expectations of VA brands as perceived from the standpoint of users, and the alignment of user and VA brand values and expectations for interaction.

LITERACY

Understanding user expectations also requires attention to literacy—specifically, the competencies users employ when navigating VA interactions. Literacy places the responsibility on users to critically engage with and adapt to VA interactions, while usability is determined by creators who design the systems to align with their intended functionality and user experience goals. Specifically, digital literacy has been defined as "a person's ability to perform tasks effectively in a digital environment" (Ilomäki et al.,

2011, p. 2), where digital refers to information primarily communicated through a computer device and literacy refers to the ability to read and interpret media, then "evaluate and apply new knowledge". Synonyms of digital literacy are often used interchangeably to describe technology-related skills, but include digital competence, information communication technology skills, technology skills, information technology skills, 21st century skills, information literacy and digital skills (Ilomäki et al., 2011).

Media can be broadly defined as any tool used to share ideas, messages and information with others (Jennings, 2018). Arguably, VAs constitute a form of media, as the ideas, messages and information conveyed through them are shaped by real people and organisations with individual beliefs and agendas. While there are various frameworks for understanding digital literacy, such as Eshet's (2004) foundations of photo-visual literacy, information literacy and social-emotional literacy, Buckingham's (2015) conceptualisation of digital literacy is relevant to how users might approach digital literacy in the context of VA interactions. These aspects of digital literacy help illuminate why users perceive and interact with VAs in particular ways, going beyond mere usability and adoption. Below is a summary of the four aspects of Buckingham's digital literacy, where I italicise my provocations for VA literacy.

- **Representation**: "Informed users of media need to be able to evaluate the material they encounter, for example by assessing the motivations of those who created it and by comparing it with other sources, including their own direct experience" (Buckingham, 2015, p. 25). As well, questioning the authority, reliability, bias, and representation of diverse voices and viewpoints is part of assessing the representation of digital media. *How might users interpret bias, authority and reliability in their VA interactions? How might users gauge sources of information provided by VAs?*
- **Language**: An awareness of grammar, different forms of communication, broader codes and conventions of communication forms. "Digital literacy must therefore involve a systematic awareness of how digital media are constructed, and of the unique rhetorics of interactive communication" (Buckingham, 2015, p. 26). *How might users interpret and manipulate language in their VA interactions?*
- **Production**: Literacy also involves understanding who is communicating to whom and why. Users need to be aware of commercial influences, the role of advertising, promotion and sponsorship, and how these forces influence the information that is available. "Awareness should also extend to non-commercial sources and interest groups, who are increasingly using the web as a means of persuasion and influence" (Buckingham, 2015, p. 26). *How might users understand the underlying connection of brands, markets, advertising and other intentions enmeshed within some of their VA interactions?*
- **Audience**: "Finally, literacy also involves an awareness of one's own position as an audience (reader or user)" (Buckingham, 2015, p. 26). Users must understand how media targets different audiences and how different audiences may respond to information. This includes how audiences access media, how they are encouraged to interact with media, and how information is taken from users. *How might VA users interpret responses from the VA? Are they part of a specific audience for interactions and skills?*

These aspects of digital literacy provide a new lens to understand how users interact with digital media. They offer insights into why a user might opt to engage with a particular form of digital media, beyond their ability to use technology in general or satisfaction with a product's usability. Deconstructing Buckingham's (2015) framework of digital literacy may help pinpoint the motivations behind users' interactions with VAs. This framework also provides a lens to explore how the foundational elements of digital literacy could manifest in users' perception and use of VAs. Another concept of literacy that may be applicable is web literacy. This concept is used to understand how users navigate and construct knowledge online using mainly visual-space-based computers or resources. Web literacy is often differentiated between Web 1.0 and Web 2.0 experiences, where the latter proposes users as co-creators, in contrast to passive viewers of content that was created for them (Cormode & Krishnamurthy, 2008). Web literacy models, such as Mozilla's Web Literacy Map (Chung et al., 2017), define three pillars of exploring (navigating the web), building (creating for the web) and connecting (participating on the web) in users' literacy of Web 2.0 practices.

Lastly, the literacy of users regarding VAs should also be examined through the lens of AI literacy. Despite VAs being considered a relatively basic, non-generative form of AI, many participants still perceived them as such. Researchers are still developing the concept of AI literacy (Long & Magerko, 2020; Ng et al., 2021) and AI literacy continues to be developed as new forms of AI emerge, like Generative AI (GenAI) chatbots like ChatGPT (Fui-Hoon Nah et al., 2023). From Long and Magerko's (2020) review on digital, computational, scientific, and data literacy, AI literacy is defined as "a set of competencies that enables individuals to critically evaluate AI technologies; communicate and collaborate effectively with AI; and use AI as a tool online, at home, and in the workplace" (p. 2). Tools to complement AI literacies are also being developed alongside a general definition of AI literacy, similar to how the CRAAP (Currency, Relevance, Authority, Accuracy, and Purpose) test might be used for information literacy and to identify potential misinformation in analysing multimedia (Gunasekara & Gerts, 2017).

To understand brands in VA interaction, I return to my findings on the audible-conversational space. As presented in an earlier chapter, VA interactions are *information* that is experienced in an *audible-conversational-virtual space* in *physical space* through a mixed-reality technology. This means that users experience information differently from how they might with visual representations of information in other virtual modalities. Considering visual computing, visual-virtual space is envisaged through symbols in the form of images, letters and words. On a laptop, the virtual space is clearly defined by the limitations of the borders of the screen, a rectangle with set dimensions. Users navigate the virtual representational space through a mouse or trackpad, their tactile interactions mapped to the visual space represented by the cursor. Users can open an internet browser by selecting a branded icon—a small fox for Mozilla, a blue compass for Safari or a multi-coloured circle for Chrome. Users will find the same long horizontal box that represents an area to enter their visual-textual query—the search bar. Small visual cues at the periphery of the salient search bar indicate to the user which provider is delivering their browsing service, for a Google, Bing, Baidu or Yahoo logo may be present. By the simple action of opening an internet browser on a visual interface, users have already aligned themselves with a global corporation.

Next, users might enter a few key terms or type a sentence to be algorithmically searched within an index of sources. A long list of search results flows down the screen, about 304,000,000 results in 0.46 seconds.

Headings, authors, logos, dates, and abstracts of webpages are presented before users. They are given a choice, or the illusion of free choice, as the results are organised with algorithmic filter bubbles, search engine optimisation (SEO) keyword manipulation, result ranking and topical relevance based on user location, trends, and keyword match relevance (*In-depth guide to how Google Search works*, 2024). Representations of choice are marked by several visual markers that fill the screen. Markers in *visual-virtual space* can give peripheral cues vital for information literacy and critical thinking.

These visual cues in visual-virtual space disappear in the context of VA interaction, where virtual space is condensed to the contents of audible sentences. When searching or browsing for information audibly, the long list of possible results and sources of information available in visual interfaces disappears, hence also taking away one's ability to "scan" the results for relevance to the query. Jen makes this distinction, comparing voice "replies" to visual "hits".

> If you did a **Google search for the same thing, you don't get replies, you do get website hits**, so I guess the Google search can be a bit more fuzzy and allows that fuzziness so it gives you an approximate match or it doesn't.
>
> Jen, 1 person, 4 device household

This difference between "results" that one can scan for "relevance" and "replies" or "responses" that one cannot control is shaped by the anthropomorphism of brands due to the audible-conversational format of VA interaction. In Jen's house, Google becomes a third conversational partner in a debate about critical thinking between her and her partner sitting on their living room couch.

> **Jen:** If I'm talking with my partner about something weird, often is the way, and he'll say, "Oh, I think that means… whatever". I'll say, "I don't think so, let's ask…" And we end up asking the device. So then the device becomes part of our conversation because I'll say, "Okay, Google, can you look up the results for this?" and she'll come back with this answer, and he'll say, "I don't agree with that, I think it's more of whatever". So I'll say, ah "Google, can you tell me the answer to that?" And then we keep going. [Jen laughs]

This excerpt from my discussion with Jen is an example of how, through the medium of VA mixed reality, brands can become more salient in the social community of the home and in the construction of users' knowledge. The illusion of choice in virtual-visual interfaces is replaced with the illusion of tacit knowledge in audible-conversational interfaces. In Jen's experience, the brand's VA persona provides the best answer based on its "perceived opinion", even though it is derived from the same algorithmic searching that is used in visual interfaces. Google VA is a conversational partner that is an authority on searching and retrieving information, has access to millions of data points and is unburdened by the limitations of the human brain. In life, a human conversational partner can disagree, but the Google VA presents information in one reply, instead of Jen and her partner being able to browse through the search results and come to a decision together. However, it is not often that one browses through internet search results together; each person may do it separately on their respective devices, which may provide different results based on their search history and customisation. The Google VA voice response, however, is a single aural response shared by both.

In another interview, Joey tells a similar story, where Google becomes an authoritative voice in a truth-seeking conversation between users. Immediate access to information allows Google to enter a conversation quickly and is taken for truth immediately based on its reputation.

Joey:	I would say the things that **mum uses it for are winning arguments**. That's about it. Sorry.
Indra:	Tell me more, Joey!
Joey:	They'll be like ... Oh, "when did... Diana die, what year?" And dad'll be like, "oh, yeah, it was this year. I remember". Mum's like, "No, it's this year". "No, no, no. It's that one", and then she'll be like, "Hey, Google. What year did Princess Diana die?" It's like "I found this from the web". Then mum's like "See, see? Huh!"

These two examples show that, by condensing the virtual space of information retrieval into audible sentences, VAs can seamlessly integrate into daily discourse, becoming an active participant in social dialogue. With VAs, the way users interact with information transforms from traditional visual experiences into something where knowledge is co-constructed as the VA persona shapes conversations in action. Through their ability to provide instant answers and contribute to ongoing debates, VAs not only shape the flow of conversation but also influence the formation of knowledge within interpersonal interactions.

Literacy in Brand-saturated Interactions

Unlike visual multimedia, which allows for review and detailed analysis, VA outputs are transient, and users must rely on voice histories accessed through secondary devices to revisit interactions. VA interactions differ significantly from traditional digital interfaces. The extensive lists of answers available in visual browsing disappear, replaced by an "illusion of tacit knowledge". The VA persona presents its response as definitive, even though the underlying processes—such as NLP, web-browser APIs, and algorithmic structures like SEO and page ranking—remain largely opaque to users. This creates a pseudo-authoritative dynamic, shaping knowledge co-construction within human–VA interactions. As Lam (2022) argues, the conceptual "black box" of AI, which obscures explainability and transparency in complex processes, parallels tacit knowledge. While developers can sometimes articulate simple AI processes, the growing complexity of data systems exacerbates the challenge of making these interactions explainable.

The limitations of audible-conversational interfaces further compound this issue. For instance, in anthropomorphic interactions, such as when Google's VA acts as a conversational partner in debates, users unknowingly integrate the VA's subjective responses into their critical thinking processes. These responses are shaped not only by the VA's NLP system but also by a network of invisible services, including the algorithms governing search engines, digital brand partnerships, and transactional exchanges. As a result, the knowledge co-constructed in human–VA interactions reflects the priorities of the digital ecosystem rather than an objective information landscape.

This interconnectedness highlights the need for research into VA literacy frameworks that address critical thinking and explainable AI. Users must navigate a landscape shaped by brand anthropomorphism, audible-conversational design, and the challenges of unexplainable AI processes. By understanding how these factors intersect, future studies can better support users in critically engaging with VAs and the broader ecosystems they operate within.

FINDINGS FEATURED IN THIS CHAPTER

TABLE 6.1 Chapter findings

Google VAs are an authoritative conversational partner in constructing knowledge	Google VA is perceived and used as an authoritative voice in truth-seeking conversations between users. Immediate access to information due to VA ubiquity allows Google to enter a conversation quickly and is often taken for truth based on Google's reputation.
Amazon VAs are an extended marketing platform and associated with retail	Aspects of Alexa's interactions were perceived as trying to sell other Amazon services to the user. This included follow-up suggestions to try an Amazon service and involvement in TV advertisements.
Participants test and compare VA brands in situ	Participants compare differences in interactions by asking the same question to multiple VAs, one after the other. This allows users to clearly identify discrepancies.
Place may inform which VA brand is used in a space	Different brands of VAs were used for specific purposes related to the meanings and uses of places.

(Continued)

TABLE 6.1 (Continued)

Participants compare tangible and intangible aspects of VA brands	The user experience of intangible characteristics, such as personality, speed, connectivity and responsiveness, might be compared to tangible aspects, such as the sensitivity of microphones or speaker quality.
Participants may use multiple brand VAs in the same space	Participants use multiple VA brands in the same space due to the perceived value and user experience offered by each brand VA (e.g. Hugo switching between Google and Alexa based on interaction needs) or specific VA interactions tied to certain places (e.g. in the car). This might include using multiple brand VA smart speakers in a space or a phone VA while another brand is available.
Participants perceived Chinese brands to be less safe	Participants commented on trusting VA-related device brands approved by Australian standards.
Users personify VA brands when communicating	Users portray brand products as entities with distinct personalities when discussing their experiences with VAs. For example, "Siri's not happy with Chinese brands where Alexa is".
Confined to singular VA brand devices	Monetary and compatibility requirements limited participants' adoption of multiple VA brand devices (this does not include IoT products).
Diversifying brand products to expand smart home capabilities	Users might opt to purchase IoT and VA products from other brands to broaden the capabilities of their smart home setup. For example, cheaper third-party IoT products, preferring Google for information retrieval and Amazon for automation.
Loyalty to a brand's digital services materialised in adoption of the brand's physical VA ecosystem	Users are inclined to use a brand's VA when acclimatised to using the brand's other digital services. For example, Avish uses Gmail and other Google Apps, so he was biased to choose the Google VA.
Exposure to products from other brands can familiarise users with VA personas	Users may interact with a brand's VA persona through another device, such as a smartphone. This may encourage or discourage adoption of the VA based on user experience. For example, Mark was displeased with his experience with Samsung's Bixby persona. This lead him to adopt a Google VA.
API-based information inconsistencies	VAs can present differing representations of information due to their connections to various API sources and relationships with other brands. For example, Siri presented different weather information to Google VA.
VA brand-to-brand relationships perceived in VA use	VA brands have established partnerships with other brands, implying a degree of selectivity in VA interactions. Users recognised that this may affect the source of VA information.

(Continued)

TABLE 6.1 (Continued)

Digital interactions manifest tangible interactions	Being integrated into digital ecosystems can tangibly expand the brand's material ecosystem. Their digital relationship with VA brands can manifest in a tangible product. For example, participants received a Google Mini VA due to their YouTube Premium subscription.
VA brand presence in third-party skills	The main VA brand, Google or Alexa, was perceived to be present in third-party interactions even when their voice is not used.
Inconsistent responses or mis-remembering commands	Spoken utterances are not reliable in retrieving consistent interactions, or participants did not use the same command, producing unintended VA interactions.
Foreign voice and personality of third-party skills emotionally impact users	Users felt uncomfortable with unfamiliar voice experiences due to the type of information asked for, the tone and speed of speech of this unfamiliar voice.

Collaborative Interaction and Compassionate Automation 7

COLLABORATIVE CHALLENGES

Some of the participants perceived that VA technology did not support collaborative interaction, considering two angles—how the device is used by multiple people at once or multiple people at different times. What sets VA interaction apart is that it lacks the familiar affordances found in other visual-based technologies, such as collaborative technologies in the home, like the television or shared desktop computer. Users have also been making compromises when sharing these visual-based devices. For instance, Netflix allows users to have separate profiles, where user data is differentiated and personalised algorithms are separated. However, in the household, users must negotiate whose turn it is to *have* the TV or whose profile they want to use to watch a film together, potentially altering their Netflix algorithm in the process. Transitioning from visual to audible-space interactions greatly alters the ways groups of people must adapt to sharing an invisible interface. Another component I have highlighted is the personification and anthropomorphism aspect of VA technology. For VA co-interaction, both aspects affect the user experience. When discussing the impact on group use of VAs, I refer to how co-interaction may deter individuals from using certain features that are more suited for individual use. Additionally, factors such as difficulty in managing multiple speakers may discourage group conversation and interaction.

Technical Barriers to Group Interaction

I begin by discussing the limitations on group interaction due to the dependence on the VA's audio interface. Phoebe tells me about the reliance on voice and distinguishing different voices of different users as an important aspect in performing certain VA interactions. In recognising different people, the VA can identify "authorised" users and allow them greater access to features.

DOI: 10.1201/9781003680840-7

> **There's not so much personalised stuff** that will only be available to one person over another or things like that, it's mostly just that there has to be authorised voices for certain features.
>
> 👤 Phoebe, 2 person, 3 device household

Phoebe's perspective revolves around the idea that the VA should not be personalised to a single user, similar to how algorithms adapt to the preferences of the primary user of a device or service. Rather, she suggests authorisation, where the devices remain unchanged but control access to certain features.

> … so certain things like **changing shopping lists** is one of the things, because like lists… Like a thing that you can build through the Google home… in order to delete lists and change lists and things like that, it has to be an authorised person… so, not anybody can just be like, "add this to the shopping list", it has to be like, "Oh, I recognise this voice as one of the authorised voices on my list of authorised voices".
>
> 👤 Phoebe, 2 person, 3 device household

Phoebe discusses the example of shopping lists, which highlights an interaction that can have material and potential cost implications. Typically, when financial information is involved, VA users remain hesitant to carry out these interactions through VAs, as I explored earlier. Phoebe notes that authorised voices do not significantly impact her and her partner's daily usage of their VAs.

> I mean, **most of the features of the way that we would use it in day-to-day is not something that's tied to the authority**, so doing music, casting things, so to speak, is something that anyone who says it clearly enough in and asking things like asking questions about the weather, asking questions for information and things like that, that's something that doesn't require that authorised voice.
>
> 👤 Phoebe, 2 person, 3 device household

This section delved into the limitations of group interaction imposed by the audio interface of VAs. Phoebe emphasised the importance of voice recognition in enabling certain VA interactions, allowing for the identification of "authorised" users who gain greater access to features. She suggested that, rather than personalisation, authorisation is key, where certain users are granted access to specific features without altering the devices.

One lack of technological support for multi-person interactions with VAs was described by participants as the lack of physical actions that communicate intent in group conversation without the need for audible sound, and the inability of VAs to identify multiple speakers or handle multiple questions or commands in a group interaction. This aligns with existing literature addressing barriers to multi-person interactions. To illustrate this, I share an excerpt regarding multi-user issues with VAs and other IoT devices as captured by Shavitt et al.'s (2021) systematic review on collaborative interaction with NUIs:

> Due to the absence of visual clues, affordances, and spatial organization, the use of natural language communication is associated with the decreased sense of control. For example, current conversational technologies (e.g., Amazon Alexa, Google home) tend to be designed for a single user input, while they are actively expanding in home spaces, which are inherently multiuser. As a result, when a situation prompts several people to interact with a conversational agent simultaneously, they either have to carefully negotiate turn-taking, or run into a danger of potentially overwriting another user's request or being ignored by the system. Unsurprisingly, such interactions tend to result in unfulfilled requests and conflicts between co-users.
>
> *(Shavitt et al., 2021, p. 2)*

Hao raises another problem for group interaction due to the medium of voice, commenting on the inability of VAs to identify multiple speakers and handle multiple questions and commands in a group interaction.

> I don't think it's designed for groups; you'd have multiple questions and multiple people asking and how does it prioritise something, and who does it talk to…
>
> Hao, 4 person, 2 device household

Hao refers to the VA device in general, then makes the association to multi-person conversations. Group conversations infer multiple users are focused on continuous interaction to command actions or share information with other people or the device. Hao comments on group interaction as he actively tries to encourage group usage with his family. Because VAs are highly personified anthropomorphic devices, users were quick to compare a pleasant group–VAs interaction to human–group interactions. Hao explains how he might navigate a conversation with a group of people to infer what he would like group–VA interaction to resemble.

> It's more the **eye contact, you walk up to someone, and you make that eye contact, and you talk to someone in a crowd**. Or you single them out, or you go, "excuse me". Whereas something like this, you know, if you don't know what its name is… [his Google device activates without hearing the wake word and Hao is interrupted and does not finish his sentence as he tells Google to stop].
>
> Hao, 4 person, 2 device household

Hao describes the physical actions that communicate intent in group conversation without the need for audible sound. Despite his efforts to encourage group usage within his family, Hao finds that VAs are tailored towards individual interactions, lacking the nuanced communication cues present in human–group interactions. Hao goes on to describe how he believes VAs are built towards person–device interactions, describing these personal interactions as more intimate.

> It's more of that tailored, intimate, I'm going to answer your question… so it's more of that 1:1 interaction that you get with an AI, **then if you want to expand it, it's more of the game stuff**.
>
> Hao, 4 person, 2 device household

Hao's response ties into an aspect of where group interactions seem to work well. He contrasts the direct, intimate nature of person–device interactions with the more expansive, game-oriented interactions that are more successful as group–VA interactions.

Social Barriers to Group Interaction

Avish also shared that he prefers to only perform this interaction while there are co-users present to elicit household bonding. Avish indicated that co-user presence affects the type of interactions users will perform. If he were to ask for a joke, it would be difficult and almost impossible to repeat the same interaction later in front of the others, as jokes are often cycled and randomised by the VA software. In addition, a joke often loses its humour when heard for the second time.

> **Indra:** When do you end up doing this interaction?
> **Avish:** Telling us a joke? Usually when we're in a silly mood, or usually when we're all together and we're getting ready for dinner or something like that. It's sort of part of family socialising, I guess.
> **Indra:** Yeah, just kind of like bonding over the funniness?
> **Avish:** Over something silly. Yeah, yeah.
> **Indra:** Do you ever ask it to tell you a joke when you're by yourself?
> **Avish:** No. Actually, I don't think I've ever done it. It's usually so that the others can hear it as well, and then we all take turns.

In some instances, the presence of co-users prevented certain participants from interacting with a VA device. Anavi and I explored the cause of her reluctance to engage with VA devices in the presence of others. Anavi described feeling "weird", "conscious", and "silly".

Anavi: Usually I'm by myself when I'm talking to her [Alexa], because I don't like talking in front of other people.
Indra: In general, or when giving commands?
Anavi: Just giving any voice assistant orders, I don't like doing that in front of other people.
Indra: Can you describe how you feel about it?
Anavi: Conscious? I think it's weird.
Indra: Can you relate another activity to this feeling?
Anavi: It's not like I'm a bad public speaker or anything, I speak a lot in class, and I talk to a lot of people. But for some reason when giving voice assistant commands I can't... in front of other people. I think that it's weird. I don't know. I think it's me, that I'm conscious of what I'm saying. The weirdness is slightly elevated because it's not a real person I'm talking to. I feel silly.

In comparison to Anavi's interactions in front of other people, group–VA interactions centred around playing games may serve as a safe space for users to engage with VAs, providing clear goals and motivations for interaction. These interactions provide clear rules and expectations, which mediate group interaction and engagement. Additionally, the presence of co-users can influence the type of interactions users engage in.

My findings also revealed that users were hyper-aware of the presence of other individuals in their environment when interacting with VAs. Participants indicated that the presence of others influenced their type of interactions, with some participants refraining from interacting with a VA device when others were present. In the literature, *social presence* is the term used to describe the sense of being with another (Biocca et al., 2003). In the context of VA usage, research on social presence typically examines the VA's perceived social presence (Sengupta et al., 2021). Prior work on VA's perceived social presence and its effects on user embarrassment has been explored in Bartneck et al.'s (2010) comparison of non-anthropomorphic and high-anthropomorphic user interfaces in an extremely personal and private health setting. Participants were asked personal health questions and to take off their clothes by a yellow robot cat named "iCat robot" or an aesthetic white and grey device, which they referred to as "e Biopac MP-150 System". Although it was a preliminary test, Bartneck et al. highlighted some notable limitations regarding the sustained use of anthropomorphic interfaces in embarrassing situations. These limitations include considerations of the environment's social context, concerns about privacy and the comparison of the anthropomorphic device to its human equivalent (in this case, a nurse). The influence of privacy can manifest differently depending on the context. It may relate to the privacy of the content being discussed during the interaction or the physical location where the interaction occurs. Both aspects—privacy of content and privacy of location—can impact how individuals perceive and engage in interactions.

Previous research on social presence typically examined users' perceived social presence of VAs (Sengupta et al., 2021), whereas my findings focus on how the presence and observation of other human users influence VA interaction. My findings confirm Cowan et al.'s (2017) findings on speaking to Siri in public environments and extend it to the social presence of other people in private spaces. Cowan et al. (2017) also found that cultural background influenced a person's expectation of audible technology etiquette, where some nationalities found it comfortable to speak loudly on the phone and, by inference, talk to Siri in the presence of others. In my study, Hugo's household illustrated this cultural difference. Thus, while studies may focus on interaction quality and trust (Kumar et al., 2021; Nasirian et al., 2017) as potential barriers to VA use, social presence from a combined perspective of space, anthropomorphism and cultural influences on technology use should also be considered. Overall, my research reveals several inhibitors to collaborative interaction with VAs, notably the lack of technological support for multi-user engagement and social presence, where the presence and observation of other human users influence interaction.

GAMIFICATION AS A SOLUTION

Some interactions are designed specifically for group play, often in the form of game skills or gamified experiences. For example, voice games like musical chairs or quiz-type games and examples of gamified skills might include interactive storytelling, where rules for interacting with the skill are communicated. In these skills, some native and some third-party developed rules and expectations are prescribed to mediate group interaction. These rules for group–VA interaction have been programmed in the skill for the VA to understand. For instance, Hao mentions the extra time players are given to respond in a game action by Google.

> ... sometimes when I get bored, we play general knowledge game, and so there's a general knowledge game on Google where you can play general knowledge and **it gives you time to answer questions and you play against four or five people**.
>
> Hao, 4 person, 2 device household

WHY GAMIFICATION WORKS FOR GROUPS

Lien agrees with the idea that group usage of VAs tends to revolve around games or gamified skills, rather than collaborative information retrieval tasks. Lien especially highlights that skills featuring less talking are more entertaining for his children, suggesting the device's ability to facilitate entertainment is more crucial than the level of verbal interaction involved in the experience.

> As in like **occasions where the whole family sit around Alexa, to play musical chair function**, the musical statue, or... We did the song quiz, we did... Some lucky trivia, but the kids are too young. for those questions. So, they're not interested, but the musical statue and their musical chair, they quite like it, the... Quite a lot of games that you can do with Alexa.
>
> Lien, 4 person, 6 device household

Some interactions are designed explicitly for group play, often in the form of game skills or gamified activities. These interactions come with rules and expectations established by the skill developer to facilitate group engagement, which the VA system can accommodate within the capabilities set by the device designers. For example, participants noted they were given additional time to respond to the VA during these group interactions. Gamification refers to "the use of game design elements in non-game contexts" (Deterding et al., 2011, p. 2). My findings indicate that group interaction was more successful during VA game skills when the rules were clearly implemented and communicated by the VA. Establishing procedures to mediate and facilitate group interaction between the VA and users further enhances the effectiveness of group interactions. Further research could explore the potential for users to teach their VAs contextual rules through conversational explanation, rather than relying on creating complex routines in secondary VA apps. This approach would be a way to apply my findings to real-world applications and enhance users' ability to customise their interaction style with VAs.

Bräuer and Mazarakis (2022, Mazarakis, 2021) confirm that gamification in VA interaction enhances user experience. They define the term audio-gamification to refer to audio feedback to communicate gamification aspects without visual representations. Their experimental design study tested the effects of audio-gamification on 81 individuals on motivation and performance to complete tasks when using a VA, implementing game elements such as a points system, time pressure, levelling, narrative and ranking into their custom Amazon skill. Perhaps more research on VA gamification may encourage VA brands to implement more gamification into general skills so they are not confined just to experimental third-party skills. However, the authors note it is "necessary to take individual needs into account when designing audio game design elements and to offer the user the possibility to adjust or switch off the elements" (Bräuer & Mazarakis, 2022, p. 10).

User-created Gamification Strategies

In non-gamified skills, participants create their own rules for group–VA interaction. In her example, Phoebe and her friend gamify their group–VA experience in retrieving information to set expectations for taking turns in interacting. In this case, building a gamified experience based on the "perceived opinion" of VAs, Phoebe and her friends create a game based on the limitations of the VA's ability to provide only singular direct responses.

> We did have some fun when a friend was over recently seeing how right the Google Home would be if we tried to obscure the ask for a song ... and then we each kind of had a thought for what the Little Mermaid song would be, whether it would be like Part of your World or Under the Sea... which one is Google going to decide is THE Little Mermaid Song. Placing bets on which one it was gonna be...
>
> Phoebe, 2 person, 3 device household

Similarly, Avish describes the turn-taking that comes with gamified interactions or interactions that have clear rules, like telling a joke. In telling a joke, the audience knows what to expect, as the VA will ask a question to the crowd and answer their question. In addition, users have some sense of when the VA will stop speaking, giving clearer timing to perform multi-user interactions.

Lastly, I raise the use of smart technology to support and provide hyper-interactive experiences, a benefit of living in a smart home.

> **Indra:** So, you've never seen your three-year-old interact with Google?
>
> **Hao:** No, no, when we read stories to her, we would go through and we'll say, so if it's a dog, a cat noise will say, "Hey Google, make a dog noise", and then that interacts with the story time and so on and so forth. So, we use it in that way.
>
> **Indra:** So, you're still telling the story, it's not the AI?
>
> **Hao:** It's the addition of being able to use the interface to add extra interactivity to what you're doing.

Hao's example illustrates how smart devices, such as Google Assistant, can be integrated into everyday activities to provide additional layers of engagement and immersion. This highlights the potential of smart home devices to enrich family interactions and create dynamic and engaging experiences, ultimately enhancing the overall quality of life within the smart home.

COMPASSIONATE AUTOMATION

In the previous section describing the relationships that formed or evolved from the presence of VAs, I shared aspects of relationships that are affected by the automation of self or others. The following section details scenarios with a commonality in that the sociality of anthropomorphic VAs emerged through participants' personal experiences and where the VA was exceptionally humanised by the perception of participants and their households, including disrupting human expressions of care, preserving human agency, and the significance of VAs in providing companionship. These interactions are novel examples of automation affecting relationships, shedding light on human–computer relationships in the context of conversational devices.

Automating Care

Earlier, I presented the manual, computing and social effort trichotomy and described scenarios where social effort was replaced with computational effort. This substitution resulted in the disruption of relationship dynamics among household members accustomed to providing support for others. In our interview, Mark recounted a confrontation with his mother after she overheard him asking Google for assistance instead of seeking help from her. The story emphasises the missed opportunity for human–human caregiving as Mark automates the tasks through his VA.

Mark: Setting reminders, setting alarms, messaging people. Starting phone calls, yeah. Yeah, I used to, quite a lot… **My mum was starting to get really upset with me…**
Indra: Why?
Mark: 'cause she'd walk past my room and hear me using the assistant, and then she'd be like, "Oh, I can wake you up at that time", and then the phone would start responding and she [mother] goes… "It's not for me".

The computational replacement is more obvious to bystanders due to the audible-conversational interaction of VAs and highlights VA interaction fields extending outside participants' concepts of space and place. With VAs using audible-conversational space, computational requests could be misconstrued as social requests by bystanders who overhear them.

Indra: So, she [Mark's mother] hears you?
Mark: She heard me asking to set an alarm and she thought I was talking to her from another room, but it was actually me talking to the phone.
Indra: That is beautiful. It… Is there any other times that's happened?
Mark: I think after that time she kind of realised that I was talking to the phone most times, so it hasn't really happened again…

It is noteworthy to observe how interactions like this may affect the relationship between Mark and his mother. Moreover, it highlights how conversational and audible interfaces expose personal computing choices to public consumption and interpretation. The prevalence of automation can alter relationship dynamics, particularly in the realm of providing care and performing acts of service within close interpersonal relationships at home. In a domestic environment, these actions carry different implications compared to performing acts of care or service in a workplace, where such actions may be expected as part of a job description, such as a nurse or hotel attendant waking someone at a set time. While care is an expression of love in the workplace and at home, the degree of intensity and intention behind this expression may vary.

Jen describes a situation in which she was open to accepting automated care from her VA. During Covid, Jen experienced long periods of isolation, living alone on her country property. She described days when she did not use her voice to speak to anyone at all. She disclosed her appreciation for being able to speak to Google when no one else was around. Jen enjoyed expressing care to her VA and receiving it in return through this small but meaningful interaction.

> You know what else I like? Which someone said to me, oh, that must drive you insane? But I actually quite like it. **When I'm going to bed at night time, I can say good night to her. Yeah, and then she tells me goodnight**, then she starts playing… Relaxation noises. Yeah, when I'm on… Yeah, you get the crickets and stuff like that, as if it's like night time and she plays it for half an hour or so, so you can go to sleep, I guess. So I think it's really cute.
>
> Jen, 1 person, 4 device household

She explained how this interaction made her feel, expressing gratitude for regaining a sense of interaction.

> I wasn't seeing anyone, so I live here on my own, I have my dogs. I go down to feed my horse, but really, I don't see that many people down there. You might see people at a distance or whatever, so sometimes actually just talking to a device sounds very pathetic, **but it was good to have that interaction back** … And as much as obviously dogs are another sentient being, so they're going to react to you, which is lovely, but don't answer you… **When you say good night to Google, she's actually quite pleasant about it, so it is like having someone saying to you in a friendly way, "Oh good night", "Have a good night's sleep, see you tomorrow"**.
>
> Jen, 1 person, 4 device household

Avish expanded on the concept of automating care and acts of service but presented a contrasting perspective on the desire to automate these values. As we came to the end of our interview, Avish and I talked about VA technology in the future. Particularly,

Avish emphasised an anti-automation culture in expressing care. He described human interactions that he would always want to have ownership of, such as food, as well as conversational and physical interactions with other people.

> I think there are still things you want to feel like I personally am in control of, like cooking is something you do, particularly for other people, and that you want to feel like you've done it, rather than you've had somebody else do it or a robot to do it or… You know, **I think there are still human interactions of which I think food is a part, conversation is a part, physical interaction, a part that you probably don't want artificial intelligence to mediate for you**.
>
> Avish, 3 person, 3 device household

Avish introduced an intriguing notion regarding automating relationships, suggesting the concept of automating oneself through VAs and future AI iterations.

> I think I feel comfortable with getting assistance in terms of looking up stuff or helping with information, but I don't know that I… at this point in my life, want artificial intelligence to do… For me. Maybe when I'm 80 and I can't do any more, I'll have a different viewpoint.
>
> Avish, 3 person, 3 device household

Avish raised the concept of ageing and the transition from self-performing care to relying on others, whether automated or not. He prompts consideration of the body's role in one's ability to interact with the world and how VAs might be a part of that story. Jen's reason to use VAs is reminiscent of the concept of automating oneself to extend ability and presence. Jen's desire is not to substitute her physical presence but to project a social presence that is indistinguishable from being physically present. She envisions a scenario using Google's broadcast feature, where her dogs would perceive her as being in the room solely based on the sound of her voice (while another human might know that technology is mediating this communication).

> Well, strangely, as I said, I kind of bought it 'cause **I wanted to use it to check on my dogs while I was at work**, and… Because obviously, I used to leave them three days a week and they'd be left for 12 hours on their own, and they were so destructive anyway. So, I had this really fun, I don't know how it would work, it actually would be interesting to see, and **I would be able to look at them and do broadcast, and say "stop that"**.
>
> Jen, 1 person, 4 device household

Compassion in Automation

A few participant experiences with VAs demonstrate preserving human authenticity in VA interactions, where aspects such as non-judgemental listening and cultural biases reflect the value of compassion. Similar to Jen's experience of Google as a listening partner, Mark comments on his appreciation of Google VA as an objective and consistent listening partner despite his tendency to mumble. Mark compares his experience with mumbling with his Google VA, compared to human conversations that have left him feeling uncomfortable about mumbling.

> There's not much consequence. Yeah**, it's [Google VA] not going to judge you for not talking properly, whereas sometimes people would be like**, "Stop mumbling blah blah blah"... Yeah but I've just come home from work. I don't need this.
>
> Mark, 4 person, 4 device household

Mark acknowledges that the machine might struggle to interpret his commands due to his unclear speech. Despite this, he remains objective and understands that, as a user, the technology may not always accurately process his attempts at interaction. Consequently, he does not place much importance on whether the VA listens to him or successfully completes the interaction.

> **Mark:** I tend to mumble a fair bit and it's normally quite good, which surprises me.
>
> **Indra:** ... Do you find then it's a better listener than real people?
>
> **Mark:** I wouldn't say... **I don't put enough weight on its responses to put value on whether it listens to me well or not**, I guess. But I find that sometimes if it's not responding correctly, I get shitty with it. I'm like "just do what I'm telling you to do it". Yeah, yeah, **I don't think I care enough about it to compare it to like a response that a normal person would give me, like if a person was like, "What did you say?... I'd happily repeat it**. I'm not too phased by it".

In contrast, Hao experiences a similar mis-interaction, but it affects him more emotionally. Specifically, he faces the issue of bias towards English words, resulting in the frequent mispronunciation of his name, noting that "Hao" is a pseudonym.

Hao: What does frustrate me with the AI stuff is it can't read out my name properly, even though you teach it… Never.
Indra: Wow. How do you teach it? How to pronounce your name.
Hao: So, you can just go learn my name, "Hey, Google learn my name", and it'll say, "Okay, pronounce your name". And then, I'll try and try and try and try, and it won't do it, Siri's the same…
Indra: Interesting. Is there a function where you can type in…
Hao: Yeah, if you type it in, even if you type in phonetically, it won't... It won't pick it up because it's a Vietnamese name. It makes it harder to pick up… It's very geared towards English-speaking people with English sounding names.

Hao's experience with VAs illustrates the emotional impact of mis-interaction and the importance of respecting the diversity of human communication, emphasising compassion in automation. Mark appreciates his VA as an objective and consistent listening partner, especially in contrast to human conversations that have made him feel uncomfortable about his tendency to mumble. Hao's frustration with VA systems mispronouncing non-English names highlights inherent biases in technology design that affect the quality of relationships with VAs. These experiences underscore the importance of compassion in addressing biases and ensuring that VAs recognise and respect the diversity of human communication.

Defining Compassionate vs Automated Compassion

My findings suggest that participants intended to use VAs to extend their caregiving capabilities to others—from assisting co-users in automating tasks to simplify their physical or cognitive efforts or provide an easy interface for accessing/interacting with music, games, or information throughout their day. I relate these experiences to social capital theory, viewing them as a form of informal caregiving. Positive and negative caregiving experiences can influence one's social capital within a community (Barrett et al., 2014; Bruhn & Rebach, 2014; Eberl, 2020). Social capital can be defined as behaviours that affect bonding and connecting for the purpose of increasing access to social mobility (Putnam, 2000). Technology and caregiving represent extensive areas of research, typically focused on supporting caregivers rather than recognising that anyone in the household can express care through technology use. Lindeman et al. (2020) highlight the emerging opportunities to leverage ubiquitous technologies for caregiver support:

> … recently the emergence of new technologies such as mobile and cloud, robotics, connected sensors, virtual/augmented/mixed reality, voice, and the evermore ubiquitous tools supported by advanced data analytics, coupled with the integration of multiple technologies through platform solutions, have opened a new era of technology-enabled interventions that can empower and support family caregivers.
>
> *(p. s41)*

Compassionate automation is a concept that has arisen from this research to describe the integration of social capital principles with smart and autonomous technology to enhance caregiving practices within households. To be specific, I offer definitions of compassionate and automated compassion. The phrase "compassionate automation" employs compassion as an adjective to describe the discourse in which users use their devices to automate tasks or interact with automated devices and other individuals in relation to VAs. Compassionate automation involves incorporating empathy, understanding and consideration for human emotions and needs into the design and implementation of automated systems and processes. In contrast, the term "automated compassion" refers to the act of automating compassionate actions, such as listening, providing acts of service or expressing emotions. Automated compassion could imply the use of automated or artificial intelligence systems to express or enact compassion in various contexts, such as Google wishing Jen goodnight. This could involve automated responses that demonstrate empathy, support or understanding in situations where a human presence is extended or absent.

Automation is defined as "a device that carries out a process independently of human intervention" (Mann & Püttmann, 2023, p. 1). Alternatively, an economics-based definition of automation infers the reduction of human presence or action, stating that "automation is often understood as a type of labor-saving technology which reduces the demand for human workers at specific tasks" (Mann & Püttmann, 2023, p. 1). The term compassionate automation could be proposed as a counter-culture concept to challenge the productivity-focused culture often associated with traditional definitions of automation. The discourse of productivity culture heavily influences discussions surrounding VA as intelligent IoT devices. My ethnographic research suggests that compassion and care towards other people drive the discourse of VA perception and use within homes.

This ethnographic view, though, focuses not simply on how people explicitly transform or programme interactive technologies, but how those technologies take on specific social meanings through their embedding within systems of practice (Dourish, 2001, p. 546).

Through ethnographic research and an embodied interaction lens in my study of VA users, I uncovered how users reshape the discourse around a product to align with their lived experiences.

CULTURAL DIMENSIONS

After learning what VA users believe about their smart homes, how does this affect how they live their daily lives and with others in their smart homes? In particular, how does the VA become a central device in operating and managing aspects across different spaces?

> I actually quite like the function that it can do, **it can sort of control everything in the house**, it's not about just the interactions of this device, **I use it as like a controller**, and I do use that drop-in function a lot, and announce function 'cause the kids could be with us, and I just say, announce dinner is ready and then they can come over o**r I drop into them, Hey, can you turn down the volume?** Things like that. So, it's sort of **like a walkie talkie within the house**.
>
> Lien, 4 person, 6 device household

Noise, Whispers, and Household Dynamics

Users must consider how their vocal interactions may affect other people. For instance, voice can be a disruptive interface in daily life. Hugo highlights a distinction between noise and being considerate of sleeping occupants in the house.

Indra: So, is it easier to just say the action to Alexa rather than using the remote?
Hugo: Yes, but the problem is with that. I mean, I do it like that. But of course, two things. Nighttime. You know, when everyone is sleeping—talking to Alexa, it will be a problem.

While Hugo appreciates the functionality of speaking commands, his awareness of others in the house and their current actions limits his VA use. When VA interaction depends on noise, users should be more considerate of how noise is expressed by individuals in the home and the issues behind different expressions or suppression of noise.

Hugo discusses the difference in country-based cultures in determining what is socially acceptable for producing noise, comparing his experience in Australia to that in South America. His family is used to shouting at each other and comfortable with making loud noises when living in South America, whereas he infers an impoliteness or inappropriateness to do so in Australia. Hugo talks about "respecting his neighbours" regarding noise—noise from conversations between occupants as well as interactions between people and Alexa.

The problem is sometimes it's 4 am and they know someone sneeze or cough and then Alexa starts speaking at 4 am. So, I need to stop that type of thing … but because **we are from South America and we are kind of a noisy family**, I would say, **you know, it's normal in there to shout**. You know, we have like a two-storey and "HEY please go to finish" [he shouts during the interview at a loud volume as if he is telling his daughters] or whatever. And I kind of tried to adjust in here where it's kind of more quiet and **try to respect neighbours** or whatever.

Hugo, 4 person, 8 device household

Hugo reflects on a personalised routine he developed to take advantage of Alexa's ability to recognise sneeze and cough-like sounds. Each time a family member would sneeze, Alexa would surprise them by remarking on the sneeze or cough. This consideration of geographical cultures affecting Hugo and his family in Australia encouraged me to reflect on how culture and tradition have stopped me from doing particular things.

> I've experienced a differentiation of culture in my lifetime, spending time in Bali, Indonesia, where my mother grew up and her family reside, and comparing that to my lifestyle and feeling like a Sydney, Australia, local. Even though I speak the native language of Indonesia, Bahasa, I still miss the cultural cues and words that they don't teach you in the language books. I learn them from living within the culture whether that is physically there geographically or replicated elsewhere in a physical or virtual space.
>
> The way we speak and the words we use may be usual or unusual in different places. For instance, I recall resting my hands on my hips when speaking to a village elder in Bali, she gave me a stern look and was not very nice to me. Afterwards I learnt that it's considered rude to pose like that when addressing someone older than you in Balinese culture—and now I'm conscious of not doing so in similar social situations.
>
> 👤 Indra

Hugo's example of cultural customs influencing his family's actions, and consequently VA interactions, sheds light on the importance of considering cultural elements in ubiquitous and anthropomorphic VA use. In designing for the issue of noise disturbances, most VAs have a whisper function that was well-known to my participants. Hugo proposes that the whispering function is the solution to late-night VA interactions. However, he runs into a different social problem with the whispering solution.

> Whispering is good, you know. The whispering function. The problem is when they whisper back… My younger daughter is scared of that one.
>
> 👤 Hugo, 4 person, 8 device household

Hugo's daughter finds the whispering function to be scary, leading to a need for consideration of family dynamics and individual preferences when using VA technology. Imagine if fears could be mapped to the user's profile to avoid unpleasant conversations. This highlights the importance of not only assessing the time and presence of others when using VA devices but also understanding the potential impact on family members, especially in households that are heavily reliant on VA functionality (e.g. needing to use VAs for basic functions like turning on lights). Is the utterance appropriate to be spoken at the volume, direction and position the user has estimated based on the status of other people in the vicinity? Is the user being observed? Is there potential to be listened to? Is the user comfortable with achieving their goal through potentially public interactions?

In other instances, I found the whisper function helped encourage VA interaction. The whisper function, which mimics the user's whispering tone, not only suggests that the VA understands the context of the conversation but also humanises the interaction, making it more comforting for the user, as seen with Anavi.

Anavi: I do prefer whispering to Alexa, especially at nighttime, or even when I know that somebody can hear [nervously giggles]. I, uh, I prefer to whisper to Alexa.
Indra: So, tell me about this, is it related to your house?
Anavi: Uh, I don't know, I think just... sometimes I don't like when people talk too loud it kind of disturbs me a little bit. I find that especially if I'm at home. At home, I like nice and quiet, peace—silence. I like whispering to Alexa because she whispers back. I prefer Alexa when it's on whisper mode.

Anavi's preference for whispering to Alexa, particularly at night or in quiet settings, highlights how the whisper function allows her to feel more at ease operating VAs in her personal space. This indicates that features like the whisper function create a more personalised and accommodating interaction environment for users.

Cultural Diversity in VA Design

Earlier, Hugo discussed the differences in culturally determined norms regarding acceptable noise levels between countries, contrasting his experiences in Australia with those of living in South America. As VA interaction relies on noise, users were mindful of how sound is expressed by individuals in the home as well as the underlying discourses behind different expressions or suppressions of noise. Cultural user interface design is a field that emphasises the consideration and integration of cultural elements into interface design, considering the specific cultural characteristics, preferences and expectations of a target user group (Kondratova & Goldfarb, 2005). Intercultural interface design is a related concept that considers multiple cultural contexts. It involves designing interfaces that can effectively accommodate users from diverse cultural backgrounds, considering potential interactions and overlaps between cultures (Heimgärtner, 2017). Research in these areas predominantly centres on GUIs, particularly webpages, as they can incorporate dynamic location-based visuals. Specifically, the concept of "culturability" (Barber & Badre, 1998)—a fusion of culture and usability in web design—is highlighted as directly influencing users' assessments of the credibility and trustworthiness of websites (Jarvenpaa et al., 1999; Marcus & Gould, 2000). For example, in the context of visual interfaces, research has shown that adapting visual icons to the culture of target users significantly impacts their perception and interface usability (Heukelman & Obono, 2009). In another instance, in a study conducted in Africa, participants mistook the music note icon (used to represent a radio application) for a bird symbol (Heukelman & Obono, 2009; Lalji & Good, 2008).

Just as cultural considerations impact the usability of visual interfaces, they could similarly affect users' interactions with VAs. Adapting the language, tone, and content of VA responses to align with the cultural expectations and preferences of target users may enhance user perception and usability. For instance, using culturally appropriate language, accents, or references in VA responses could contribute to a more intuitive and engaging user experience. Based on my findings within the context of a Western English-speaking country, where interviews were conducted in English, future research involving geographically and culturally diverse participants would be necessary to further investigate cultural and intercultural design considerations in VAs. There may be an opportunity within the third-party skill market to develop voice skills that are culturally tailored to specific countries. Additionally, the base Amazon or Google VA intelligence could potentially incorporate cultural knowledge relevant to the region in which the user is located.

FINDINGS FEATURED IN THIS CHAPTER

TABLE 7.1 Chapter findings

Strategic selection of smart objects	Users expressed selective purchasing strategies of VA and related IoT devices to elevate their lifestyle, ensuring optimal longevity and functionality (e.g. users chose to purchase a smart light switch instead of a smart lightbulb. Though both items would automate the task, one was seen as an option with more longevity).
Noise expectations and nighttime interactions	Participants discussed different attitudes towards noise in the home. This affected participants' ability to interact with their VAs at night.
Cultural expectations of noise influencing VA use	Users must consider how vocal interactions with VAs affect others, with cultural differences shaping what is considered acceptable noise, as highlighted by Hugo's experiences in Australia and South America.
Fear as a barrier to interaction	Participants described household members fearing aspects of VA interaction, e.g. Hugo's daughter found the whisper function of VA technology scary. This emphasised the importance of assessing the timing, presence of others and potential impact on family members in households that rely heavily on VA devices.
Adding engagement and immersion during storytelling	Participants noted using VAs to add interactive audio elements like animal sounds to their storytelling activities.
Comparing group–VA interactions to human–group conversations	Because VAs are highly personified anthropomorphic devices, users were quick to compare a pleasant group–VA interaction to human–group interactions. Users compared differences in group interactions.
Geared towards user–VA over group–VA interactions	Participants perceived VAs to be tailored towards individual interactions, lacking the nuanced communication cues present in human–group interactions.

(*Continued*)

TABLE 7.1 (Continued)

Gamified experiences enable group use	Group usage of VAs tended to revolve around games or gamified skills, rather than collaborative information retrieval tasks. Group–VA interactions centred around playing games may serve as a safe space for users to engage with VAs.
Users gamified their VA experience to enable group–VA participation	Participants were shown to gamify their VA experiences for group use and would create rules for group–VA interaction, providing clear goals and motivations for interaction.
Human presence a barrier to VA interaction	The presence of other people prevented certain participants from interacting with a VA device.
Computational replacement of caregiving	Participants described missed opportunities for human–human caregiving as they automate tasks through their VAs. The prevalence of automation can alter relationship dynamics, particularly in the realm of providing care and performing acts of service within close interpersonal relationships at home.
Appreciating automated care	Participants described situations in which they were open to accepting automated care from their VAs. Participants expressed gratitude for regaining a sense of contact through VA interaction during self-isolation for Covid-19.
Extending presence and influence	Participants discussed the desire to project a social presence that is indistinguishable from being physically present in a space.
VA as an objective listening partner	Participants expressed appreciation for their VA as an objective and consistent listening partner. Perceiving the technology may not always accurately process their attempts at interaction, instead of other social factors that constrain human interaction.
VA English bias	Participants noted bias towards English words, resulting in the frequent mispronunciation of non-English names.

Before They Walk In

8

THE TIMELINE IS IMMINENT

The transition from stationary VAs to mobile humanoid robots is no longer speculative. Technology companies are actively preparing for domestic deployment of embodied robots powered by generative AI. These developments signal a significant shift in the role of AI within domestic settings, moving from disembodied voice interfaces to physically present, interactive companions that can move, gesture, and physically inhabit domestic space in new ways.

Many of the tensions explored in this book—ownership, co-use, brand perception, and spatial negotiation—are likely to be present and exacerbated by robot bodies that walk, follow, and even see. By understanding how families already negotiate with, adapt to, and resist today's AI, we gain valuable foresight into how to design for what's next.

Looking ahead to future trends, including humanoid robots and increasingly adaptive AI, it poses final questions about how households, policymakers, and designers might proactively prepare for a world where robots are integral members of our households.

The contributions of this research are particularly timely in the context of the rapid integration of GenAI technologies, such as LLM-powered chatbots, robots, and other AI-driven systems, into homes and everyday life. The current "AI Arms Race" (Chow & Perrigo, 2023) has led to an accelerated push to market AI technologies, often at the expense of accuracy and accountability. This includes concerns over the hallucination of inaccurate information by GenAI models (Siontis et al., 2024), as well as ethical and environmental challenges such as underpaid labour for data review (Perrigo, 2023) and the substantial ecological footprint of AI technologies, including energy consumption, carbon emissions, and resource extraction (Jiang et al., 2024).

This research highlights the complex interplay between humans, conversational UI domestic technologies, and their physical and social environments. It situates VAs within the broader transition from personal monolithic computing to collaborative ubiquitous computing in the home. By providing empirical insights into these dynamics, the research contributes to ongoing conversations about ethical design, user-centred development, and the role of AI in everyday life. It calls for placing user needs and well-being at the forefront of technological innovation, rather than prioritising the marketing and commercial interests of developers.

DOI: 10.1201/9781003680840-8

The research addressed the intersection of anthropomorphism and ubiquitous conversational voice-user interfaces with embodied interaction theory. By synthesising ideas from a literature review and empirical data, the study explored how the human-like characteristics of VAs influence user perceptions and interactions. The focus extended beyond technical functionality to consider socio-cultural understandings and material collaborative interactions that shape the holistic VA experience. The book examined the affordances of anthropomorphised and ubiquitous VAs, not solely through how users tangibly interact in space, place and time, but also examining the implications of social computing that considers the emotional, social and cultural aspects of everyday use in the home. The study provided a nuanced understanding of how anthropomorphic features impact the usability and acceptability of VAs in daily life, contributing to the broader discourse on human–computer, human–AI, and human–robot interaction.

Here's what we learnt, and the final frameworks that emerged to capture the overall cycle of VA interaction.

FRAMEWORKS FOR UNDERSTANDING EMBODIED DOMESTIC AI

The Effort Triad: Manual, Computing, and Social Pathways

When Lien is inspired to interact with his VA, he and other users process a few steps before even formulating a question to achieve his goal. I use the term goal, instead of "action", "task", "interaction", "question", or "command", as reaching an end state may consist of many actions, tasks, questions, and commands to complete. Interaction is useful to describe the user experiences and the computer reaching the end state. For instance, a goal I might have is to continue reading a book in my warm bed and turn the light off when I am about to fall asleep. I might move to do so (action), interact with a VA (interaction/command) or ask my sister to help me (question)—while comparing social and computing efforts. I present the manual, computing and social effort trichotomy for satisfying short-term goals when a VA is available to use. While evaluation might be based on human desires, space, place and technical affordances also drive the consideration of effort.

Comparing manual and computing effort

Vincent illustrates the process of coming up with a clear goal and the important step of evaluating the goal against the computing and manual effort. The goal in Vincent's example is to turn lights off in different rooms of the house. He rationalises using his VA device over the app on his phone, theorising that the effort of interacting with both computing systems, one more physically demanding than the other.

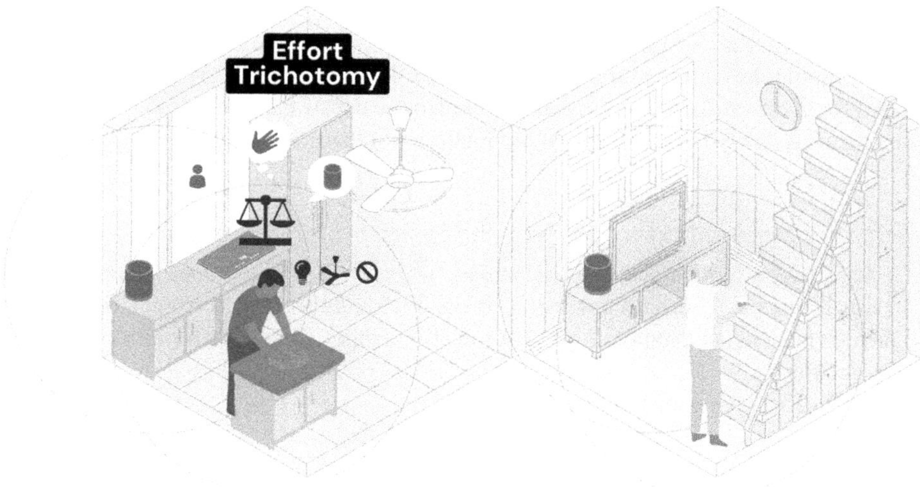

FIGURE 8.1 Effort Trichotomy showing the distribution of conversational effort across user, device, and automated tasks

> Usually, I will talk to Google before I use the app. It's only convenient if I'm already on my phone anyway. I could just turn it off that way, but I feel like it's much more effort to actually use the app, 'cause you have to unlock the app, you have to find the app and then turn it off. Whereas I could just say, I could just call Google and just tell it to basically turn off the light
>
> Vincent, 2 person, 4 device household

Other participants spoke about justifying energy expenditure in manually performing the action instead of their VAs; however, Vincent rationalises another aspect in manually performing the action himself—interrupting or disabling the IoT system by turning off the lights from the energy source, meaning that IoT devices will not be able to connect to the device to control it. So, he is dependent on continuing interactions to maintain the computerised systems he has set up in his home.

> I know that I can physically press the button [light switch] to flick it off [the light]. But because I have all the light switches already on [due to the IoT requirements of being able to control the lights through VAs], I'd rather use Google to turn them off [if he switches them off from the wall, Google will be unable to control them later].
>
> Vincent, 2 person, 4 device household

The other side to this is that reliance on VA technology can mean less use of other technologies, but not in the same sense of creating complex IoT systems that exclude other technologies in their design protocols. In this situation, the setup of the Alexa system for controlling their TV has not excluded the use of the remote, but the pleasure of using a VA has led to the eventual elimination of other tools over time.

> I can change the channel; I can increase or decrease the volume. I can mute, I can… just say, "Turn on channel 7 on the TV" and then it will trigger. See, we haven't been using a remote for a very long time, that's why… We haven't stopped using Alexa.
>
> Lien, 4 person, 6 device household

More reliance on VA systems, as other systems are not maintained and less available, demonstrates that the computing effort of VA systems is perhaps more pleasurable than other, more physical computing tools such as remotes and keyboards.

> Yeah, so the battery is flat for the TV remote, and we haven't replaced it.
>
> Lien, 4 person, 6 device household

Vincent's example sheds light on the process of setting clear goals and evaluating them in terms of computing and manual effort. Although his example uses physical effort in the sense of tapping his smartphone, the manual effort of tactile interfaces consumes more computing in comparison to voice interaction. A clear example of manual effort might be getting up, walking and turning off the light switch without the help of any automation. Vincent's and Lien's stories illustrate the dependency on continued computerised interactions to maintain their smart home setup, where reliance on VA technology gradually replaces other tools like remotes, reflecting a broader trend of increased dependence on VAs.

Comparing social and computing effort

Another factor in evaluating the goal of the interaction against computing and manual effort is the social effort as another avenue of completing the goal—asking someone else to complete the action for you. I wrote about this experience in my researcher autoethnography, which also uses the example of turning the light off.

> I have my lamp that I can control through Alexa; however, I must remember to turn the ceiling light off before I jump into bed. So, I can only turn the ceiling light off through physical or social interactions, doing it myself or asking someone else to do it for me. Sometimes, when I'm warm and settled in bed, I do not want to extract myself from my bed to turn the light off. It would be convenient for me if someone were to walk by and turn it off on their way. A series of questions go through my mind as I contemplate asking someone else to do this for me.
>
> I think about how comfortable I am, who is home, and whom I would feel comfortable asking, where are they in the home and what the likelihood of them passing by my room at this time of day is—based on their habitual patterns? For example, my stepdad is in bed by 8 pm, so I cannot hope for him to walk by after 8 to turn my light off for me. My sister stays at her boyfriend's house two nights a week, is it one of those nights? Will she be home later to turn it off in the next few hours, I guess I could wait an hour or so... Or how loud do I need to shout when an available person walks by to turn my light off for me if they don't hear me—do I want to shout again? Is that worth not getting out of bed for?
>
> 👤 Indra

In considering the effort involved in completing a task, I recognised social effort as an alternative avenue for achieving a goal. Despite having the capability to control my lamp through Alexa, the ceiling light requires my manual actions or the assistance of someone else. This decision-making process involves weighing factors such as comfort, the availability of others in the household and their likelihood of passing by my room. It prompts a series of questions regarding timing, habitual patterns and the potential discomfort of requesting assistance. This example illustrates how social dynamics influence considerations of effort and convenience in everyday interactions in the home.

Another VA embodied interaction process presented in the book identified the cognitive decision-making involved in evaluating the effort of computing through VAs compared to using other computers (computing effort), physically performing the interaction (manual effort) or asking another human who knows the information or can perform the action (social effort). I referred to this as the manual, computing and social effort trichotomy. Computational offloading is a term used to describe delegating or outsourcing some computationally intensive tasks to dedicated infrastructure (Flores et al., 2017); cognitive offloading is "the use of physical action to alter the information processing requirements of a task so as to reduce cognitive demand" (Risko & Gilbert, 2016, p. 676). Social offloading has been proposed as, "any shared task-based situation in which an individual is able to leverage agents in the social world (either implicitly or explicitly) to facilitate their own cognitive performance" (Tufft & Richardson, 2020, p. 859). While computational offloading is not what is being performed here, cognitive and social offloading do not capture the physical trade-offs, such as the manual activity of walking to switch off a light. So, perhaps effort-expectancy theory is better, as it captures the process of comparing the effort required in computational, manual and social pathways to task completion.

Effort-expectancy theory is commonly used in evaluating VA usage, perception, and adoption, but is mostly framed to capture the effort in learning to use VAs (Zhong et al., 2022) or setting up their VAs and IoT ecosystems (Kessler & Martin, 2017), instead of the effort of performing routine interactions once set up and in regular use.

In considering effort expectancy in computational, manual or social interaction regarding a potential VA interaction, two out of these three actions require conversational interaction, either with the VA or another human to perform the task. Different factors are associated with each. With the VA, is this utterance correct? Can the VA perform this task? Is the IoT connected and working? When asking another human, are they busy? Are they in the mood? Will they judge me? Are they available to start a conversation? Also, in potential VA interactions that are purely information-based, such as seeking intelligence, the manual effort route remains, but it is filtered to physically interacting with other technologies, such as a phone or computer, to manually type and click towards an answer. This could be explored in future research that evaluates the manual, computing and social efforts in information-based goals. So, in action-based potential interactions, I infer that three avenues of interaction may be considered by the user in the manual, computing and social effort trichotomy.

The Embodied Interaction Heuristic

Users perform a set of checks to engage in a VA interaction. This framework considers tangible and social computing aspects, including orientation, distance, technical or social availability of a device, social expectations of other users in the vicinity, construction of utterance and evaluating the success of the interaction.

During the analysis of my conversations with participants through the lens of embodied interaction theory, a holistic process of VA interaction emerged from the data. I started to identify steps in a semi-linear process where physical and social behaviours might deter an interaction and consideration of space and place manifesting through different "checks". My conversation with Lien below highlighted how the space and place dichotomy affects how VA interactions are performed from an embodied interaction perspective. This mapped process may be useful in considering human–VA interactions or other human–UbiComp interactions as it considers the computer's placement in the environment, space and context of place.

Indra: Do you have an idea in your head how far away you are where it can't hear you?

Lien: Yeah, sort of. I can, I know where they are, so if I'm shouting, I'm shouting in that direction, to where the closest Alexa is.

From my conversations with participants, embodied interaction aspects regarding the navigation of space and place in VA use emerged, such as mapping the general location of the devices, singling out the closest/most convenient device, orientation towards a device, and considering volume to reach across distance. Lien focuses on the device's location in relation to where he stands. Not only must he mentally map the distance to the device and its direction, but he must also consider which of his devices he is currently closest to. Lien involuntarily considers all these factors before deciding how loudly he can speak based on the cultural expectations of the house, for example, no shouting while others are sleeping, or if the closest device is in someone's bedroom and the door is closed. This is all before putting together the best possible utterance based on their experience in voice information seeking, familiarity, and repetition with achieving their goal.

After describing the considerations a person might go through before initiating a VA request, I describe the complete process of choosing to solve a goal through VA computing. These steps have been informed by the observations of participants during interviews, their retellings of interactions and my experiences with VAs. Some steps may be interchangeable depending on the context of the user's experience, the space/place composition of their home, the number/type of VA devices owned, individual preferences, experience, confidence and VA literacy. Also, the interaction can end at any point in this process; for example, at step 2, the user chooses to manually turn on the TV instead of using their VA based on a poor history of that interaction. Or the user may stop at step 8, where they feel the room is too crowded to complete a goal or ask a question. The process could pivot in intention or location at any step, and users may revisit steps to complete a thorough check before performing the interaction.

From observations and conversations throughout the research, I map the process of initiating VA interaction as steps.

I call this process the VA Embodied Interaction Heuristic (VA EIH), which illustrates the holistic understanding participants have discovered about interacting with their VA. This heuristic describes a concentrated, macro view of a single VA interaction, mapping significant checks that may stop or discourage interaction. By taking a micro lens to interaction, the VA EIH could inform macro-VA processes, like general adoption and use. Cho et al. (2019) identified five phases of Amazon Alexa adoption consisting of pre-adoption, adoption, adaptation, stagnation and acceptance. VA EIH could help to inform the adaptation, stagnation and acceptance stages of Cho et al.'s proposed VA adoption process. The VA EIH could also inform hardware and system design, as it considers cultural and spatial-related data points. Designers can leverage the VA EIH to ideate novel technical aspects, such as elevating microphones and sound processing algorithms, such as ones that support user localisation. Also, anthropomorphic aspects of conversational interaction improve steps in VA EIH that rely on utterance formulation, confidence in performing in busy spaces and understanding VA feedback, by bettering the design of VA conversational space.

I acknowledge that the VA EIH is a remnant of a user journey map, which is used in interaction design to identify user experience and pain points. User journey maps may include additional qualitative information, such as what the user is thinking and feeling at each stage of the process. This could add value to the VA EIH to help researchers identify issues users have in their spaces or with performing interactions. Researchers have also used user journey maps to identify pain points that could be solved by the mediation of a VA, such as the work presented by Hemn et al. (2021) on accessibility with e-commerce platforms. User journey maps and VA EIH can help to map the steps in a process, particularly to highlight blocks and barriers to interaction. In VA EIH,

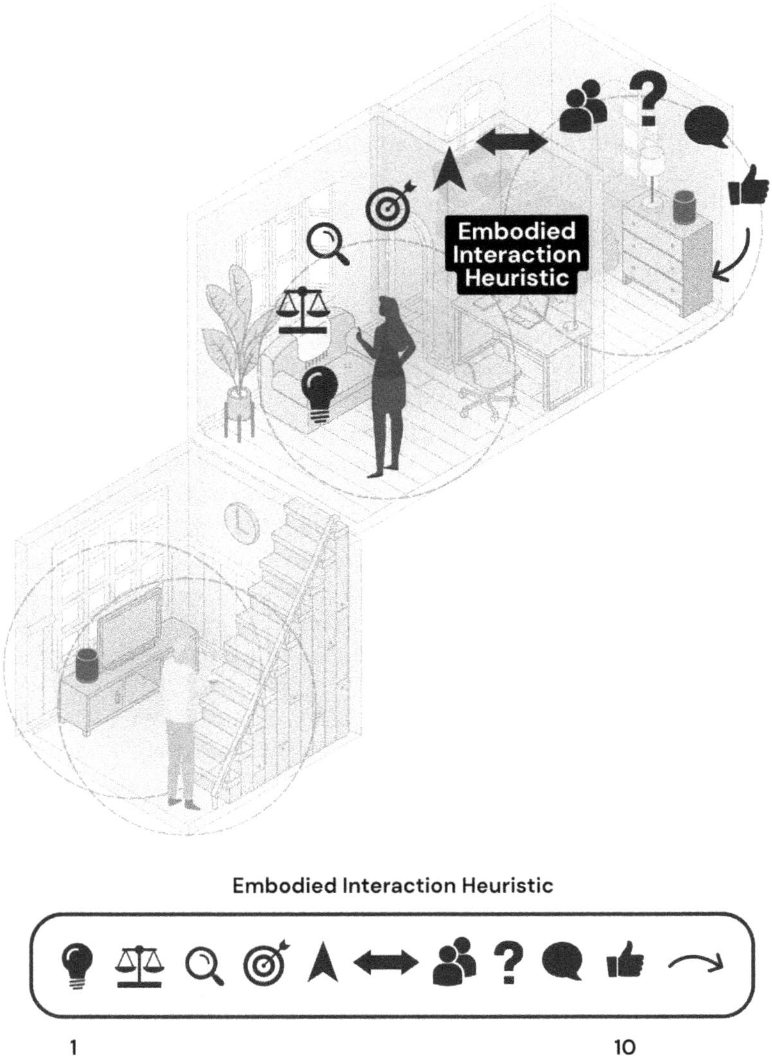

FIGURE 8.2 Embodied Interaction Heuristic showing evaluation dimensions for VA use in the domestic environment

I note that the first interaction of a new goal might take considerably longer to perform checks, compared to a habitual interaction that is performed daily or the interactions performed after successfully initiating a VA. As the user will have more experience and confidence that the checks are successful in repeat interactions, some aspects may require less effort, such as formulating an utterance or locating an available VA device for habitual interactions. This is further evidenced by users' ability to plan future interactions, where Joey knew to speak an identical command in the same spot at the exact timing of his nighttime routine.

The framework of the VA EIH

1. **Think of the goal**: Can this be completed via VA interaction? Have I used a VA to complete this goal before?

> I wish you could do things like... Especially when I was fiddling around with my lights and stuff like that, I had a setting which was getting ready for bed or something like that, and two lights above my bed would turn on and dim right down.
>
> 👤 Mark, 4 person, 4 device household

2. **Evaluate if the goal is worth the effort**: Is the convenience of voice interaction worth the computing effort (using an automated tool to complete the goal) or is the manual option less effort (manually performing the action or manually interacting through other computers, including turning on devices, typing and browsing for information or applications), or are there better social opportunities available (asking someone else to complete the action or if they know the information)?

> ... with the lights in my old room, I just found that process just took too long. Like you'd say, "Okay, turn on the lights" and then you'd be waiting five seconds for the lights to turn on. It's like you could just flick the light switch and the lights will turn on. That's the only time where I did stop using a specific instruction.
>
> 👤 Mark, 4 person, 4 device household

3. **Recall all VA availability, accessibility and status**: Are devices available—are any broken, unplugged, behind closed doors, already in use or do I feel I cannot use a device that does not belong to me?

> I have two Google Minis, which, one is behind me at the moment, although it's meant to be in my bedroom. So, everything is a little bit displaced at the moment because of everything being packed up.
>
> 👤 Jen, 1 person, 4 device household

4. **Recall the closest VA device**: Where am I situated? Which device will be most convenient to interact with? In which room is the device? Do I need to move to the vicinity of the device?

> I think sometimes, as much as I could just grab my phone and open the BOM app and have a look, I think sometimes it's a bit of laziness and now I can just be walking past the device and say, "Can you tell me what the weather's like?"
>
> 👤 Jen, 1 person, 4 device household

5. **Estimate orientation to closest VA device**: Am I facing the device? Do I need to see the device to complete the goal? Do I need to see the device to evaluate the success of the interaction (based on my experience with completing the goal in the past)?

> If I'm talking at her direction… That's when she hears it.
>
> 👤 Anavi, 3 person, 3 device household

6. **Estimate distance to closest VA device**: How far away from the device am I? Can I shout loud enough to reach the device? Do I need to move closer?

> I'll be in the kitchen, and I'll yell out… And I think there's no way she's gonna hear that [the Google in the living room], and then I'll hear her in the distance go, "Okay, it's been set", so I go "Oh, okay good".
>
> 👤 Jen, 1 person, 4 device household

7. **Formulate utterance**: Form my input based on my experience with conversational information seeking and past repetition and performance of the goal and utterance.

> With the Google Home Mini, it works better if you actually are asking a question rather than just being like "Brad Pitt".
>
> 👤 Phoebe, 2 person, 3 device household
>
> I showed her [Mark's mother], so like the first few times I was like, […] you have to say, "Okay Google or Hey"—you have to say the words and then just ask of what you wanted to do, either say, "Play Elvis on Spotify" or "listen to country radio" or something like that. And yeah, it could be that she [Mark's mother] just doesn't know how to give it instructions well.
>
> 👤 Mark, 4 person, 4 device household

8. **Estimate appropriate interaction based on cultural expectations within the given environment**: Is my utterance appropriate to be spoken at this volume, direction and position I have estimated based on the status of other people in the vicinity? Am I being observed? Is there potential to be listened to? Am I comfortable with achieving my goal through potentially public interactions?

> ... now and then, if I just want a funny bit of interaction, or if I'm at home alone and if it's there, I'll just go, "Hey, Google, play me something?"
> 👤 Lien, 4 person, 6 device household

9. **Perform interaction**: Remember to speak the VA's wake word, then repeat the utterance formed in my mind without interruptions at the estimated volume and direction. Interruptions may include stumbling over words, coughing, loud background sounds, pausing, forgetting and spoken interruptions from other users that may mix into the recorded audio and create unreadable inputs for NLP extraction.

> It's mainly when the kids are very noisy and you try to turn off the TV [using Alexa] and they keep shouting, and so you need to go closer to Alexa.
> 👤 Lien, 4 person, 6 device household
> Google is anticipating that you talk like you would to a normal person, they're not anticipating that you draw out your words and your syllables, so maybe that confuses the speaker [Google] maybe, 'cause she [Mark's mother] talks quite slowly
> 👤 Mark, 4 person, 4 device household

10. **Evaluate interaction success**: Did I complete the goal? A correct response may look like this:

Chosen VA will light up when listening, responding and/or actioning the request correctly.

If incorrect, evaluate at which step my estimation was incorrect based on the VA response.

> I ask her a really straightforward question and she just keeps saying things like... "Sorry, I didn't understand the question". And I always think was a really simple question and you don't understand it, how did you not understand that? So, I'll try and rephrase it.
> 👤 Jen, 1 person, 4 device household

By interviewing long-term users and becoming one myself, I mapped a comprehensive embodied process based on their repeated use and adoption of VA activity. This process could be appropriate to understand other robotic devices that operate through predominantly voice interaction and have some physical presence in the home—whether that is a stationary device or a mobile robot. These steps are illustrated in Figure 8.2, encapsulating the tangible and social computing aspects of embodied interaction theory leading up to VA interaction.

I also raise the concept of heuristics in my presentations of models of VA interaction as a concept as to why users may not be aware of performing the VA EIH. A heuristic "is a procedure for decision-making under uncertainty. It ignores information to make decisions faster, more frugally, and/or more accurately than complex procedures" (Gigerenzer & Gaissmaier 2011, p. 454). Gigerenzer uses the example of catching a ball to visualise a smart heuristic, which focuses on the frugality of information to make a decision. As the person catching the ball might not have the capacity to measure its initial velocity, distance and angle, the catcher can instead rely on a simplified point of reference—in this case, the gaze of the ball—to automatically adjust their speed, trajectory and target (Gigerenzer, 2007, 2021). This example is now categorised as a gaze heuristic that disposes the act of looking at an object to ascertain information about an action. Gaze heuristics "requires the ability to hold one's gaze on an object, to run, and to adjust one's running speed. These abilities are learned early in development" (Gigerenzer, 2021, p.5). Gaze heuristics could be applied to shortcut VA EIH, in that gazing at the VA can instantly provoke information, and the user can perceive their distance, directionality and adjust volume or positioning based on their gaze. Gaze heuristics are a type of embodied heuristic, which is defined as "innate or learned rules of thumb that exploit evolved sensory and motor abilities in order to facilitate superior decisions" (Gigerenzer, 2021, p.1). While smart, gaze, and embodied heuristics are a way of understanding user's shortcuts to interacting in situ, understanding the invisible overlooked steps of VA EIH may help developers improve VA interaction so there are fewer variables to potentially failed interactions as users simplify their interactions through heuristics.

Common causes of interaction failure

This list describes common reasons for not achieving a goal through VA computing. Interaction failure is connected to the VA EIH.

Users are forced to hypothesise failed interactions

Users described a lack of feedback mechanisms, leading them to hypothesise strategies based on their understanding of VA hardware and software capabilities.

This section examines the evaluation of interaction success in the embodied VA interaction process framework. Drawing from personal experiences and participant interviews, it identifies potential points of interaction failure. I feature the lack of feedback cues from VAs and how this complicates user understanding and interaction, emphasising the need for clearer feedback mechanisms to enhance user experience.

In this section, I expand on Step 10 of the VA EIH, "Evaluate interaction success", by offering common VA failures and how these can be addressed by the VA embodied interaction process. At the end of the embodied VA interaction process, if the interaction was not successful, the device gives clues about where the interaction went wrong. I note them here based on my experiences and from the participant interviews:

1. **Chosen VA did not light up in listening mode**: User is not in the VA's interaction field—recall personal and VA positions, and adjust orientation, volume and distance. The user should go back to step 3.
2. **Chosen VA lit up but no vocal response**: Check if the device is broken or connected to the internet. Recall all VA locations and status. The user should go back to step 3.
3. **Unintended VA responded**: User was not in the required VA's interaction field. The user should go back to step 3, recall personal and VA positions, and adjust orientation and distance.
4. **Incorrect answer was given**: Reformulate utterance as the word choice did not reflect the goal in the conditions of the VA system. The user should go back to step 7.
5. **Not understood response was given**: Either reformulate utterance (the input did not match the mapping of the device's conditions) or replicate the interaction without interruptions (the audio recording of the input was of poor quality). The user should go back to step 7.

The type of feedback received from the VA is open to interpretation. For Lien, the lack of specificity on the point of failure for his interaction forces him to repeat the process.

> I try once and shout, and if they don't respond I try again.
> 👤 Lien, 4 person, 6 device household

Feedback mechanisms in robotics, AI and specifically machine learning are a large field of study. The concepts of interpretability and explainability are used to infer the quality of feedback in human–machine interactions (Kaur et al., 2022). *Attention system* is the term used by Amazon to describe the universal colours, sounds and animations to be used across any Alexa product to maintain a sense of familiarity with this brand across different embodiments (AVS UX attention system, 2023). However, the current attention system may not provide enough feedback to users to encourage trust in future interactions. Baughan et al. (2023) studied user trust after VA interaction failures and found that "different types of failures do differentially impact users' trust, which in turn affects intention to use their VAs for tasks in the future" (p.14). The authors found different types of failed interaction, i.e. incorrect action executed, missed triggers or over-capturing audio. Overall, the ambiguity of how VAs work, in their AI and hardware design, provides room for users to invent explanations for any absurd interactions they experience based on the interplay of technical and anthropomorphic variables, rather than counting it as a failed interaction.

When Lien tries again, he might iterate the process only to hypothesise what mistake was made. Did the question not make sense to the VA, or was the voice pointed in the incorrect direction? A common pattern from all my participants was repeating failed interactions and tweaking a part of the process, as Lien says, "If they don't respond I try again". By mapping this embodied interaction process, I highlight that there are many roadblocks in VA interaction that designers may not have considered or do not know how to solve. However, even though there are many steps in a human–VA interaction, I also argue that human–human conversations are even more complex. However, the agency of both sides in a human–human conversation means that repair is on both participants. The lack of feedback cues from a lower agency conversation partner means a lack of information for users to deploy their interaction repair. The outcome of poor interactions is, as Lien and Vincent have put it, shouting repetitively at the VA, or as Jen says, "I'll try to rephrase it".

Vincent:	… I just scream at it again, just tell it to turn on the hallway lights, but… Yeah.
Indra:	Do you just say the same thing over again?
Vincent:	Yeah, essentially, yeah.
Indra:	Okay, so you think it's more of it—it's like it didn't hear you kind of thing, rather than what you said?
Vincent:	I think so. I think it only captured it probably just… hears "living room" and then associates that with just turning on the living room. I noticed that sometimes I would say "turn off the living room". I'll turn off, I think the living room lights … I don't know if that they can do that or if it's just… Yeah, I'm not too sure.

Vincent indicated the lack of feedback information from his VA is confusing and leads to users theorising about the capabilities of the VA system. Based on personal experiences and participant interviews, potential points of failure were identified in the evaluation of interaction success within the embodied VA interaction process framework.

The embodied process of user interactions also involved processing their devices' availability, locations, the user's spatial orientation and distance to an available device, and the cultural appropriateness of interacting with a device. Interaction models are discussed in VA literature in describing custom interaction model designs within experiments (as seen in Santos et al., 2020). Otherwise, models describing plug-and-play VAs are limited to short objective descriptions of input and output, such as the model illustrating voice input and output by Kadali et al. (2020) or modelling the system's architecture, interfaces, systems and APIs, such as the social robot architecture employing VA by Alonso et al. (2020). Mental models are discussed in relation to contributing to how users perceive and use VAs, including cultural aspects such as trust, confidence and curiosity (Chiang et al., 2020).

Some models of VA interaction have been ascribed to different ways people use their VAs, such as Kim and Lim's (2019) mental models of VA interaction: the Getting-Things-Done Agent and Companion Agent models. Studies have found that "mental models influenced what and how the participants wanted the system to communicate, and how they would assess, diagnose, and subsequently improve it" (Chiang et al., 2020, p. 1). My research evidences some mental models developed by participants over time in domestic settings that are based on their informal research, observations and testing. Could designers address some of these mental models through better feedback, indication and instructional strategies? I found that users rely on self-theorising to develop their mental models or understanding due to the lack of feedback mechanisms and ambiguity of the hardware (microphones and speakers) and software (AI) composition of VAs. I found that users are forced to hypothesise failed interactions, and from my ethnography work, I provide common causes of interaction failure as a secondary part of the VA EIH. Sensemaking is the overarching process through which users may theorise and test assumptions while building an explanation to resolve a gap or inconsistency of knowledge (Odden & Russ, 2019). Data collection is a vital step where the user collects internal information, such as memory and past experiences (tacit), and external information, such as from books, people and the internet (explicit) (Langen et al., 2022). However, what is shown in my findings is that users are forced to guess or hypothesise failed interactions due to a lack of external data points, support or communication. Improved feedback mechanisms may help inform the internal data collection for users in their sensemaking.

Users left guessing

I identified that the lack of feedback cues from VAs can lead to confusion and speculation among users regarding what VAs can do and how they work. The reporting of self-observations is a sign that the audio processing capabilities of VAs are not well communicated. "I've noticed" and "I think" indicate Anavi's hypotheses, experimentation and conclusion from her time as a VA owner, to the point where participant explanations of how their VAs listened sounded like conspiracy theories. They had not researched or confirmed their assumptions through Alexa's or Google's documentation (even the information on the microphone range I summarised above was sourced from developer-focused and jargon-heavy knowledge bases). Anavi also compares her VA experience to other technologies with which she has interacted; interestingly, the concept of directional microphone technology is explained through her experience with smartphones.

Anavi: I've noticed that if I'm talking to her and if I'm talking in her direction… That's when she hears it. I think it has that technology where it can tell which direction the sound is coming from because I know that iPhones have that as well.

…

Indra: Where did you… did you read that somewhere or something?

Anavi: No, I've noticed it a lot, because sometimes I'll be doing my makeup and looking in the mirror, and I say, "Alexa", she can't hear me. Like even now, she didn't respond. But if I look at her and I say "Alexa"… [Anavi mumbles the word Alexa to not wake the device], yeah.

This conversation reveals more complexity because Anavi anthropomorphises Alexa by assigning gender, but she also directs her gaze and expects Alexa to detect and respond to her visual focus of attention (VFOA). Anavi does not gaze at Alexa to listen to a response, but directs her attention to Alexa to indicate to her conversational partner to actively listen. VFOA is a common conversational cue in human conversation, which could have different implications if Alexa or Google were given a face (human-like or not). Anavi thinks it is her responsibility, perhaps, to activate Alexa's microphones by assimilating conventional human conversational cues like VFOA. Overall, there is conflict in how she describes the algorithm of the smartphone's microphone's orientation vs the humanism of Alexa listening from her gaze.

> I try once and shout, and if they don't respond I try again.
> Lien, 4 person, 6 device household

> I mean on the phone, I can see what I'm saying, I can see how they're understanding what I'm trying to say.
> Anavi, 3 person, 3 device household

Anavi refers to text appearing in real-time as the computer processes the audio input and displays what the VA "hears". She compares this to the disorientation she feels as she tries to gauge the success of her interaction. It is less about whether the VA has heard her, but whether the VA has heard her correctly. The flickering or flashing light cue and the ping sound are indicators of her VA listening but not indications that the NLP and audio processing algorithms have worked correctly. Anavi compares the lack of feedback from her VAs to the expressions that convey signs and meaning during conversation.

> **Anavi:** But with Alexa, I'm a little clueless until she responds, I can't see... For example, if I'm saying something to Google and some of the words are just not ... it's kind of like seeing the confusion on someone's face or if someone is understanding you.
> **Indra:** So... true. What does that look like?...
> **Anavi:** It's the same as looking someone's face and they're like, they have the eyebrow up and they're just like, "What?" But with Alexa, I don't know if she's understood me until she gives me an answer.

My conversation with Mark extends Anavi's example of implied humanism in how the VA machines express conversational etiquette. Mark has three VA-enabled devices in his bedroom: his Google phone, Google Nest Hub Mini and Google clock. Because their interaction fields intersect in a small space, every device's listening is activated when Mark uses the Google wake word. Each device indicates they are listening to his utterance by showing the corresponding visual cue (a light on his clock or Mini, or the animation and audio cue from his phone). However, Mark explains that only one device will respond to him. He explains this phenomenon carefully, and we nervously laugh through the retelling, feeling the uncanny reaction to the devices showing social intelligence beyond their question and answer capabilities. I remember being in awe; as a VA user, I had not experienced this phenomenon.

Indra: When you verbally give a command out loud, both of the machines pick up your voice? And do you have two speaking at the same time or?
Mark: No, I don't know how it works, but both machines turn on and start registering my voice but only one will respond.
Indra: Is it different every time? Or is it…
Mark: It's normally which I am closest to, because I have a Google phone as well, and even the phone will start listening to me [both nervously laugh].
Indra: So, how close do you think you have to be to a machine… A device, for it to be the one to respond?
Mark: Well, um, I mean, I could be probably five metres away and it would respond, but if I was closer to another device, like maybe a metre, I don't know, I don't have much space to work with here [referring to his small bedroom—gesturing with his hands to the room around him in the Zoom video call].

Mark also picks up some potential acoustic echo cancellation in practice and attributes it to Google's ability to understand him, instead of an invisible algorithm instantly and automatically scanning and deleting noise pollution.

> I've also found it performs quite well with ambient noise around. Like my phone especially, if I'm at a restaurant, there's music playing, people talking everywhere. It [Google VA] really understands what I'm telling it. Which is surprising to me.
> 👤 Mark, 4 person, 4 device household

On the other hand, device specificity, orientation and the idea of balancing multiple device fields are juxtaposed by the metaphor of a central intelligence or centralised system. However, there is a distinction between devices in the home and the connected system. For his family and the layout of his home, Lien appoints a device that is symbolic of a central physicality to access the invisible Alexa system. He refers to the space of his home, in appointing a centralised location for the device. "Middle of the house", he declares, referring to the living room later.

Lien: When you can get everything onto the one device and control, it's just… handy.
Indra: Yeah, so when you say the one device do you mean like your phone and the seven Alexas in the house? So, I guess device, does that mean just like one…
Lien: Like I said, yeah, when we're in the living room, we always refer to the Echo Show, so that's sort of like a centralised device to me to use the device. But yeah, the whole system, I would say, yeah. Just the whole connected system.

Another hypothesis comes from Hugo, who refers to the age of the device in assuming its poor receptivity. This is an established phenomenon in that new models are comparatively an improvement on previous ones, and the concept of planned obsolescence is popular in describing this. However, Hugo has decided the older generation device is better than the new generation model, strengthening the concept of self-hypothesising in VA interaction based on their everyday experiences.

> I noticed that the second generation, from my point of view, has a better speaker and is better in terms of capturing what I'm saying. So, I left one 2nd generation in the living room because I think that's working a lot better than the 3rd generation. I don't know why. Because the reviews they're not saying that, but.
>
> 👤 Hugo, 4 person, 8 device household

This sparks the thought that, although technology works on a new model basis and a device can be improved through firmware or software updates, hardware can only be replaced manually, either by bringing it to an expert who could hack and upgrade parts or the new version that is offered by manufacturers. Hardware is an important factor in AI-based technologies, as the capabilities of the microphone and speaker have a large effect on how users perceive and use their VA devices.

APPLYING LESSONS TO HUMANOID ROBOTS

In my interview with Mark, we began speculating about his VA Google having a humanoid body and what that experience might look like. Our conversation began with a description of its form, and Mark describes a classically humanoid-looking device, using imagery and motives from popular culture to communicate his mental image.

> I… I feel like it'd be really cyborg like, not really emotive, very computational, like classic Terminator movie type thing, but not so aggressive. Good intentions, but not quite there… I don't think it would turn against you, I think it would be just very like master-servant thing, which I would not be interested in having, which is… Yeah, actually a very interesting point, if it was like a human being that was waiting for your instructions, that would make me feel more uncomfortable—because it's an inanimate object, I guess that makes it okay for me for some reason.
>
> 👤 Mark, 4 person, 4 device household

Mark describes feeling uncomfortable in making a human wait for you, compared to an inanimate object. By inanimate, I believe Mark is referring to the current VA device shell and system.

Indra: Well, what would make you feel more comfortable it was doing when waiting for your instructions?
Mark: I don't know if it'd want it walking around the house… And if it was just sitting there waiting. That would be weird.

We imagine together what it would be like to have Google Home walking around. My imagination flicks between a robot walking through the corridors of my house, then sitting in the corner of Mark's room that I can see through my Zoom screen. We talk about the robot bearing the burden of maintaining Giusti et al.'s (2022) potential interest, where the moving Google Assistant would be the one to chase our interaction field. We talk about feeling safe knowing the device is stationary, compared to feeling hunted and stalked.

Mark: Imagine if it was like a Google Assistant Roomba, it followed you to listen… Now, that would be creepy. People wouldn't like it.
Indra: No, if it followed you to listen to you…
Mark: Like you were just in the lounge room and it would move into the room… Or something terrible. Pretty high level tech, but… creepy.

Our conversation turns to thinking about space, occupying and sharing it.

Just imagining another being walking around this room just really aggravates me 'cause I didn't have enough room to walk around myself, so the fact that it's taking up space and moving around the room would really be like, "No get out, like go find somewhere else".
Mark, 4 person, 4 device household

Speculating on the potential physicality of a VA robot not only highlights the intimate relationship between technology and the spaces it occupies but also illustrates the embodiment of time. Waiting for and passing time between interactions—when given a moving body, what would a VA do with time? Considering how a VA would navigate time when not actively engaged in interactions adds complexity to my understanding of how users might perceive and use VAs.

WHEN THEY WALK IN: HOW THE FRAMEWORKS TRANSFORM

This research offers practical insights that can inform the design and development of VAs and similar technologies, particularly in domestic and multi-user settings. The findings highlight challenges and opportunities in multi-user scenarios, such as turn-taking, shared use, and collaborative tasks. Designers can enhance functionality by incorporating advanced voice recognition, personalised user profiles, and customised responses. Context-aware systems that distinguish whether users are addressing one another or the VA could help reduce disruptions in human-to-human interactions, creating a more seamless and collaborative experience. Ethical design practices must balance commercial interests with user needs, ensuring that VAs prioritise meaningful engagement over marketing agendas. These considerations are vital for fostering a secure and trustworthy relationship between users and their devices.

The findings may extend to the design of domestic robots, offering guidance on integrating context awareness and supporting collaborative, socially attuned interactions. Designers can draw from this research to create technologies that avoid reinforcing stereotypes or limiting roles, instead focusing on adaptability to diverse household needs. This aligns with user-centred design principles, which emphasise the importance of involving users in the development process. Participatory and ethnographic design practices can lead to more intuitive, culturally sensitive, and contextually relevant VA features by ensuring the technology is deeply informed by users' lived experiences. Additionally, the study highlights the spatial and social dynamics of VA use, offering opportunities to rethink how these technologies are integrated into domestic environments. Considerations such as VA placement, interaction fields, and shared usage scenarios can inform ergonomic and spatial design in smart homes, optimising the physical and social interaction spaces for all household members. By documenting the lived experiences of VA users, this research provides actionable insights for aligning product designs with real-world user needs. These improvements could increase user satisfaction, trust, and long-term adoption of VAs and similar technologies, ensuring that they better serve the households of the future.

Embodied Technologies in Embodied Interaction

There is a lack of research on VAs that uses embodied interaction theory to understand users; rather, the term embodiment from the standpoint of the VA embodying humanness or a body is its current perspective. Embodiment plays a large part in VA interaction as the casing or body of the AI may determine how one may use or decide to ask the VA, as well as the physical embodiment of hardware components. For example, the amount, quality of construction and placement of the microphone, speakers, screens and buttons on the device might have some effect on user–VA interaction. Other than the VA speaker models that participants of this study owned, VAs are now available in other technological forms, such as televisions, cars, fridges, watches and even glasses. Being within the body of another technology, which has a completely different set of expectations of use by the user, further complicates the embodiment of VAs.

VA conversation is available through many electronic mediums, and the extent of these conversations may be influenced by the AI's embodiment. For example, if the VA is contained within a television, it will have the ability to connect to functions such as turning it off or on. If it is contained within a fridge, it may be able to adjust the temperature. More considerations of embodied technology-based contexts would be needed to understand these interactions, as well as the different ways a person uses a non-VA embodied version of these technologies. Even more, if many devices in the house contain or are connected through a VA programme, users can control the different embodiments of the VAs from other devices—the basis of a connected smart home. So, how will these interplays of embodiment within different metal and plastic bodies affect how participants engage with VAs in their lives? I do not focus on the complex issue of VAs embodied in other devices, but it would be a good area for further research, and some researchers have investigated the role of VAs in televisions (Ferraz de Abreu et al., 2019; Noor & Sayyidati, 2020), smartwatches (Efthymiou & Halvey, 2016), fridges (Fujiwara et al., 2018) and more. However, these studies do not consider an embodied interaction theory perspective that might lead to understanding the holistic process of voice interaction with an object in a domestic setting. This is why there is a distinct need for research like mine that uses embodied interaction theory.

Chapter Application to Humanoid Speculations

The findings from studying stationary voice assistants offer a foundation for thinking about what happens when domestic AI becomes mobile. Shifting the question from how people live with voice-only devices to how they'll navigate shared space with walking

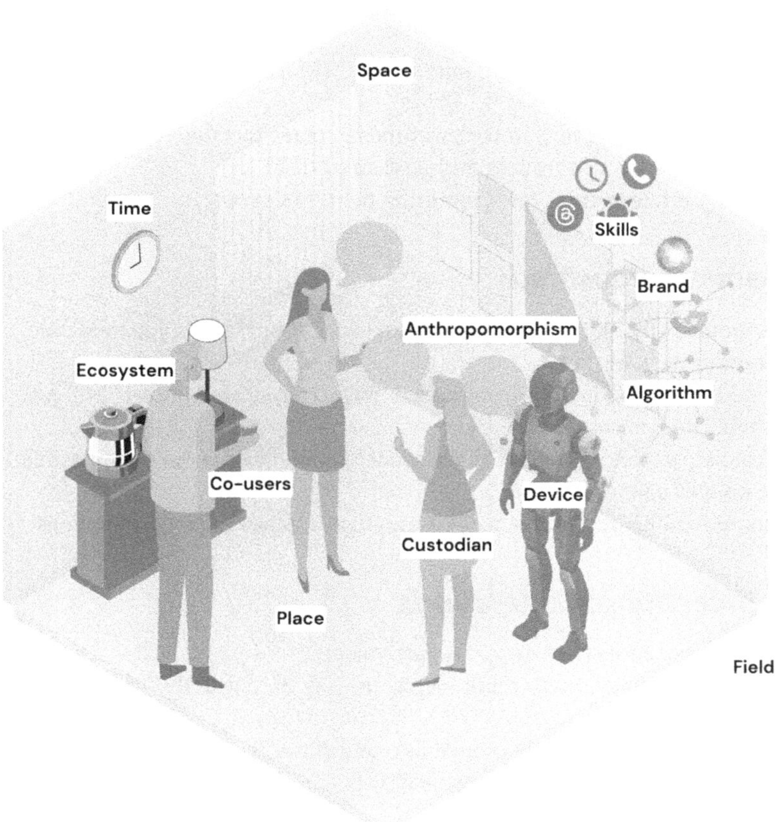

FIGURE 8.3 Extended Domestic VA Interaction Framework showing contextual elements applied to an embodied humanoid AI device

robots. The frameworks developed in this research—brand anthropomorphism, space and place, effort pathways, custodianship—don't disappear when the robot gains legs; they transform. What follows applies each chapter's findings to consider how mobility and physical form change the dynamics already documented with VAs. This isn't prediction, but rather an exploration of how existing patterns might evolve. Understanding VAs has given us a vocabulary and a set of observations about domestic AI; here's how that groundwork translates when the device can follow you from room to room.

Spatial dynamics transformed

- Interaction fields become pursuit zones (Giusti et al.'s potential interest inverts)
- Place-tied behaviours are disrupted (the robot follows you from the kitchen to the bedroom)
- Spatial manipulation tactics evolve (Hugo's closed bedroom door won't stop it)
- Robots taking up more physical space (Mark's concern becomes real)

Temporal dynamics

- What does the robot DO between interactions? (Mark's discomfort: "just sitting there waiting")
- Phantom interactions (ghost in the machine becomes footsteps in the hall)
- Interaction pauses (robot freezes mid-gesture or task)
- Planned future interactions (programming the robot's route)

Social dynamics intensified

- Compassionate automation through physical acts (robot brings you medicine, not just reminds you)
- Automated compassion takes embodied form (physical comfort, not just "goodnight")
- Custodianship expands (who locks the robot in at night and who's responsible when it knocks something over?)
- The "computational replacement of caregiving" extends to physical actions

Cultural & diversity considerations

- Hugo's noise concerns (footsteps, not just voice)
- Hao's name pronunciation (robot needs to say it correctly while looking at him)
- Whisper mode (does the robot crouch or come closer?)
- Cultural, religious or other perceptions of robots and humanoid beings

Group interaction challenges amplified

- Multiple people, one walking robot (whose request does it prioritise?)
- Physical turn-taking (not just verbal interactions)
- Co-user presence anxiety (Anavi won't want the robot watching her)
- Gamification might help (robots as NPCs in family activities)

Brand anthropomorphism embodied

- Google/Amazon logos on humanoid bodies
- Physical design choices reveal corporate values
- Can you "boycott" a robot living in your house?
- Third-party "skills" become physical capabilities

CONCLUSION: WHAT WE LEARNT AND WHAT IT MEANS

The study highlights how the audible-conversational format, with its semi-ephemeral outputs, poses challenges for users in critically evaluating information. I answer the question: How does the format of voice-conversational interaction and form of ubiquitous anthropomorphism impact perception and use of VAs? Overall, VAs create an "illusion of tacit knowledge", presenting their responses as authoritative while obscuring the complexities of their underlying algorithms and branded partnerships. This lack of transparency limits users' ability to assess the reliability of the information provided. Additionally, anthropomorphic elements, such as the VA acting as a conversational partner, embed the device into human-like roles. These roles influence user perceptions by fostering relational dynamics that frame the VA as more than a functional tool, shaping how users interpret and engage with these systems.

Something I also answered was: how do users physically interact with their bodies, with VAs, other people and the spaces they share interactions? Ultimately, my study found that users' physical interactions with VAs are significantly shaped by spatial orientation, device placement, and the embodied effort required to initiate interactions. The VA EIH model offers a comprehensive understanding of these dynamics by considering factors such as device availability, spatial arrangement, and cultural appropriateness. The study also highlights the role of social dynamics within the household, with the presence of co-users influencing the nature and type of interactions. This intersection of physical and social presence reveals how VAs mediate individual and shared engagement within domestic spaces, emphasising the importance of context in shaping interaction patterns.

I also asked: how is interaction with VAs social, and how does this affect perception and use? How does it influence relationships with other people, including developers, brands, communities and co-users of VAs? Well, VA interactions are shown to reshape social dynamics within households and extend to relationships with external entities, such as brands and developers. Brand anthropomorphism plays a crucial role, with users perceiving VAs as extensions of global corporations, which influences their behaviour, including loyalty and resistance. Third-party skills introduce further complexities, as users navigate their functionality within the broader VA ecosystem. The study also documents the concept of VA custodians, who manage and maintain smart ecosystems, particularly in collaborative or parenting contexts. Social presence is identified as a key factor, with co-user interactions influencing the types of activities performed, while challenges in multi-user support reveal barriers to fully collaborative engagement. These findings underscore the intricate social dimensions of VA use and the importance of socialogical investigation of future forms of embodied social AI.

References

Abercrombie, G., Curry, A. C., Pandya, M., & Rieser, V. (2021). Alexa, Google, Siri: What are your pronouns? Gender and anthropomorphism in the design and perception of conversational assistants. *Arxiv, arXiv:2106.02578*. https://doi.org/10.18653/v1/2021.gebnlp-1.4

Adamopoulou, E., & Moussiades, L. (2020). An overview of chatbot technology. In *IFIP international conference on artificial intelligence applications and innovations* (pp. 373–383). Springer, Cham. https://doi.org/10.1007/978-3-030-49186-4_31

Adler, P. A., & Adler, P. (1987). *Membership roles in field research*. Sage. https://doi.org/10.4135/9781412984973

Aggarwal, P., & McGill, A. L. (2012). When brands seem human, do humans act like brands? Automatic behavioral priming effects of brand anthropomorphism. *Journal of Consumer Research*, *39*(2), 307–323. https://doi.org/10.1086/662614

Agnew, J. (2011). Space and place. In J. Agnew & D. Livingstone (Eds.), *The SAGE handbook of geographical knowledge*. SAGE Publications Ltd. http://dx.doi.org/10.4135/9781446201091

Alaieri, F., & Vellino, A. (2016). Ethical decision making in robots: Autonomy, trust and responsibility. In *Social Robotics: 8th international conference, ICSR 2016, Kansas City, MO, USA, November 1–3, 2016 proceedings 8* (pp. 159–168). Springer International Publishing. https://doi.org/10.1007/978-3-319-47437-3_16

Alonso, R., Concas, E., & Reforgiato, D. (2020). A flexible and scalable social robot architecture employing voice assistant technologies. In *CEUR workshop proceedings* (Vol. 2724, pp. 36–40).

Alshehri, A., Salem, M. B., & Ding, L. (2020, December). Are smart home devices abandoning IPV victims? In *2020 IEEE 19th International conference on trust, security and privacy in computing and communications (TrustCom)* (pp. 1368–1375). IEEE. https://doi.org/10.1109/TrustCom50675.2020.00184

Ammari, T., Kaye, J., Tsai, J. Y., & Bentley, F. (2019). Music, search, and IoT: How people (really) use voice assistants. *ACM Transactions on Computer-Human Interaction (TOCHI)*, *26*(3), 1–28. https://doi.org/10.1145/3311956

Anderson, C., Hübener, I., Seipp, A. K., Ohly, S., David, K., & Pejovic, V. (2018). A survey of attention management systems in ubiquitous computing environments. *Proceedings of the ACM on Interactive, Mobile, Wearable and Ubiquitous Technologies*, *2*(2), 1–27. https://doi.org/10.1145/3214261

Anderson, L. (2006). Analytic autoethnography. *Journal of contemporary ethnography*, *35*(4), 373–395. https://doi.org/10.1177/0891241605280449

Anderson, M. (2017). How Burger King revealed the hackability of voice assistants. *AP News*. Retrieved April 26, 2024, from https://apnews.com/general-news-2d8036d742504890b2f9edc3f98c77ef

André, E., Klesen, M., Gebhard, P., Allen, S., & Rist, T. (1999, October). Integrating models of personality and emotions into lifelike characters. In *International workshop on affective interactions* (pp. 150–165). Springer, Berlin Heidelberg. https://doi.org/10.1007/10720296_11

Aranda, J., Ali-Hasan, N., & Baig, S. (2016, September). I'm just trying to survive: An ethnographic look at mobile notifications and attention management. In *Proceedings of the 18th international conference on human-computer interaction with mobile devices and services adjunct* (pp. 564–574).

Ardanuy, M. C., Nanni, F., Beelen, K., Hosseini, K., Ahnert, R., Lawrence, J., McDonough, K., Tolfo, G., Wilson, D.C.S. & McGillivray, B. (2020). Living machines: A study of atypical animacy. *arXiv, arXiv:2005.11140.*

Aronson, J. (1995). A pragmatic view of thematic analysis. *The Qualitative Report*, *2*(1), 1–3. https://doi.org/10.46743/2160-3715/1995.2069

Atkinson, P., & Barker, R. (2021). 'Hey Alexa, what did I forget?': Networked devices, Internet search and the delegation of human memory. *Convergence*, *27*(1), 52–65. https://doi.org/10.1177/1354856520925740

Audio Hardware Configurations. (2023). Developer.amazon.com. Retrieved April 26, 2024, from https://developer.amazon.com/en-US/docs/alexa/alexa-voice-service/audio-hardware-configurations.html

AVS UX Attention System. (2023). Developer.amazon.com. Retrieved April 26, 2024, from https://developer.amazon.com/de-DE/docs/alexa/alexa-voice-service/ux-design-attention.html

Baker, J. E. (2020). Being together in place: Indigenous coexistence in a more than human world: By Soren C. Larsen and Jay T. Johnson, Minneapolis, University of Minnesota Press, 2017. *Journal of Cultural Geography*, *37*(1), 111–113. https://doi.org/10.1080/08873631.2019.1704376

Balasuriya, S. S., Sitbon, L., Bayor, A. A., Hoogstrate, M., & Brereton, M. (2018, December). Use of voice activated interfaces by people with intellectual disability. In *Proceedings of the 30th australian conference on computer-human interaction* (pp. 102–112). https://doi.org/10.1145/3292147.3292161

Baldota, S., & Malathy, C. (2021). Classification of ultrasound thyroid nodule images by computer-aided diagnosis: A technical review. In *Computational vision and bio-inspired computing: ICCVBIC 2020* (pp. 353–368). https://doi.org/10.1007/978-981-33-6862-0_30

Ballmer, T. T. (1980). The role of pauses and suprasegmentals in a grammar. In H. W. Dechert & M. Raupach (Eds.), *Temporal variables in speech: Studies in honour of Frieda Goldman-Eisler* (pp. 211–220). De Gruyter Mouton. https://doi.org/10.1515/9783110816570.211

Barber, W., & Badre, A. (1998, June). Culturability: The merging of culture and usability. In *Proceedings of the 4th conference on human factors and the web* (Vol. 7, No. 4, pp. 1–10).

Barrett, P., Hale, B., & Butler, M. (2014). *Family care and social capital: Transitions in informal care.* Springer Science & Business Media. https://doi.org/10.1007/978-94-007-6872-7

Bartholomew, K., Henderson, A. J. Z., & Marcia, J. E. (2000). Coding semi-structured interviews in social psychological research. In H. Reis & C. M. Judd (Eds.), *Handbook of research methods in social and personality psychology* (pp. 286–312). Cambridge University Press.

Bartneck, C., Bleeker, T., Bun, J., Fens, P., & Riet, L. (2010). The influence of robot anthropomorphism on the feelings of embarrassment when interacting with robots. *Paladyn*, *1*, 109–115. https://doi.org/10.2478/s13230-010-0011-3

Barzilai, G., & Rampino, L. (2020, July). Just a natural talk? The rise of intelligent personal assistants and the (hidden) legacy of ubiquitous computing. In *International conference on human-computer interaction* (pp. 18–39). Springer International Publishing, Cham. https://doi.org/10.1007/978-3-030-49760-6_2

Battarbee, K. (2003a, April). Co-experience: The social user experience. In *CHI'03 extended abstracts on Human factors in computing systems* (pp. 730–731). https://doi.org/10.1145/765891.765956

Battarbee, K. (2003b, June). Defining co-experience. In *Proceedings of the 2003 international conference on Designing pleasurable products and interfaces* (pp. 109–113). https://doi.org/10.1145/782896.782923

Battarbee, K. (2004). *Co-experience: Understanding user experiences in interaction.* Aalto University.

Battarbee, K., & Koskinen, I. (2005). Co-experience: User experience as interaction. *CoDesign*, *1*(1), 5–18. https://doi.org/10.1080/15710880412331289917

Battarbee, K., & Koskinen, I. (2008). Co-experience: Product experience as social interaction. In H. Schifferstein & P. Hekkert (eds.). *Product experience* (pp. 461–476). Elsevier. https://doi.org/10.1016/B978-008045089-6.50022-8

Baughan, A., Wang, X., Liu, A., Mercurio, A., Chen, J., & Ma, X. (2023, April). A mixed-methods approach to understanding user trust after voice assistant failures. In *Proceedings of the 2023 CHI conference on human factors in computing systems* (pp. 1–16). https://doi.org/10.1145/3544548.3581152

Baxter, P., & Jack, S. (2008). Qualitative case study methodology: Study design and implementation for novice researchers. *The Qualitative Report, 13*(4), 544–559.

Beneteau, E., Boone, A., Wu, Y., Kientz, J. A., Yip, J., & Hiniker, A. (2020, April). Parenting with Alexa: Exploring the introduction of smart speakers on family dynamics. In *Proceedings of the 2020 CHI conference on human factors in computing systems* (pp. 1–13). https://doi.org/10.1145/3313831.3376344

Beneteau, E., Richards, O. K., Zhang, M., Kientz, J. A., Yip, J., & Hiniker, A. (2019, May). Communication breakdowns between families and Alexa. In *Proceedings of the 2019 CHI conference on human factors in computing systems* (pp. 1–3). https://doi.org/10.1145/3290605.3300473

Bentley, R., Hughes, J. A., Randall, D., Rodden, T., Sawyer, P., Shapiro, D., & Sommerville, I. (1992). Ethnographically-informed systems design for air traffic control. In *Proceedings of the 1992 ACM conference on computer-supported cooperative work* (pp. 123–129). https://doi.org/10.1145/143457.143470

Biermann, M., Schweiger, E., & Jentsch, M. (2019). Talking to stupid?!? Improving voice user interfaces. In H. Fischer & S. Hess (Eds.), *Mensch und computer 2019—usability professionals*. Hamburg.

Biocca, F., Harms, C., & Burgoon, J. K. (2003). Toward a more robust theory and measure of social presence: Review and suggested criteria. *Presence: Teleoperators & Virtual Environments, 12*(5), 456–480. https://doi.org/10.1162/105474603322761270

Bogdan, R., Tatu, A., Crisan-Vida, M. M., Popa, M., & Stoicu-Tivadar, L. (2021). A practical experience on the Amazon Alexa integration in smart offices. *Sensors, 21*(3), 734. https://doi.org/10.3390/s21030734

Bolino, M., Long, D., & Turnley, W. (2016). Impression management in organizations: Critical questions, answers, and areas for future research. *Annual Review of Organizational Psychology and Organizational Behavior, 3*, 377–406. https://doi.org/10.1146/annurev-orgpsych-041015-062337

Brain, W. R. (1941). Visual orientation with special reference to lesions of the right cerebral hemisphere. *Brain, 64*, 244–272. https://doi.org/10.1093/brain/64.4.244

Brandtzaeg, P. B., Skjuve, M., & Følstad, A. (2022). My AI friend: How users of a social chatbot understand their human–AI friendship. *Human Communication Research, 48*(3), 404–429. https://doi.org/10.1093/hcr/hqac008

Branham, S. M., & Mukkath Roy, A. R. (2019, October). Reading between the guidelines: How commercial voice assistant guidelines hinder accessibility for blind users. In *Proceedings of the 21st international ACM SIGACCESS conference on computers and accessibility* (pp. 446–458). https://doi.org/10.1145/3308561.3353797

Bräuer, P., & Mazarakis, A. (2022). "Alexa, can we design gamification without a screen?"-Implementing cooperative and competitive audio-gamification for intelligent virtual assistants. *Computers in Human Behavior, 135*, 107362. https://doi.org/10.1016/j.chb.2022.107362

Braun, V., & Clarke, V. (2006). Using thematic analysis in psychology. *Qualitative research in psychology, 3*(2), 77–101. https://doi.org/10.1191/1478088706qp063oa

Bruhn, J.G. & Rebach, H.M. (2014). *The sociology of caregiving.* Springer, Heidelberg. https://doi.org/10.1007/978-94-017-8857-1

Bründl, S., Matt, C., & Hess, T. (2017). Consumer use of social live streaming services: The influence of co-experience and effectance on enjoyment. In *Proceedings of the 25th European Conference on Information Systems (ECIS), Guimarães, Portugal, June 5–10, 2017* (pp. 1775–1791).

Buckingham, D. (2015). Defining digital literacy: What do young people need to know about digital media?. *Nordic Journal of Digital Literacy, 10*(Jubileumsnummer), 21–35. https://doi.org/10.18261/ISSN1891-943X-2015-Jubileumsnummer-03

Burton, N. G., & Gaskin, J. (2019). "Thank you, Siri": Politeness and intelligent digital assistants. In *Proceedings twenty-fifth Americas conference on information systems* (pp. 1–10).

Cafaro, A., Vilhjálmsson, H. H., & Bickmore, T. (2016). First impressions in human-agent virtual encounters. *ACM Transactions on Computer-Human Interaction (TOCHI), 23*(4), 1–40. https://doi.org/10.1145/2940325

Cambre, J., & Kulkarni, C. (2019). One voice fits all? Social implications and research challenges of designing voices for smart devices. *Proceedings of the ACM on human-computer interaction, 3*(223), 1–19. https://doi.org/10.1145/3359325

Cambridge Dictionary. (n.d.) *Personality.* Retrieved April 26, 2024, from https://dictionary.cambridge.org/dictionary/english/personality

Carvalho, V. M., & Rodrigues, M. A. F. (2023, August). Investigating and comparing the perceptions of voice interaction in digital games: Opportunities for health and wellness applications. In *2023 IEEE 11th international conference on serious games and applications for health (SeGAH)* (pp. 1–8). IEEE. https://doi.org/10.1109/SeGAH57547.2023.10253798

Catania, F., Spitale, M., & Garzotto, F. (2021, May). Toward the introduction of Google assistant in therapy for children with neurodevelopmental disorders: An exploratory study. In *Extended abstracts of the 2021 CHI conference on human factors in computing systems* (pp. 1–7). https://doi.org/10.1145/3411763.3451666

Cecchinato, M., & Harrison, D. (2017, February). Degrees of agency in owners and users of home IoT devices. In *CHI'17 workshop: Making home: Asserting agency in the age of IoT.* Association for Computing Machinery (ACM), Athens, Greece.

Cecchinato, M. E., Cox, A. L., & Bird, J. (2017). Always on (line)? User experience of smartwatches and their role within multi-device ecologies. In *Proceedings of the 2017 CHI conference on human factors in computing systems* (pp. 3557–3568). https://doi.org/10.1145/3025453.3025538

Cha, I., Kim, S. I., Hong, H., Yoo, H., & Lim, Y. K. (2021, May). Exploring the use of a voice-based conversational agent to empower adolescents with autism spectrum disorder. In *Proceedings of the 2021 CHI conference on human factors in computing systems* (pp. 1–15). https://doi.org/10.1145/3411764.3445116

Chambers, D. (2020). Domesticating the "smarter than you" home. Gendered agency scripts embedded in smart home discourses. *M&K Medien & Kommunikationswissenschaft, 68*(3), 304–317. https://doi.org/10.5771/1615-634X-2020-3-304

Chan, S. (2021). The interplay between relational and transactional psychological contracts and burnout and engagement. *Asia Pacific Management Review, 26*(1), 30–38. https://doi.org/10.1016/j.apmrv.2020.06.004

Chen, G.M. (2013). Don't call me that: A techno-feminist critique of the term mommy blogger. *Mass Communication and Society, 16*(4), 510–532. https://doi.org/10.1080/15205436.2012.737888

Chen, S., Liu, T., Gao, F., Ji, J., Xu, Z., Qian, B., Wu, H., & Guan, X. (2017). Butler, not servant: A human-centric smart home energy management system. *IEEE Communications Magazine, 55*(2), 27–33. https://doi.org/10.1109/MCOM.2017.1600699CM

Chiang, Y. S., Chang, R. C., Chuang, Y. L., Chou, S. Y., Lee, H. P., Lin, I. J., Chen, J-H. J. & Chang, Y. J. (2020, April). Exploring the design space of user-system communication for smart-home routine assistants. In *Proceedings of the 2020 CHI conference on human factors in computing systems* (pp. 1–14). https://doi.org/10.1145/3313831.3376501

Cho, M., Lee, S.-S., & Lee, K.-P. (2019). Once a kind friend is now a thing: Understanding how conversational agents at home are forgotten. In *Proceedings of the 2019 ACM Designing Interactive Systems Conference (DIS 2019)* (pp. 107–121). https://doi.org/10.1145/3322276.3322332

Chow, A. R., & Perrigo, B. (2023, February 13). The AI arms race is changing everything. *Time.* https://time.com/6255952/ai-impact-chatgpt-microsoft-google/

Chung, A. M., Bond Gill, I., & O'Byrne, I. (2017). *Web Literacy 2.0 [report].* https://nowcomment.com/documents/webliteracy

Conway, J. C., & Rubin, A. M. (1991). Psychological predictors of television viewing motivation. *Communication Research, 18*(4), 443–463. https://doi.org/10.1177/009365091018004001

Cormode, G. & Krishnamurthy, B. (2008). Key differences between Web 1.0 and Web 2.0. *First Monday, 13*(6). https://doi.org/10.5210/fm.v13i6.2125

Cowan, B. R., Pantidi, N., Coyle, D., Morrissey, K., Clarke, P., Al-Shehri, S., Earley, D. & Bandeira, N. (2017, September). "What can I help you with?" Infrequent users' experiences of intelligent personal assistants. In *Proceedings of the 19th international conference on human-computer interaction with mobile devices and services* (pp. 1–12). https://doi.org/10.1145/3098279.3098539

Cox-George, C., & Bewley, S. (2018). I, Sex Robot: The health implications of the sex robot industry. *BMJ Sexual & Reproductive Health, 44*(3), 161–164. https://doi.org/10.1136/bmjsrh-2017-200012

Cuadra, A., Li, S., Lee, H., Cho, J., & Ju, W. (2021). My bad! Repairing intelligent voice assistant errors improves interaction. *Proceedings of the ACM on Human-Computer Interaction, 5*(CSCW1), 1–24. https://doi.org/10.1145/3449101

Cunningham, S. J., & Jones, M. (2005). Autoethnography: A tool for practice and education. In *Proceedings of the 6th ACM SIGCHI New Zealand chapter's international conference on Computer-human interaction: Making CHI natural* (pp. 1–8). https://doi.org/10.1145/1073943.1073944

Dai, Q., & Zhu, L. (2018). Verbal-spatial and visuospatial coding of power–space interactions. *Consciousness and Cognition, 63*, 151–160. https://doi.org/10.1016/j.concog.2018.05.003

Degenhard, J. (2024). *Percentage of households with internet access in Australia from 2014 to 2029.* Statista. Falcao, C., Lemos, A. C., & Soares, M. (2015). Evaluation of natural user interface: A usability study based on the leap motion device. *Procedia Manufacturing, 3*, 5490–5495. https://doi.org/10.1016/j.promfg.2015.07.697

Delacote, P. (2009). On the sources of consumer boycotts ineffectiveness. *The Journal of Environment & Development, 18*(3), 306–322. https://doi.org/10.1177/1070496509338849

Denisova, A. (2023). The impact of negative media coverage, brand-hate, or consumer boycotts on the employer brand (in the example of Amazon) [Masters thesis, Aalto University]. Altodoc. https://aaltodoc.aalto.fi/items/d0c000bb-d88c-4f54-8b16-3649acbd20e4

Denzin, N. K., & Lincoln, Y. S. (2008). *The landscape of qualitative research.* Sage.

Deshmukh, A. M., & Chalmeta, R. (2024). User experience and usability of voice user interfaces: A systematic literature review. *Information, 15*(9), 579. https://doi.org/10.3390/info15090579

Deterding, S., Dixon, D., Khaled, R., & Nacke, L. (2011, September). From game design elements to gamefulness: Defining "gamification". In *Proceedings of the 15th international academic MindTrek conference: Envisioning future media environments* (pp. 9–15). https://doi.org/10.1145/2181037.2181040

DeVito, M. A. (2021). Adaptive folk theorization as a path to algorithmic literacy on changing platforms. *Proceedings of the ACM on Human-Computer Interaction, 5*(CSCW2), 1–38. https://doi.org/10.1145/3476080

DeVito, M. A., Gergle, D., & Birnholtz, J. (2017, May). "Algorithms ruin everything" #RIPTwitter, folk theories, and resistance to algorithmic change in social media. In *Proceedings of the 2017 CHI conference on human factors in computing systems* (pp. 3163–3174). https://doi.org/10.1145/3025453.3025659

Dey, A. K. (2001). Understanding and using context. *Personal and Ubiquitous Computing*, *5*, 4–7.

Dourish, P. (1999). Embodied interaction: Exploring the foundations of a new approach to HCI. *Work*, *1*(1), 1–16.

Dourish, P. (2001). *Where the action is: The foundations of embodied interaction*. MIT Press. https://doi.org/10.7551/mitpress/7221.001.0001

Dourish, P. (2006). Implications for design. In *Proceedings of the SIGCHI conference on Human Factors in computing systems* (pp. 541–550). https://doi.org/10.1145/1124772.1124855

Dourish, P., & Button, G. (1998). On "technomethodology": Foundational relationships between ethnomethodology and system design. *Human-computer interaction*, *13*(4), 395–432. https://doi.org/10.1207/s15327051hci1304_2

Druga, S., Williams, R., Breazeal, C., & Resnick, M. (2017, June). "Hey Google is it ok if I eat you?" Initial explorations in child-agent interaction. In *Proceedings of the 2017 conference on interaction design and children* (pp. 595–600). https://doi.org/10.1145/3078072.3084330

Dubbels, B. (2011). Cognitive ethnography: A methodology for measure and analysis of learning for game studies. *International Journal of Gaming and Computer-Mediated Simulations (IJGCMS)*, *3*(1), 68–78. https://doi.org/10.4018/jgcms.2011010105

Eberl, A. (2020). The effect of informal caregiving on social capital investments. *Social Science Research*, *85*(102319), 1–23. https://doi.org/10.1016/j.ssresearch.2019.06.010

Edwards, A., Edwards, C., Fortunati, L., Manganelli, A. M., & de Luca, F. (2024). Mass robotics: How do people communicate with, use, and feel about Alexa? A cross-cultural, user perspective. *Computers in Human Behavior: Artificial Humans*, *2*(1), 1–9. https://doi.org/10.1016/j.chbah.2024.100060

Efthymiou, C., & Halvey, M. (2016). Evaluating the social acceptability of voice based smartwatch search. In *Information retrieval technology: 12th Asia information retrieval societies conference, AIRS 2016, Beijing, China, November 30–December 2, 2016, proceedings 12* (pp. 267–278). Springer International Publishing. https://doi.org/10.1007/978-3-319-48051-0_20

Ehrenberg, N., & Keinonen, T. (2021, May). The technology is enemy for me at the moment: How smart home technologies assert control beyond intent. In *Proceedings of the 2021 CHI conference on human factors in computing systems* (pp. 1–11). https://doi.org/10.1145/3411764.3445058

Ellis, C. & Bochner, A.P. (2000). Autoethnography, personal narrative, reflexivity: Researcher as subject. In N. K. Denzin & Y. S. Lincoln (eds), *Handbook of qualitative research* (2nd ed., pp. 733–768). Sage Publications.

Epley, N., Waytz, A., & Cacioppo, J. T. (2007). On seeing human: A three-factor theory of anthropomorphism. *Psychological Review*, *114*(4), 864. https://doi.org/10.1037/0033-295X.114.4.864

Erickson, T., & Kellogg, W. A. (2000). Social translucence: An approach to designing systems that support social processes. *ACM Transactions On Computer-Human Interaction (TOCHI)*, *7*(1), 59–83. https://doi.org/10.1145/344949.345004

Eshet, Y. (2004). Digital literacy: A conceptual framework for survival skills in the digital era. *Journal of Educational Multimedia and Hypermedia*, *13*(1), 93–106.

Eslami, M., Karahalios, K., Sandvig, C., Vaccaro, K., Rickman, A., Hamilton, K., & Kirlik, A. (2016, May). First I "like" it, then I hide it: Folk theories of social feeds. In *Proceedings of the 2016 CHI conference on human factors in computing systems* (pp. 2371–2382). https://doi.org/10.1145/2858036.2858494

Esquivel, P., Gill, K., Goldberg, M., Sundaram, S. A., Morris, L., & Ding, D. (2024). Voice assistant utilization among the disability community for independent living: A rapid review of recent evidence. *Human Behavior and Emerging Technologies*, *2024*. https://doi.org/10.1155/2024/6494944

Evans, J. (2020). Social computing unhinged. *Journal of Social Computing*, *1*(1), 1–13. https://doi.org/10.23919/JSC.2020.0002

Falcao, C., Lemos, A. C., & Soares, M. (2015). Evaluation of natural user interface: A usability study based on the leap motion device. *Procedia Manufacturing*, *3*, 5490–5495. https://doi.org/10.1016/j.promfg.2015.07.697

Ferraz de Abreu, J., Santos, R., Silva, T., Marques, T., & Cardoso, B. (2019). Proactivity: The next step in voice assistants for the TV ecosystem. In *Iberoamerican conference on applications and usability of interactive TV* (pp. 103–116). Springer International Publishing. https://doi.org/10.1007/978-3-030-56574-9_7

Fetterman, D.M. (2008). 'Emic/Etic perspective. In L. Given (Ed.), *The SAGE encyclopedia of qualitative research methods* (pp. 1–3). Thousand Oaks.

Fink, J. (2012, October). Anthropomorphism and human likeness in the design of robots and human-robot interaction. In *International conference on social robotics* (pp. 199–208). Springer. https://doi.org/10.1007/978-3-642-34103-8_20

Flores, H., Hui, P., Nurmi, P., Lagerspetz, E., Tarkoma, S., Manner, J., Kostakos, V., Li, Y. & Su, X. (2017). Evidence-aware mobile computational offloading. *IEEE Transactions on Mobile Computing*, *17*(8), 1834–1850. https://doi.org/10.1109/TMC.2017.2777491

Flury, T., Privat, G., & Ramparany, F. (2004). OWL-based location ontology for context-aware services. In *Proceedings of the artificial intelligence in mobile systems (AIMS 2004)* (pp. 52–57), Saarbrücken, Germany.

Følstad, A., & Brandtzæg, P. B. (2017). Chatbots and the new world of HCI. *Interactions*, *24*(4), 38–42. https://doi.org/10.1145/3085558

Ford, M., & Palmer, W. (2019). Alexa, are you listening to me? An analysis of Alexa voice service network traffic. *Personal and Ubiquitous Computing*, *23*, 67–79. https://doi.org/10.1007/s00779-018-1174-x

Fota, A., & Schramm-Klein, H. (2024). The impact of digital voice assistants on the everyday life of physically disabled users: Barriers, drivers and potential for improvement. In *Proceedings of the 57th Hawaii international conference on system sciences.* (pp. 3637–3646), Honolulu, Hawaii.

Froding, B., & Peterson, M. (2021). Friendly AI. *Ethics and Information Technology*, *23*(3), 207–214. https://doi.org/10.1007/s10676-020-09556-w

Fui-Hoon Nah, F., Zheng, R., Cai, J., Siau, K., & Chen, L. (2023). Generative AI and ChatGPT: Applications, challenges, and AI-human collaboration. *Journal of Information Technology Case and Application Research*, *25*(3), 277–304. https://doi.org/10.1080/15228053.2023.2233814

Fujiwara, M., Moriya, K., Sasaki, W., Fujimoto, M., Arakawa, Y., & Yasumoto, K. (2018). A smart fridge for efficient foodstuff management with weight sensor and voice interface. In *Workshop proceedings of the 47th international conference on parallel processing* (pp. 1–7). https://doi.org/10.1145/3229710.3229727

Gao, Y., Pan, Z., Wang, H., & Chen, G. (2018, October). Alexa, my love: Analyzing reviews of Amazon Echo. In *2018 IEEE SmartWorld, ubiquitous intelligence & computing, advanced & trusted computing, scalable computing & communications, cloud & big data computing, internet of people and smart city innovation* (pp. 372–380). IEEE. https://doi.org/10.1109/SmartWorld.2018.00094

Garfinkel, H. (1967). *Studies in ethnomethodology*. Prentice-Hall.

Garfinkel, H. (2023). Studies in ethnomethodology. In *Social theory re-wired* (pp. 58–66). Routledge.

Garg, R., Cui, H., Seligson, S., Zhang, B., Porcheron, M., Clark, L., Cowan, B. R., & Beneteau, E. (2022). *The last decade of HCI research on children and voice-based conversational agents. Proceedings of the 2022 CHI conference on human factors in computing systems* (pp. 1–19). https://doi.org/10.1145/3491102.3502023

Garg, R., & Moreno, C. (2019). Understanding motivators, constraints, and practices of sharing internet of things. *Proceedings of the ACM on Interactive, Mobile, Wearable and Ubiquitous Technologies*, *3*(2), 1–21. https://doi.org/10.1145/3328915

Garg, R., & Sengupta, S. (2020). He is just like me: A study of the long-term use of smart speakers by parents and children. *Proceedings of the ACM on Interactive, Mobile, Wearable and Ubiquitous Technologies*, *4*(1), 1–24. https://doi.org/10.1145/3381002

Gaver, W. W. (1991). Technology affordances. In *Proceedings of the SIGCHI conference on Human factors in computing systems* (pp. 79–84). https://doi.org/10.1145/1015530.1015555

Gaver, W. W., Boucher, A., Pennington, S., & Walker, B. (2004). Cultural probes and the value of uncertainty. *Interactions*, *11*(5), 53–56. https://doi.org/10.1145/1015530.1015555

Gebhart, A. (2017). Google Home gets an edge on Alexa with multi-user support. *CNET*. https://www.cnet.com/news/google-home-gets-an-edgeon-alexa-with-multi-user-support/

Gebru, B., Zeleke, L., Blankson, D., Nabil, M., Nateghi, S., Homaifar, A., & Tunstel, E. (2022). A review on human–machine trust evaluation: Human-centric and machine-centric perspectives. *IEEE Transactions on Human-Machine Systems*, *52*(5), 952–962. https://doi.org/10.1109/THMS.2022.3144956

Gehlhaus, D., & Mutis, S. (2021). The US AI Workforce [report]. *Center for Security and Emerging Technology*. https://cset.georgetown.edu/wp-content/uploads/US-AI-Workforce_Brief-1.pdf

Gergen, K.J. (1999). *An invitation to social construction*. Sage.

Ghazali, E., Mutum, D. S., & Lun, N. K. (2024). Expectations and beyond: The nexus of AI instrumentality and brand credibility in voice assistant retention using extended expectation-confirmation model. *Journal of Consumer Behaviour*, *23*(2), 655–675. https://doi.org/10.1002/cb.2228

Gigerenzer, G. (2007). *Gut feelings: The intelligence of the unconscious*. Viking Press.

Gigerenzer, G. (2021). Embodied heuristics. *Frontiers in Psychology*, *12*, 711289. https://doi.org/10.3389/fpsyg.2021.711289

Gigerenzer, G., & Gaissmaier, W. (2011). Heuristic decision making. *Annual Review of Psychology*, *62*, 451–482. https://doi.org/10.1146/annurev-psych-120709-145346

Giusti, L., Bedal, L., Hayashi, E., Yamanaka, J., Oyedeji, T., Bay, C., & Poupyrev, I. (2022). Fields: Towards socially intelligent spatial computing. *eprint arXiv:2211.09933*. https://doi.org/10.48550/arXiv.2211.09933

Glasser, A., Mande, V., & Huenerfauth, M. (2020, July). Accessibility for deaf and hard of hearing users: Sign language conversational user interfaces. In *Proceedings of the 2nd conference on conversational user interfaces* (pp. 1–3). https://doi.org/10.1145/3405755.3406158

Goffman, E. (2002). Front and back regions of everyday life [1959]. In B. Highmore (Ed.), *The everyday life reader* (pp. 50–57).

Gottlieb, B. (2018). *Digital materialism: Origins, philosophies, prospects*. Emerald Publishing Limited. https://doi.org/10.1108/9781787436688

Govindarajan, V., & Damodharan, S. (2023, December). Virtual personal assistant by using hand gesture and voice assistant for disabilities. In *2023 intelligent computing and control for engineering and business systems (ICCEBS)* (pp. 1–6). IEEE. https://doi.org/10.1109/ICCEBS58601.2023.10448922

Grover, Y., Mishra, S. G., Kumar, S., Verma, P., & Nayak, S. R. (2022, September). Computer vision-based smart helmet with voice assistant for increasing driver safety. In *International conference on advances and applications of artificial intelligence and machine learning* (pp. 203–216). Springer Nature Singapore, Singapore. https://doi.org/10.1007/978-981-99-5974-7_18

Grudin, J., & Poltrock, S. (2012). Taxonomy and theory in computer supported cooperative work. In S. W. J. Kozlowski (Ed.), *The Oxford handbook of organizational psychology* (pp. 1323–1348). Oxford University Press.

Gunasekara, C., & Gerts, C. (2017). Enabling authentic assessment: The essential role of information literacy. *Journal of the Australian Library and Information Association*, *66*(4), 393–405. https://doi.org/10.1080/24750158.2017.1399014

Gunawardena, C. N. (1995). Social presence theory and implications for interaction and collaborative learning in computer conferences. *International Journal of Educational Telecommunications*, *1*(2), 147–166.

Gunawardena, C. N., & Zittle, F. J. (1997). Social presence as a predictor of satisfaction within a computer-mediated conferencing environment. *American Journal of Distance Education, 11*(3), 8–26. https://doi.org/10.1080/08923649709526970

Halevy, N., Chou, E. Y., & Galinsky, A. D. (2011). A functional model of hierarchy: Why, how, and when vertical differentiation enhances group performance. *Organizational Psychology Review, 1*(1), 32–52. https://doi.org/10.1177/2041386610380991

Hannerz, U. (1992). *Cultural complexity: Studies in the social organization of meaning.* Columbia University Press.

Harari, Y. N. (2014). *Sapiens: A brief history of humankind.* Random House.

Harrington, C. N., Garg, R., Woodward, A., & Williams, D. (2022, April). "It's kind of like code-switching": Black older adults' experiences with a voice assistant for health information seeking. In *Proceedings of the 2022 CHI conference on human factors in computing systems* (pp. 1–15). https://doi.org/10.1145/3491102.3501995

Harrison, S. R., & Dourish, P. (1996). Re-Place-Ing Space: The roles of place and space in collaborative systems. *Proceedings of the 1996 ACM Conference on Computer Supported Cooperative Work.* https://doi.org/10.1145/240080.240193

Heimgärtner, R. (2017). Using converging strategies to reduce divergence in intercultural user interface design. *Journal of Computer and Communications, 5*(04), 84. https://doi.org/10.4236/jcc.2017.54006

Heitkaemper, J., Narayanan, A., Shabestary, T. Z., Panchapagesan, S., Walker, J., Gajare, B., … & Gruenstein, A. (2024, April). Improving acoustic echo cancellation for voice assistants using neural echo suppression and multi-microphone noise reduction. In *ICASSP 2024–2024 IEEE international conference on acoustics, speech and signal processing (ICASSP)* (pp. 736–740). IEEE. https://doi.org/10.1109/ICASSP48485.2024.10447477

Hemn, B. A., Lu, Z., & Yuantu, Z. (2021). A new approach of e-commerce web design for accessibility based on game accessibility in Chinese market. *International Journal of Advanced Computer Science and Applications, 12*(8), 1–8. https://doi.org/10.14569/IJACSA.2021.0120801

Heukelman, D., & Obono, S. E. (2009, October). Exploring the African village metaphor for computer user interface icons. In *Proceedings of the 2009 annual research conference of the South African institute of computer scientists and information technologists* (pp. 132–140). https://doi.org/10.1145/1632149.1632167

Hirvonen, N., Jylhä, V., Lao, Y., & Larsson, S. (2023). Artificial intelligence in the information ecosystem: Affordances for everyday information seeking. *Journal of the Association for Information Science and Technology. 2023*, 1–14. https://doi.org/10.1002/asi.24860

Hoffner, C. A., & Bond, B. J. (2022). Parasocial relationships, social media, & well-being. *Current Opinion in Psychology, 45*, 101306. https://doi.org/10.1016/j.copsyc.2022.101306

Hofstadter, D. R. (1995). *Fluid concepts and creative analogies: Computer models of the fundamental mechanisms of thought.* Basic Books.

Hopkins, N., & Dixon, J. (2006). Space, place, and identity: Issues for political psychology. *Political Psychology, 27*(2), 173–185. https://doi.org/10.1111/j.1467-9221.2006.00001.x

Horstmann, A. C., Strathmann, C., Lambrich, L., & Krämer, N. C. (2023, September). Alexa, what's inside of you: A qualitative study to explore users' mental models of intelligent voice assistants. In *Proceedings of the 23rd ACM international conference on intelligent virtual agents* (pp. 1–10). https://doi.org/10.1145/3570945.3607335

Horton, D., & Richard Wohl, R. (1956). Mass communication and para-social interaction: Observations on intimacy at a distance. *Psychiatry, 19*(3), 215–229. https://doi.org/10.1080/00332747.1956.11023049

Hoskins, J. (2013). *Biographical objects: How things tell the stories of peoples' lives.* Routledge. https://doi.org/10.4324/9781315022598

How Google's Knowledge Graph works. (n.d.). *Knowledge Panel Help.* https://support.google.com/knowledgepanel/answer/9787176?hl=en

Hoy, M. B. (2018). Alexa, Siri, Cortana, and more: An introduction to voice assistants. *Medical reference services quarterly*, *37*(1), 81–88. https://doi.org/10.1080/02763869.2018.1404391

Hsieh, S. H., & Lee, C. T. (2021). Hey Alexa: Examining the effect of perceived socialness in usage intentions of AI assistant-enabled smart speaker. *Journal of Research in Interactive Marketing*, *15*(2), 267–294. https://doi.org/10.1108/JRIM-11-2019-0179

Huang, L., & Wang, C. (2020, June). WalkID: Towards context awareness of smart home by identifying walking sounds. In *2020 IEEE 6th World Forum on Internet of Things (WF-IoT)* (pp. 1–6). IEEE. https://doi.org/10.1109/WF-IoT48130.2020.9221184

Huang, Y., Obada-Obieh, B., & Beznosov, K. (2020, April). Amazon vs. my brother: How users of shared smart speakers perceive and cope with privacy risks. In *Proceedings of the 2020 CHI conference on human factors in computing systems* (pp. 1–13). https://doi.org/10.1145/3313831.3376529

Hutchby, I. (2001). Technologies, texts and affordances. *Sociology*, *35*(2), 441–456. https://doi.org/10.1177/S0038038501000219

Hutchins, E. (2020). The distributed cognition perspective on human interaction. In S. C. Levinson & N. J. Enfield (Eds.), *Roots of human sociality* (pp. 375–398). Routledge. https://doi.org/10.4324/9781003135517-19

Iliadis, A., & Ford, H. (2023). Fast facts: Platforms from personalization to centralization. *Social Media+ Society*, *9*(3), 20563051231195546. https://doi.org/10.1177/20563051231195546

Ilomäki, L., Kantosalo, A., & Lakkala, M. (2011). What is digital competence. *Linked Portal*, 1–12.

In-depth guide to how Google Search works. (2024). Developers.google.com. Retrieved April 26, 2024 from https://developers.google.com/search/docs/fundamentals/how-search-works

Ischen, C., Araujo, T. B., Voorveld, H. A., Van Noort, G., & Smit, E. G. (2022). Is voice really persuasive? The influence of modality in virtual assistant interactions and two alternative explanations. *Internet Research*, *32*(7), 402–425. https://doi.org/10.1108/INTR-03-2022-0160

Jacobs, M., Cramer, H., & Barkhuus, L. (2016, November). Caring about sharing: Couples' practices in single user device access. In *Proceedings of the 2016 ACM international conference on supporting group work* (pp. 235–243). https://doi.org/10.1145/2957276.2957296

Jaffe, J., & Anderson, S. W. (1979). Communication rhythms and the evolution of language. In A. W. Siegman (Ed.), *Of speech and time: Temporal speech pattern in interpersonal contexts* (pp. 17–22). Lawrence Erlbaum.

Jander, R. (1975). Ecological aspects of spatial orientation. *Annual Review of Ecology and Systematics*, *6*(1), 171–188. https://doi.org/10.1146/annurev.es.06.110175.001131

Janes, B., Crawford, H., & O'Connor, T. J. (2020, May). Never ending story: Authentication and access control design flaws in shared IoT devices. In *2020 IEEE Security and Privacy Workshops (SPW)* (pp. 104–109). IEEE. https://doi.org/10.1109/SPW50608.2020.00033

Jarvenpaa, S. L., Tractinsky, N., & Saarinen, L. (1999). Consumer trust in an Internet store: A cross-cultural validation. *Journal of Computer-Mediated Communication*, *5*(2). https://doi.org/10.1111/j.1083-6101.1999.tb00337.x

Jennings, B. J. (2018). *What is Media?* Capstone.

Jiang, L., Zhou, W., Ren, Z., & Yang, Z. (2022). Make the apps stand out: Discoverability and perceived value are vital for adoption. *Journal of Research in Interactive Marketing*, *16*(4), 494–513. https://doi.org/10.1108/JRIM-03-2021-0076

Jiang, P., Sonne, C., Li, W., You, F., & You, S. (2024). Preventing the immense increase in the life-cycle energy and carbon footprints of LLM-powered intelligent chatbots. *Engineering*, *40*, 202–210. https://doi.org/10.1016/j.eng.2024.04.002

Jones, O., & Cloke, P. (2008). Non-human agencies: Trees in place and time. *Material Agency: Towards a Non-anthropocentric Approach, 79–96*. https://doi.org/10.1007/978-0-387-74711-8_5

Joo, H., Simon, T., Cikara, M., & Sheikh, Y. (2019). Towards social artificial intelligence: Nonverbal social signal prediction in a triadic interaction. In *Proceedings of the IEEE/CVF conference on computer vision and pattern recognition* (pp. 10873–10883). https://doi.org/10.1109/CVPR.2019.01113

Kadali, B., Prasad, N., Kudav, P., & Deshpande, M. (2020). Home automation using chatbot and voice assistant. In *ITM Web of Conferences, 32*(01002). https://doi.org/10.1051/itmconf/20203201002

Kaur, H., Adar, E., Gilbert, E., & Lampe, C. (2022, June). Sensible AI: Re-imagining interpretability and explainability using sensemaking theory. In *Proceedings of the 2022 ACM conference on fairness, accountability, and transparency* (pp. 702–714). https://doi.org/10.1145/3531146.3533135

Kempt, H. (2022). *Synthetic friends: A philosophy of human-machine friendship.* Springer International Publishing. https://doi.org/10.1007/978-3-031-13631-3

Kessler, S. K., & Martin, M. (2017). *How do potential users perceive the adoption of new technologies within the field of Artificial Intelligence and Internet-of-Things?- A revision of the UTAUT 2 model using voice assistants* [Master's thesis, Lund University]. Lund University Libraries. https://lup.lub.lu.se/student-papers/search/publication/8909840

Kim, D. & Lim, Y. (2019). Co-performing agent: Design for building user-agent partnership in learning and adaptive services. In *Proceedings of the 2019 CHI conference on human factors in computing systems (CHI '19)* (pp. 1–14). https://doi.org/10.1145/3290605.3300714

Klein, N. (2000). *No logo: No space no choice no jobs.* Flamingo.

Kocaballi, A. B., Coiera, E., & Berkovsky, S. (2020, April). Revisiting habitability in conversational systems. In *Extended abstracts of the 2020 CHI conference on human factors in computing systems* (pp. 1–8). https://doi.org/10.1145/3334480.3383014

Koenecke, A., Nam, A., Lake, E., Nudell, J., Quartey, M., Mengesha, Z., Toups, C., Rickford, J.R., Jurafsky, D., & Goel, S. (2020). Racial disparities in automated speech recognition. *Proceedings of the National Academy of Sciences, 117*(14), 7684–7689. https://doi.org/10.1073/pnas.1915768117

Koku, P.S. (2012). On the effectiveness of consumer boycotts organized through the internet: The market model. *Journal of Services Marketing, 26*(1), 20–26. https://doi.org/10.1108/08876041211199698

Koku, P.S. (2022). Are ethical boycotts merely signaling value? The financial effect of ethical boycotts. In J. Allen, B. Jochims, & S. Wu (Eds.), *Celebrating the past and future of marketing and discovery with social impact. AMSAC-WC 2021. Developments in marketing science: Proceedings of the academy of marketing science* (pp. 493–501). Springer, Cham. https://doi.org/10.1007/978-3-030-95346-1_165

Koller, M., Bauer, D., de Pagter, J., Papagni, G., & Vincze, M. (2019, March). A pilot study on determining the relation between gaze aversion and interaction experience. In *2019 14th ACM/IEEE International Conference on Human-Robot Interaction (HRI)* (pp. 644–645). IEEE. https://doi.org/10.1109/HRI.2019.8673237

Kondratova, I., & Goldfarb, I. (2005, June). Cultural visual interface design. In *EdMedia+ Innovate Learning* (pp. 1255–1262). Association for the Advancement of Computing in Education (AACE).

Koschmann, T. (2019). Tracing the seminal notion of accountability across the Garfinkelian œuvre. *Human Studies, 42*(2), 239–252. https://doi.org/10.1007/s10746-019-09513-7

Koski, J.E., Xie, H.E. & Olson, I.R. (2015). Understanding social hierarchies: The neural and psychological foundations of status perception, *Social Neuroscience, 10*(5), 527–550. https://doi.org/10.1080/17470919.2015.1013223

Kujala, S., Miron-Shatz, T., & Jokinen, J. J. (2019). The cross-sequential approach: A short-term method for studying long-term user experience. *Journal of Usability Studies, 14*(2), 105–116.

Kumar, B., Singh, A. V., & Agarwal, P. (2021). AI based computational trust model for intelligent virtual assistant. *Journal of Information Systems and Telecommunication (JIST), 4*(32), 263. https://doi.org/10.29252/jist.8.32.263

Lalji, Z., & Good, J. (2008). Designing new technologies for illiterate populations: A study in mobile phone interface design. *Interacting with Computers, 20*(6), 574–586. https://doi.org/10.1016/j.intcom.2008.09.002

Lam, N. (2022). Explanations in AI as claims of tacit knowledge. *Minds and Machines*, *32*(1), 135–158. https://doi.org/10.1007/s11023-021-09588-1
Langen, T., Ali, H. B., & Falk, K. (2022). A conceptual framework for data sensemaking in product development—A case study. *Technologies*, *11*(1), 4. https://doi.org/10.3390/technologies11010004
Larsen, S. C., & Johnson, J. T. (2017). *Being together in place: Indigenous coexistence in a more than human world.* U of Minnesota Press. https://doi.org/10.5749/minnesota/9781517902216.001.0001
Lau, J., Zimmerman, B., & Schaub, F. (2018). Alexa, are you listening?: Privacy perceptions, concerns and privacy-seeking behaviors with smart speakers. *In Proceedings of the ACM on human-computer interaction, 2(CSCW)*, 1–31. https://doi.org/10.1145/3274371
Lee, K., Lee, K. Y., & Sheehan, L. (2019). Hey Alexa! A magic spell of social glue?: Sharing a smart voice assistant speaker and its impact on users' perception of group harmony. *Information Systems Frontiers*, *22*, 1–21. https://doi.org/10.1007/s10796-019-09975-1
Lee, O.-K. D., Ayyagari, R., Nasirian, F., & Ahmadian, M. (2021). Role of interaction quality and trust in use of AI-based voice-assistant systems. *Journal of Systems and Information Technology*, *23*(2), 154–170. https://doi.org/10.1108/JSIT-07-2020-0132
LeFebvre, R. (2017). Amazon's Alexa can recognize the voices of multiple users. *Engadget.* https://www.engadget.com/2017/10/11/amazon-alexamultiple-users/
Lentzsch, C., Shah, S. J., Andow, B., Degeling, M., Das, A., & Enck, W. (2021). Hey Alexa, is this skill safe?: Taking a closer look at the Alexa skill ecosystem. In *Network and distributed systems security (NDSS) symposium 2021.* https://doi.org/10.14722/ndss.2021.23111
Li, A. (2022). Google removing third-party Assistant voice apps and Nest Hub games amid Android focus. *9 to 5 Google*. Retrieved April 26, 2024, from https://9to5google.com/2022/06/13/google-assistant-voice-apps/
Liang, Y., Xu, Q., & Jin, L. (2021). The effect of smart and connected products on consumer brand choice concentration. *Journal of Business Research*, *135*, 163–172. https://doi.org/10.1016/j.jbusres.2021.06.039
Lin, Y., Liu, Q., Qi, D., Zhang, J., & Ding, Z. (2022). Smartphone embodiment: The effect of smartphone use on body representation. *Current Psychology*, *42*, 1–19. https://doi.org/10.1007/s12144-022-03740-5
Lindeman, D. A., Kim, K. K., Gladstone, C., & Apesoa-Varano, E. C. (2020). Technology and caregiving: Emerging interventions and directions for research. *The Gerontologist*, *60*(Supplement_1), S41–S49. https://doi.org/10.1093/geront/gnz178
Long, D., & Magerko, B. (2020, April). What is AI literacy? Competencies and design considerations. In *Proceedings of the 2020 CHI conference on human factors in computing systems* (pp. 1–16). https://doi.org/10.1145/3313831.3376727
Lopatovska, I., & Williams, H. (2018, March). Personification of the Amazon Alexa: BFF or a mindless companion. In *Proceedings of the 2018 conference on human information interaction & retrieval* (pp. 265–268). https://doi.org/10.1145/3176349.3176868
Lottridge, D., Chignell, M., & Jovicic, A. (2011). Affective interaction: Understanding, evaluating, and designing for human emotion. *Reviews of Human Factors and Ergonomics*, *7*(1), 197–217. https://doi.org/10.1177/1557234X11410385
Lovchik, C. S., & Diftler, M. A. (1999, May). The robonaut hand: A dexterous robot hand for space. In *Proceedings 1999 IEEE international conference on robotics and automation* (Vol. 2, pp. 907–912). IEEE.
Luger, E., & Sellen, A. (2016, May). "Like having a really bad PA" The gulf between user expectation and experience of conversational agents. In *Proceedings of the 2016 CHI conference on human factors in computing systems* (pp. 5286–5297). https://doi.org/10.1145/2858036.2858288
Lunardi, G. M., Al Machot, F., Shekhovtsov, V. A., Maran, V., Machado, G. M., Machado, A., Mayr, H. C. & de Oliveira, J. P. M. (2018). IoT-based human action prediction and support. *Internet of Things*, *3*, 52–68. https://doi.org/10.1016/j.iot.2018.09.007

Luther, D., & Ali, R. (2022, August 25). *Scenario planning: Strategy, steps and practical examples.* Oracle NetSuite. Retrieved April 26, 2024, from https://www.netsuite.com/portal/resource/articles/financial-management/scenario-planning.shtml

MacLeod, A., Cameron, P., Ajjawi, R., Kits, O., & Tummons, J. (2019). Actor-network theory and ethnography: Sociomaterial approaches to researching medical education. *Perspectives On Medical Education*, *8*(3), 177–186. https://doi.org/10.1007/S40037-019-0513-6

Major, D., Huang, D. Y., Chetty, M., & Feamster, N. (2021). Alexa, who am I speaking to?: Understanding users' ability to identify third-party apps on Amazon Alexa. *ACM Transactions on Internet Technology (TOIT)*, *22*(1), 1–22. https://doi.org/10.1145/3446389

Mande, V., Glasser, A., Dingman, B., & Huenerfauth, M. (2021, May). Deaf users' preferences among wake-up approaches during sign-language interaction with personal assistant devices. In *Extended abstracts of the 2021 CHI conference on human factors in computing systems* (pp. 1–6). https://doi.org/10.1145/3411763.3451592

Mann, K., & Püttmann, L. (2023). Benign effects of automation: New evidence from patent texts. *Review of Economics and Statistics*, *105*(3), 562–579. https://doi.org/10.1162/rest_a_01083

Manzanillo, C., Chettiar, R., Soroushmojdehi, R., Ying, L., & Dong, J. (2024, January). Soft speech, loud world: Bone conduction microphones enhance voice assistant interaction. In *2024 IEEE International Conference on Consumer Electronics (ICCE)* (pp. 1–5). IEEE. https://doi.org/10.1109/ICCE59016.2024.10444140

Marcus, A., & Gould, E. W. (2000, June). Cultural dimensions and global web user-interface design: What? So what? Now what. In *Proceedings of the 6th conference on human factors and the web* (Vol. 19), Austin, Texas.

Martin, B., & Hanington, B. (2018). Design ethnography. *In 100 ways to research complex problems, develop innovative ideas, and design effective solutions.* Rockport Publishers.

Martin, T. (2017). How to add multiple accounts to Google Home. *CNET.* https://www.cnet.com/home/smart-home/how-to-add-multiple-accounts-to-google-home/

Mayan M. J. (2001). *An introduction to qualitative methods.* Qual Institute Press.

Mazarakis, A. (2021). Gamification reloaded: Current and future trends in gamification science. *I-com*, *20*(3), 279–294. https://doi.org/10.1515/icom-2021-0025

McDaniel, B. T., & Coyne, S. M. (2016). "Technoference": The interference of technology in couple relationships and implications for women's personal and relational well-being. *Psychology of Popular Media Culture*, *5*(1), 85. https://doi.org/10.1037/ppm0000065

McGill, M., McGookin, D., Wilson, G., & Brewster, S. (2020). Acoustic transparency and the changing soundscape of auditory mixed reality. In *CHI '20: Proceedings of the 2020 CHI conference on human factors in computing systems* (pp. 1–16). https://doi.org/10.1145/3313831.3376702

McIntosh, M. J., & Morse, J. M. (2015). Situating and constructing diversity in semi-structured interviews. *Global Qualitative Nursing Research*, *2*, 1–12. https://doi.org/10.1177/2333393615597674

McLean, G., & Osei-Frimpong, K. (2019). Hey Alexa… examine the variables influencing the use of artificial intelligent in-home voice assistants. *Computers in Human Behavior*, *99*, 28–37. https://doi.org/10.1016/j.chb.2019.05.009

McLean, G., Osei-Frimpong, K., & Barhorst, J. (2021). Alexa, do voice assistants influence consumer brand engagement? Examining the role of AI powered voice assistants in influencing consumer brand engagement. *Journal of Business Research*, *124*, 312–328. https://doi.org/10.1016/j.jbusres.2020.11.045

McTear, M. F. (2002). Spoken dialogue technology: Enabling the conversational user interface. *ACM Computing Surveys (CSUR)*, *34*(1), 90–169. https://doi.org/10.1145/505282.505285

Meng, N., Keküllüoğlu, D., & Vaniea, K. (2021). Owning and sharing: Privacy perceptions of smart speaker users. *Proceedings of the ACM on Human-Computer Interaction*, *5*(CSCW1), 1–29. https://doi.org/10.1145/3449119

Merriam-Webster. (n.d.). Custodian. In *Merriam-Webster.com dictionary.* Retrieved April 26, 2024, from https://www.merriam-webster.com/dictionary/custodian

Mesch, G. S. (2006). Family relations and the Internet: Exploring a family boundaries approach. *The Journal of Family Communication*, *6*(2), 119–138. https://doi.org/10.1207/s15327698jfc0602_2

Miksik, O., Munasinghe, I., Asensio-Cubero, J., Bethi, S. R., Huang, S. T., Zylfo, S. X. Liu, T., Nica, A., Mitrocsak, S., Mezza, R., Beard, R., Shi, R., Ng, P., Mediano, Z., Fountas, S-H., Lee, J., Medvesek, H., Zhuang, Y., Rogers & Swietojanski, P. (2020). Building proactive voice assistants: When and how (not) to interact. *arXiv* preprint arXiv:2005.01322. https://doi.org/10.48550/arXiv.2005.01322

Millen, D. R. (2000). Rapid ethnography: Time deepening strategies for HCI field research. In *Proceedings of the 3rd conference on Designing interactive systems: Processes, practices, methods, and techniques* (pp. 280–286). https://doi.org/10.1145/347642.347763

Moon, A., Hashmi, M., Loos, H. M. V. D., Croft, E. A., & Billard, A. (2021). Design of hesitation gestures for nonverbal human-robot negotiation of conflicts. *ACM Transactions on Human-Robot Interaction (THRI)*, *10*(3), 1–25. https://doi.org/10.1145/3418302

Moon, Y., Jeong, Y., & Seo, E. (2019, September). I'm listening: The effect of cue difference to elicit user's continuous turn-taking with AI agent in TV. In *Adjunct proceedings of the 2019 ACM international joint conference on pervasive and ubiquitous computing and proceedings of the 2019 ACM international symposium on wearable computers* (pp. 153–156). https://doi.org/10.1145/3341162.3343848

Morse J. M., Richards L. (2002). *Readme first for a user's guide to qualitative methods*. Sage.

Mueller, A. E., & Segal, D. L. (2014). Structured versus semistructured versus unstructured interviews. *The Encyclopedia of Clinical Psychology, 1–7.* https://doi.org/10.1002/9781118625392.wbecp069

Muncey, T. (2005). Doing autoethnography. *International Journal of Qualitative Methods*, *4*(1), 69–86. https://doi.org/10.1177/160940690500400105

Murad, C. (2019, October). Tools to support voice user interface design. In *Proceedings of the 21st international conference on human-computer interaction with mobile devices and services* (pp. 1–5). https://doi.org/10.1145/3338286.3344424

Murtazina, M. S., & Avdeenko, T. V. (2020, September). An ontology-based knowledge representation in the field of cognitive functions assessment. In *IOP Conference Series: Materials Science and Engineering*, 919(5), 052013. IOP Publishing. https://doi.org/10.1088/1757-899X/919/5/052013

Murthy, D. (2008). Digital ethnography: An examination of the use of new technologies for social research. *Sociology*, *42*(5), 837–855. https://doi.org/10.1177/0038038508094565

Myers, C., Furqan, A., Nebolsky, J., Caro, K., & Zhu, J. (2018, April). Patterns for how users overcome obstacles in voice user interfaces. In *Proceedings of the 2018 CHI conference on human factors in computing systems* (pp. 1–7). https://doi.org/10.1145/3173574.3173580

Narayan, B. (2013). From everyday information behaviours to clickable solidarity in a place called social media. *Cosmopolitan Civil Societies: An Interdisciplinary Journal*, *5*(3), 32–53.

Nasirian, F., Ahmadian, M., & Lee, O. K. D. (2017). AI-based voice assistant systems: Evaluating from the interaction and trust perspectives. In *Twenty-third Americas Conference on Information Systems*. https://aisel.aisnet.org/amcis2017/AdoptionIT/Presentations/27

Nerenberg, J. (2020). *Divergent mind: Thriving in a world that wasn't designed for you.* HarperOne.

Newman, J., Bornik, A., Pustka, D., Echtler, F., Huber, M., Schmalstieg, D., & Klinker, G. (2007). Tracking for distributed mixed reality environments. In *Workshop on trends and issues in tracking for virtual environments at the IEEE virtual reality conference (VR'07)*, Charlotte, North Carolina.

Ng, D. T. K., Leung, J. K. L., Chu, S. K. W., & Qiao, M. S. (2021). Conceptualizing AI literacy: An exploratory review. *Computers and Education: Artificial Intelligence*, *2*(100041), 1–11. https://doi.org/10.1016/j.caeai.2021.100041

Noor, A., & Sayyidati, R. (2020). Development of internet-based (IOT) smart tv assistant prototype. In *Journal of physics: Conference series* (Vol. 1450, No. 1, p. 012070). IOP Publishing. https://doi.org/10.1088/1742-6596/1450/1/012070

Noor, N., Rao Hill, S., & Troshani, I. (2022). Artificial intelligence service agents: Role of para-social relationship. *Journal of Computer Information Systems*, *62*(5), 1009–1023. https://doi.org/10.1080/08874417.2021.1962213

Nordstrom, S. N. (2013). Object-interviews: Folding, unfolding, and refolding perceptions of objects. *International Journal of Qualitative Methods*, *12*(1), 237–257. https://doi.org/10.1177/160940691301200111

Norum, K. E. (2008). Reality and multiple realities. In L. Given (Ed.), *The SAGE encyclopedia of qualitative research methods* (pp. 1–8). Thousand Oaks.

Nunez-Pacheco, C., & Loke, L. (2014, June). Crafting the body-tool: A body-centred perspective on wearable technology. In *Proceedings of the 2014 conference on Designing interactive systems* (pp. 553–566). https://doi.org/10.1145/2598510.2598546

Odden, T. O. B., & Russ, R. S. (2019). Defining sensemaking: Bringing clarity to a fragmented theoretical construct. *Science Education*, *103*(1), 187–205. https://doi.org/10.1002/sce.21452

Oh, J., Kim, W., Kim, S., Im, H., & Lee, S. (2024, May). Better to ask than assume: Proactive voice assistants' communication strategies that respect user agency in a smart home environment. In *Proceedings of the 2024 CHI conference on human factors in computing systems* (pp. 1–17). https://doi.org/10.1145/3613904.3642193

Pacchierotti, E., Christensen, H. I., & Jensfelt, P. (2005, August). Human-robot embodied interaction in hallway settings: A pilot user study. In *ROMAN 2005. IEEE international workshop on robot and human interactive communication.* (pp. 164–171). IEEE.

Pal, D., Arpnikanondt, C., Funilkul, S., & Varadarajan, V. (2019, July). User experience with smart voice assistants: The accent perspective. In *2019 10th international conference on computing, communication and networking technologies (ICCCNT)* (pp. 1–6). IEEE. https://doi.org/10.1109/ICCCNT45670.2019.8944754

Palanica, A., Thommandram, A., Lee, A., Li, M., & Fossat, Y. (2019). Do you understand the words that are comin outta my mouth? Voice assistant comprehension of medication names. *NPJ Digital Medicine*, *2*(1), 55. https://doi.org/10.1038/s41746-019-0133-x

Papadogiorgaki, M., Grammalidis, N., Grammatikopoulou, A., Apostolidis, K., Bei, E. S., Grigoriadis, K., Zafeiris, S., Livanos, G., Mezaris, V. & Zervakis, M. E. (2023). An integrated support system for people with intellectual disability. *Electronics*, *12*(18), 3803. https://doi.org/10.3390/electronics12183803

Patompak, P., Jeong, S., Nilkhamhang, I., & Chong, N. Y. (2020). Learning proxemics for personalized human–robot social interaction. *International Journal of Social Robotics*, *12*, 267–280. https://doi.org/10.1007/s12369-019-00560-9

Patrizi, M., Šerić, M., & Vernuccio, M. (2024). Hey Google, I trust you! The consequences of brand anthropomorphism in voice-based artificial intelligence contexts. *Journal of Retailing and Consumer Services*, *77*, 103659. https://doi.org/10.1016/j.jretconser.2023.103659

Patrizi, M., Vernuccio, M., & Pastore, A. (2021). "Ok, Google!" are my data safe? The mediated effect of perceived privacy risk on brand trust. In *Proceedings of 20th international marketing trends conference 2021 Venice, ed. Jean-Claude Andreani and Umberto Collesei, Paris-Venice marketing trends association* (pp. 1–5).

Pennebaker, J. W., Boyd, R. L., Jordan, K., & Blackburn, K. (2015). *The development and psychometric properties of LIWC2015.* University of Texas at Austin.

Pennington, M. C. & Doi, T. (1989). Hesitation phenomena in the interlanguage discourse of Japanese learners of English. *University of Hawai'i Working Papers in ESL*, *8*(2), 171–205.

Perrigo, B. (2023, January 18). Exclusive: OpenAI used Kenyan workers on less than $2 per hour to make ChatGPT less toxic. *Time*. https://time.com/6247678/openai-chatgpt-kenya-workers/

Porcheron, M., Fischer, J. E., Reeves, S., & Sharples, S. (2018, April). Voice interfaces in everyday life. In *Proceedings of the 2018 CHI conference on human factors in computing systems* (pp. 1–12). https://doi.org/10.1145/3173574.3174214

Possati, L. M. (2023). Psychoanalyzing artificial intelligence: The case of Replika. *AI & Society, 38*(4), 1725–1738. https://doi.org/10.1007/s00146-021-01379-7

Pradhan, A., Findlater, L., & Lazar, A. (2019). "Phantom Friend" or "just a box with information" personification and ontological categorization of smart speaker-based voice assistants by older adults. *Proceedings of the ACM on Human-Computer Interaction, 3*(CSCW), 1–21. https://doi.org/10.1145/3359316

Publish your skill to the Alexa Skills Store. (n.d.). Blueprints Amazon. Retrieved April 26, 2024, from https://blueprints.amazon.com.au/help/publish-your-skill

Purington, A., Taft, J. G., Sannon, S., Bazarova, N. N., & Taylor, S. H. (2017, May). "Alexa is my new BFF". Social roles, user satisfaction, and personification of the Amazon Echo. In *Proceedings of the 2017 CHI conference extended abstracts on human factors in computing systems* (pp. 2853–2859). https://doi.org/10.1145/3027063.3053246

Putnam, R. D. (2000). *Bowling alone: The collapse and revival of American community.* Simon and Schuster. https://doi.org/10.1145/358916.361990

Rafferty, J., Nugent, C. D., Liu, J., & Chen, L. (2017). From activity recognition to intention recognition for assisted living within smart homes. *IEEE Transactions on Human-Machine Systems, 47*(3), 368–379. https://doi.org/10.1109/THMS.2016.2641388

Raine, R. (2009, November). Making a clever intelligent agent: The theory behind the implementation. In *2009 IEEE international conference on intelligent computing and intelligent systems* (Vol. 3, pp. 398–402). IEEE. https://doi.org/10.1109/ICICISYS.2009.5358137

Rapp, A. (2018). Autoethnography in human-computer interaction: Theory and practice. In M. Filimoqicz & V. Tzankova (Eds.), *New directions in third wave human-computer interaction: Volume 2-Methodologies*, Human–Computer Interaction Series, 25–42. https://doi.org/10.1007/978-3-319-73374-6_3

Reed-Danahay D. E. (1997). *Auto/ethnography: Rewriting the self and the social.* Berg.

Riemer, M., Bogon, J., Russwinkel, N., Henze, N., Wiese, E., Halbhuber, D., & Thomaschke, R. (2023). Time and timing in human-computer interaction. In *Mensch und computer 2023 – workshopband*, Rapperswil, Switzerland.

Risko, E. F., & Gilbert, S. J. (2016). Cognitive offloading. *Trends in cognitive sciences, 20*(9), 676–688. https://doi.org/10.1016/j.tics.2016.07.002

Rizzolatti, G., Fadiga, L., Fogassi, L., & Gallese, V. (1997). The space around us. *Science, 277*(5323), 190–191. https://doi.org/10.1126/science.277.5323.190

Sa, N., & Yuan, X. (2020). Examining users' partial query modification patterns in voice search. *Journal of the Association for Information Science and Technology, 71*(3), 251–263. https://doi.org/10.1002/asi.24238

Sabir, A., Lafontaine, E., & Das, A. (2022, April). Hey Alexa, who am I talking to?: Analyzing users' perception and awareness regarding third-party Alexa skills. In *Proceedings of the 2022 CHI conference on human factors in computing systems* (pp. 1–15). https://doi.org/10.1145/3491102.3517510

Sack, R. D. (1997). *Homo geographicus.* Johns Hopkins University Press.

Santos, R., Abreu, J., Beça, P., Rodrigues, A., & Fernandes, S. (2020). Voice interaction on TV: Analysis of natural language interaction models and recommendations for voice user interfaces. *Multimedia Tools and Applications, 79*, 35689–35716. https://doi.org/10.1007/s11042-020-08710-2

Sarker, I. H. (2022). AI-based modeling: Techniques, applications and research issues towards automation, intelligent and smart systems. *SN Computer Science, 3*(2), 158. https://doi.org/10.1007/s42979-022-01043-x

Schiefer, M. (2015, May). Smart home definition and security threats. In *2015 9th international conference on IT security incident management & IT forensics* (pp. 114–118). IEEE. https://doi.org/10.1109/IMF.2015.17

Schiller, A., & McMahon, J. (2019). Alexa, alert me when the revolution comes: Gender, affect, and labor in the age of home-based artificial intelligence. *New Political Science*, *41*(2), 173–191. https://doi.org/10.1080/07393148.2019.1595288

Schmalstieg, D., & Höllerer, T. (2016). *Augmented reality: Principles and practice.* Addison-Wesley Professional.

Schuler, D. (1994). Community networks: Building a new participatory medium. *Communications of the ACM*, *37*(1), 38–51. https://doi.org/10.1145/175222.175225

Schweitzer, F., Belk, R., Jordan, W., & Ortner, M. (2019). Servant, friend or master? The relationships users build with voice-controlled smart devices. *Journal of Marketing Management*, *1–23*. https://doi.org/10.1080/0267257X.2019.1596970

Sciuto, A., Saini, A., Forlizzi, J., & Hong, J. I. (2018, June). "Hey Alexa, what's up?" A mixed-methods studies of in-home conversational agent usage. In *Proceedings of the 2018 designing interactive systems conference* (pp. 857–868). https://doi.org/10.1145/3196709.3196772

Scott, J. W. (1991). The evidence of experience. *Critical Inquiry*, *17*(4), 773–797. https://doi.org/10.1086/448612

Sengupta, R., Chatterjee, L., & Parker, J. (2021). The effect of anticipated embarrassment on the preference for using chatbots [report]. *Marketing Science Institute*. https://www.msi.org/wp-content/uploads/2021/09/MSI_Report_21-135.pdf

Šerić, A., & Fong, C. Y. (2017). Gender in domestic AI and humanoid robots. In D. Popova, S. Ejrnæs, C. Joann Koh, R. Das, T. Allen, A. O'Donnell, K. Taft, R. Alfaro, L. Boye Danielsen, & E. Newall (Eds.), *Gender in science & technology: A collection of theses from the Physics Department at Lund University 2017.* (pp. 34–43). Lund University. ISBN 978-91-7753-883-7.

Sezer, O. B., Dogdu, E., & Ozbayoglu, A. M. (2017). Context-aware computing, learning, and big data in internet of things: A survey. *IEEE Internet of Things Journal*, *5*(1), 1–27. https://doi.org/10.1109/JIOT.2017.2773600

Shao, C., & Kwon, K. H. (2021). Hello Alexa! Exploring effects of motivational factors and social presence on satisfaction with artificial intelligence-enabled gadgets. *Human Behavior and Emerging Technologies*, *3*(5), 978–988. https://doi.org/10.1002/hbe2.293

Sharkey, A. (2017). Can robots be responsible moral agents? And why should we care? *Connection Science*, *29*(3), 210–216. https://doi.org/10.1080/09540091.2017.1313815

Shavitt, C., Kuzminykh, A., Ridel, I., & Cauchard, J. R. (2021). Naturally together: A systematic approach for multi-user interaction with natural interfaces. *Proceedings of the ACM on Human-Computer Interaction*, *5*(349), 1–31. https://doi.org/10.1145/3476090

Shen, S., Chen, D., Wei, Y. L., Yang, Z., & Choudhury, R. R. (2020, April). Voice localization using nearby wall reflections. In *Proceedings of the 26th annual international conference on mobile computing and networking* (pp. 1–14). https://doi.org/10.1145/3372224.3380884

Silverio-Fernández, M., Renukappa, S., & Suresh, S. (2018). What is a smart device?-a conceptualisation within the paradigm of the internet of things. *Visualization in Engineering*, *6*(1), 1–10. https://doi.org/10.1186/s40327-018-0063-8

Simonite, T. (2018, September). Amazon wants Alexa to hear your whispers and frustration. *Wired*. https://www.wired.com/story/amazon-alexa-upgrades-whisper-alexa-guard/

Siontis, K. C., Attia, Z. I., Asirvatham, S. J., & Friedman, P. A. (2024). ChatGPT hallucinating: Can it get any more humanlike? *European Heart Journal*, *45*(5), 321–323. https://doi.org/10.1093/eurheartj/ehad766

Skjuve, M., Følstad, A., Fostervold, K. I., & Brandtzaeg, P. B. (2021). My chatbot companion-a study of human-chatbot relationships. *International Journal of Human-Computer Studies*, *149*, 102601. https://doi.org/10.1016/j.ijhcs.2021.102601

Smith, L. T. (1999). *Decolonizing methodologies: Research and indigenous peoples.* University of Otago Press.

Someshwar, D., Bhanushali, D., Chaudhari, V., & Nadkarni, S. (2020, July). Implementation of virtual assistant with sign language using deep learning and TensorFlow. In *2020 second international conference on inventive research in computing applications (ICIRCA)* (pp. 595–600). IEEE. https://doi.org/10.1109/ICIRCA48905.2020.9183179

Sparkes, A.C. (2000). Autoethnography and narratives of self: Reflections on criteria in action. *Sociology of Sport Journal, 17*(1), 21–43. https://doi.org/10.1123/ssj.17.1.21

Strengers, Y. (2013). *Smart energy technologies in everyday life: Smart utopia?* Springer. https://doi.org/10.1057/9781137267054

Strengers, Y., & Kennedy, J. (2020). *The smart wife: Why Siri, Alexa, and other smart home devices need a feminist reboot.* MIT Press. https://doi.org/10.7551/mitpress/12482.001.0001

Sugawara, T., Cyr, B., Rampazzi, S., Genkin, D., & Fu, K. (2020). Light commands: Laser-Based audio injection attacks on Voice-Controllable systems. In *29th USENIX security symposium (USENIX security 20)* (pp. 2631–2648).

Sundén, J. (2012). Desires at play: On closeness and epistemological uncertainty. *Games and Culture, 7*(2), 164–184. https://doi.org/10.1177/1555412012451124

Swan, E. (2008). Let's not get too personal: Critical reflection, reflexivity and the confessional turn. *Journal of European Industrial Training, 32*(5), 385–399. https://doi.org/10.1108/03090590810877102

Ta, V., Griffith, C., Boatfield, C., Wang, X., Civitello, M., Bader, H., DeCero, E., & Loggarakis, A. (2020). User experiences of social support from companion chatbots in everyday contexts: Thematic analysis. *Journal of Medical Internet Research, 22*(3), e16235. https://doi.org/10.2196/16235

Tabassum, M., Kosinski, T., & Lipford, H. R. (2019). "I don't own the data": End user perceptions of smart home device data practices and risks. In *Fifteenth symposium on usable privacy and security (SOUPS 2019)* (pp. 435–450) Santa Clara, California.

Takeuchi, A., & Naito, T. (1995, May). Situated facial displays: Towards social interaction. In *Proceedings of the SIGCHI conference on Human factors in computing systems* (pp. 450–455). https://doi.org/10.1145/223904.223965

Talip, B. A., & Narayan, B. (2020). Co-experience on Twitter: A study of information technology professionals. *Information Research, 25*(1).

Talja, S., Tuominen, K. & Savolainen, R. (2005). "'Isms" in information science: Constructivism, collectivism and constructionism'. *Journal of documentation, 61*(1), 79–101. https://doi.org/10.1108/00220410510578023

Tam, K. P., Lee, S. L., & Chao, M. M. (2013). Saving Mr. Nature: Anthropomorphism enhances connectedness to and protectiveness toward nature. *Journal of Experimental Social Psychology, 49*(3), 514–521. https://doi.org/10.1016/j.jesp.2013.02.001

Tanenbaum, J., Tanenbaum, K., Antle, A. N., & Bizzocchi, J. (2011). *Understanding narrative and embodied interactions with "present-at-mind". The 29th ACM international conference on human factors in computing systems*, ACM, Vancouver, British Columbia.

Tondu, B. (2012). Anthropomorphism and service humanoid robots: An ambiguous relationship. *The Industrial Robot, 39*(6), 609–618. https://doi.org/10.1108/01439911211268840

Tufft, M., & Richardson, D. C. (2020, July). Social offloading: Just working together is enough to remove semantic interference. In *Proceedings of CogSci 2020* (pp. 859–865).

Turkle, S. (2005). *The second self: Computers and the human spirit.* MIT Press. https://doi.org/10.7551/mitpress/6115.001.0001

Van den Hoven, E., Orth, D., & Zijlema, A. (2021). Possessions and memories. *Current Opinion in Psychology, 39*, 94–99. https://doi.org/10.1016/j.copsyc.2020.08.014

Vanian, J. (2017). This is Amazon's latest effort to get alexa into more devices. *Fortune Magazine.* http://fortune.com/2017/08/17/amazon-alexa-devices-software-kit/

Varis, P. (2016). Digital ethnography. In T. Spilioti & A. Georgakopoulou (Eds.), *The Routledge handbook of language and digital communication* (pp. 55–68).

Vernuccio, M., Patrizi, M., & Pastore, A. (2020). Brand anthropomorphism and brand voice: The role of the name-brand voice assistant. In *Advances in digital marketing and eCommerce: First international conference, 2020* (pp. 31–39). Springer International Publishing. https://doi.org/10.1007/978-3-030-47595-6_5

Vernuccio, M., Patrizi, M., & Pastore, A. (2023a). Delving into brand anthropomorphisation strategies in the experiential context of name-brand voice assistants. *Journal of Consumer Behaviour, 22*(5), 1074–1083. https://doi.org/10.1002/cb.1984

Vernuccio, M., Patrizi, M., Šerić, M., & Pastore, A. (2023b). The perceptual antecedents of brand anthropomorphism in the name-brand voice assistant context. *Journal of Brand Management, 30*(4), 302–317. https://doi.org/10.1057/s41262-022-00305-6

Wall, S. (2008). Easier said than done: Writing an autoethnography. *International Journal of Qualitative Methods, 7*(1), 38–53. https://doi.org/10.1177/160940690800700103

Wei, J., Tag, B., Trippas, J. R., Dingler, T., & Kostakos, V. (2022, April). What could possibly go wrong when interacting with proactive smart speakers? A case study using an ESM application. In *Proceedings of the 2022 CHI conference on human factors in computing systems* (pp. 1–15). https://doi.org/10.1145/3491102.3517432

Weiser, M. (1991). The computer for the 21st century. *Scientific American, 265*(3), 94–104. https://doi.org/10.1038/scientificamerican0991-94

Whitehead, T.L. (2004). What is ethnography? Methodological, ontological, and epistemological attributes. In *Ethnographically informed community and cultural assessment research systems (EICCARS) working paper series*, University of Maryland, College Park, Maryland.

Whitmore, A., Agarwal, A., & Da Xu, L. (2015). The Internet of Things—A survey of topics and trends. *Information Systems Frontiers, 17*, 261–274. https://doi.org/10.1007/s10796-014-9489-2

Wiener, H. J., & Chartrand, T. L. (2014). The effect of voice quality on ad efficacy. *Psychology & Marketing, 31*(7), 509–517. https://doi.org/10.1002/mar.20712

Wienrich, C., Carolus, A., Markus, A., Augustin, Y., Pfister, J., & Hotho, A. (2023). Long-term effects of perceived friendship with intelligent voice assistants on usage behavior, user experience, and social perceptions. *Computers, 12*(4). https://doi.org/10.3390/computers12040077

Williams, K. (2015). An anxious alliance. In *Proceedings of the fifth decennial aarhus conference on critical alternatives* (pp. 121–131). https://doi.org/10.7146/aahcc.v1i1.21146

Williams, R. F. (2006). Using cognitive ethnography to study instruction. In I. S. Barab, K. E. Hay, & D. T. Hickey (Eds.), Using cognitive ethnography to study instruction. International Society of the Learning Sciences.

Woods, H.S. (2018). Asking more of Siri and Alexa: Feminine persona in service of surveillance capitalism. *Critical Studies in Media Communication, 35*(4), 334–349. https://doi.org/10.1080/15295036.2018.1488082

Woodward, I. (2001). Domestic objects and the taste epiphany: A resource for consumption methodology. *Journal of Material Culture, 6*(2), 115–136. https://doi.org/10.1177/135918350100600201

Wu, T., He, S., Liu, J., Sun, S., Liu, K., Han, Q. L., & Tang, Y. (2023). A brief overview of ChatGPT: The history, status quo and potential future development. *IEEE/CAA Journal of Automatica Sinica, 10*(5), 1122–1136. https://doi.org/10.1109/JAS.2023.123618

Xu, J., & Montague, E. (2013). Working with an invisible active user: Understanding trust in technology and co-user from the perspective of a passive user. *Interacting with Computers, 25*(5), 375–385. https://doi.org/10.1093/iwc/iws022

Xu, Z., Hua, R., Juang, J., Xia, S., Fan, J., & Hwang, C. (2021). Inaudible attack on smart speakers with intentional electromagnetic interference. *IEEE Transactions on Microwave Theory and Techniques, 69*(5), 2642–2650. https://doi.org/10.1109/TMTT.2021.3058585

Yin, R. K. (2003). *Case study research: Design and methods* (3rd ed.). Sage.

Youn, S., & Jin, S. V. (2021). "In AI we trust?" The effects of parasocial interaction and technopian versus luddite ideological views on chatbot-based customer relationship management in the emerging "feeling economy". *Computers in Human Behavior, 119*, 106721. https://doi.org/10.1016/j.chb.2021.106721

Young, K. (2021). Scrape, brush, flick: The phenomenology of sound. In H. M. Berger, F. Riedel, & D. VanderHamm (Eds.), *The Oxford handbook of the phenomenology of music cultures* (pp. 375–404). Oxford University Press. https://doi.org/10.1093/oxfordhb/9780190693879.013.16

Zargham, N., Bonfert, M., Porzel, R., Doring, T., & Malaka, R. (2021, May). Multi-agent voice assistants: An investigation of user experience. In *Proceedings of the 20th international conference on mobile and ubiquitous multimedia* (pp. 98–107). https://doi.org/10.1145/3490632.3490662

Zhang, M. R., Wang, R., Xu, X., Li, Q., Sharif, A., & Wobbrock, J. O. (2021, May). Voicemoji: Emoji entry using voice for visually impaired people. In *Proceedings of the 2021 CHI Conference on Human Factors in Computing Systems* (pp. 1–18). https://doi.org/10.1145/3411764.3445338

Zhong, R., Ma, M., Zhou, Y., Lin, Q., Li, L., & Zhang, N. (2022). User acceptance of smart home voice assistant: A comparison among younger, middle-aged, and older adults. *Universal Access in the Information Society*, *23*, 275–292. https://doi.org/10.1007/s10209-022-00936-1

Zijlema, A., van den Hoven, E., & Eggen, B. (2016). Companions: Objects accruing value and memories by being a part of our lives. In *Proceedings of the 28th Australian conference on computer-human interaction* (pp. 170–174). https://doi.org/10.1145/3010915.3010958

Zinko, R., Ferris, G. R., Blass, F. R., & Laird, M. D. (2007). Toward a theory of reputation in organizations. In J. J. Martocchio (Ed.), *Research in personnel and human resources management* (pp. 163–204). JAI Press/Elsevier Science. https://doi.org/10.1016/S0742-7301(07)26004-9

Zoghaib, A. (2017). The contribution of a brand spokesperson's voice to consumer-based brand equity. *Journal of Product & Brand Management*, *26*(5), 492–502. https://doi.org/10.1108/JPBM-06-2016-1230

Zoghaib, A. (2019). Persuasion of voices: The effects of a speaker's voice characteristics and gender on consumers' responses. *Recherche et Applications en Marketing (English Edition)*, *34*(3), 83–110. https://doi.org/10.1177/2051570719828687

Index

Note: Pages in *italics* refer to figures and pages in **bold** refer to tables.

B

C

D

E

F

G

H

T

U

V

W

For Product Safety Concerns and Information please contact our EU
representative GPSR@taylorandfrancis.com
Taylor & Francis Verlag GmbH, Kaufingerstraße 24, 80331 München, Germany

www.ingramcontent.com/pod-product-compliance
Ingram Content Group UK Ltd.
Pitfield, Milton Keynes, MK11 3LW, UK
UKHW020200200926
475702UK00004B/551
* 9 7 8 1 0 4 1 1 5 7 0 5 2 *